# CATHOLIC PENTECOSTALISM

Anybody with the gift of tongues
speaks to God,
but not to other people;
because nobody understands him
(St. Paul, 1 Co. 14:2)

# CATHOLIC PENTECOSTALISM

*René Laurentin*

TRANSLATED
BY
MATTHEW J. O'CONNELL

*Doubleday & Company, Inc.*
*Garden City, New York*
*1977*

Original edition:
*Pentecôtisme chez les Catholiques: Risques et Avenir,*
© Éditions Beauchesne, 1974.


Excerpts from *The Jerusalem Bible,*
copyright © 1966
by Darton, Longman & Todd, Ltd. and Doubleday & Company, Inc.
Used by permission of the publisher.

LIBRARY OF CONGRESS CATALOGING IN PUBLICATION DATA

Laurentin, René.
Catholic Pentecostalism.

Translation Pentecôtisme chez les catholiques.
Bibliography: p. 204
1. Pentecostalism—Catholic Church.  I. Title.
BX2350.57.L3613     282
ISBN: 0-385-12129-6
Library of Congress Catalog Card Number 76–18358

# Contents

O Holy Spirit . . . who art present in the Church
and dost infallibly guide it,
pour forth, we pray, the fullness of Thy gifts
upon the Ecumenical Council. . . .
Renew Thy wonders in this our day
as by a new Pentecost.[1]

POPE JOHN XXIII

Jesus is preparing for his Church
great things
that we cannot even imagine.
Perhaps you will see the beginnings of it all.
The Holy Spirit is invisibly at work.
We must have unconditional confidence
in the work of the Holy Spirit.[2]

JACQUES MARITAIN

The fresh breath of the Spirit . . .
has come to awaken
latent energies
within the Church,
to stir up dormant charisms,
and to infuse
a sense of vitality and joy . . .
which makes the Church youthful . . .
in every age.[3]

POPE PAUL VI

# *Introduction*

---

"They speak in other tongues."[1] They go in for "healing." They are followers, more or less, of the "pentecostal sects." Such are some of the most common impressions abroad of the Catholic Neo-Pentecostal movement, which is called "The Charismatic Renewal" in the United States and "Renewal in the Spirit" or "Spiritual Renewal" in France. The most accurate names for the movement have come in for criticism and therefore been more or less abandoned. The result? A confusion that is all the greater, since "charismatic group" today can refer to people of quite varying allegiances.

We must try to dissipate the confusion and focus clearly on one important point: After less than ten years, Catholic pentecostalists number a half million in about a hundred countries. You hear of the gathering near where you live—in the Montparnasse chapel, in the crypt of Saint-Sulpice, or in a neighbor's house in Paris or elsewhere in the country. Somewhat uneasy about approaching a group of initiates and wondering whether you may be getting involved in unusual rites, you go to observe them. You find no reticence, a warm welcome, no prejudice shown, no questions asked.

Chairs are set up in concentric circles, the innermost having about a dozen chairs and stools. After the greeting, the meeting gets under way, not following a preconceived plan or externally imposed direction, but depending for its course on what the members contribute. Scripture readings, brief exhortations or teachings, and witnessings alternate with singing and spontaneous prayer. All express themselves freely, whether individually or in groups, in words or in song, and yet no one ever interrupts anyone else—not even in France! At times all speak or sing at once, each with his own rhythm and in his own tongue, but this happens by common consent. The harmony that marks these improvisations is surprising. Is it a grace flowing from the receptiveness of each person to the others? Or from the presence of the Spirit to whom each member of the group is attending? At times, the group you visit may be one that has established a community in which everything is shared: money, housing, projects.

The more penetrating studies conducted by psychologists, theologians, pastors of various confessions, and bishops (especially by several national episcopal conferences) have concluded with positive judgments on the movement, even though those conducting the studies may often have begun with a strong bias against it. I was struck by the favorable, even enthusiastic reaction of a physician-psychoanalyst who asked if he might accompany me to a meeting. And yet those who look at the movement from outside feel apprehensive and even fearful about it. Theirs is the reaction people often have to novelties that promise to be permanent and threaten to cause changes in their lives.

At the same time, these negative judgments can be quite contrary to one another. The traditionalists fear destructive innovations, the establishment of a charismatic hierarchy, new "ecumenical confusions," and the manipulation of these naïve groups by political leftists. The progressives, on the contrary, fear that the mysticism of the charismatics may lead to a dispersal of forces, or enable conservative clerics to gain control again, or even become the Trojan horse of traditionalism.

Integrists see the movement as the means of Anglo-Saxon Protestant infiltration. But American Protestant circles see it rather as a marginal manifestation of the counterculture: "Just another 'revival' in a long series, all of them ephemeral because based on collective emotion. Another example of sentimental womanish mysticism."[2] In such a judgment we can see the usual armory of epithets being brought to bear: fundamentalism, illuminism, emotionalism, elitism, etc.

Does the movement with its impressive growth have a purely psychological explanation? Is it from God? From the devil? All three hypotheses have been defended.

Is it a new delusion, or the new Pentecost that John XXIII anticipated at the beginning of the Council?

This book has been written to answer these questions.

But why still another book? The writer must admit right off that
it satisfies a long-frustrated urge of his. After the Council, when I
was looking about for "signs of the times," I became interested in
Catholic Pentecostalism as early as 1967, the very year of its birth.
On August 8 of that year, I spoke with Father Edward O'Connor of
Notre Dame, one of the founders of the movement, at the Mari-
ological Congress in Lisbon, and he told me: "I see in this movement the future of the Church."

He had me believing him. But then he became so discreet as to
say nothing more about the movement. I asked for further information, but he simply sent me his article on the subject, published in
the fall of 1967, with a covering note: "I let you have this provided
you do not say anything about it in print." The reason for his
reserve was that if news about the movement spread too soon, it
might militate against the slow germination of an experience that is
so difficult for the outsider to appreciate. The result was that I
remained quiet and kept my eye on what was happening.

I came into direct contact with the movement again and took
part in charismatic gatherings on my journeys to the United States
(1970) and England (1971) as well as in France itself. Once the
whole business became public knowledge, I published two articles
on it in *Le Figaro* (January 21 and February 18, 1974). Letters to
me raised a lot of questions, especially since a third article was not
published and the first two had appeared only in abridged form. In
June 1974, I felt I had to return to the fountainhead of the movement and so I attended the international conference at Notre Dame,
at which thirty thousand charismatics gathered (June 14–16). From
there I went to visit charismatic communities at Ann Arbor, New
Orleans, Houston, and in Canada.

As I went about seeking information, I was also engaged in theological reflection on the Holy Spirit in preparation for an (unpublished) course at Quebec (July 1974). In the course I tried to
show the convergence of three approaches to the Spirit: that of
dogma, that of symbolism (especially biblical symbolism), and that
of practice (from the Pauline Church of Corinth down to contemporary movements). The theme was a new one, and quite fascinat-
ing, since with few exceptions (and even these were less serene than

they appeared on the surface) the movements centering on the Spirit had never been placid affairs. They have always found it difficult to strike a balance between radicalism and dullness, rebellion and the status quo.

I intend this book as a contribution from a theologian and historian who is also a professional religious journalist. I want to bring together the many scattered items of information and to deal with them historically and doctrinally, while also being open to the interdisciplinary contributions of the human sciences (sociology, psychology, linguistics). My aim is to discover the meaning and direction of the movement.

Previous studies have usually been written inside and for the movement itself. The present book presents the viewpoint of a participating observer (in this matter, participation is a prerequisite for understanding), while keeping the distance needed for objective investigation.

Where did the Catholic Neo-Pentecostal movement come from? What do Church authorities think of it? (Chapters 1 and 2).

Which is more fundamental: baptism in the Spirit or experience of the charisms? (Chapter 3).

What of the two most striking charisms: speaking in tongues (Chapter 4) and healings (Chapter 5)?

What are the historical antecedents of the new movement? (Chapter 6).

How explain the movement? (Chapter 7).

What are the risks it runs? (Chapter 8).

In what direction is it moving? (Chapter 9).

These are the questions that need answering.

# Chapter 1

# THE BIRTH
# OF
# CATHOLIC PENTECOSTALISM

The Catholic Pentecostal movement, now to be found in almost a hundred countries, came into existence at the beginning of 1967, at Duquesne University, a Pittsburgh foundation of the Holy Ghost Fathers. The circumstances were as follows.

## 1. ORIGINS[1]

In August 1966, some lay professors of Duquesne University attended the Congress of the Cursillo movement. They were looking for something that would activate in them the full power of faith and evoke a total generosity, and they hoped to find it in this movement for spiritual formation that had started in Spain before the Council. They had already been involved in the liturgical, ecumenical, apostolic, and peace movements, and been disillusioned with all of them.

At the Cursillo Congress they met Steve Clark and Ralph Martin, who are now the leaders of the Ann Arbor community, and who at that time were co-ordinators of student activities in St. John's Parish, East Lansing, Michigan. Steve had just been reading a book that he found both moving and disconcerting: *The Cross and the Switchblade*, by David Wilkerson.[2] This is the autobiographical story of a Protestant pastor who was led by strong inner impulses to abandon the life of a salaried parish minister and embark on a dangerous mission to the delinquents and drug addicts of Brooklyn, in neighborhoods into which the average American would not venture at night, or even by day, for that matter.

Chapter 21 of the book penetrated to the heart of the pastor's, and others', experience: "The Holy Spirit is what you need." Here the professors found what they had been looking for and had failed to find, once again, in the Cursillo movement: the Bible, the Holy Spirit, the Spirit's charisms. For two months Wilkerson's book provided the basis for their prayer and discussions, while they tried to apply its lessons to their daily living. Then one of them, Ralph Keifer, came across another book on pentecostalism: John Sherrill's *They Speak in Other Tongues*, which offered practical ways and means of attaining an experience of the Spirit.

In the fall, the group met for a period of deeper prayer, during which the recitation of the "Come, Holy Spirit," the Catholic hymn to the Holy Spirit, was given an important place.

These Catholic laymen asked themselves whether it might not be time to discuss matters with some pentecostalists, despite the reputation of the latter for extremism and anti-Catholicism. W. Lewis, an Episcopalian priest, put them in touch with one of his women parishioners who was involved in the charismatic movement. The meeting on Epiphany, January 6, 1967, brought them an invitation to take part in a prayer meeting the following Friday, January 13. As the Catholics noted, this was the day when their Church's liturgy celebrated the baptism of Jesus by the Holy Spirit in the waters of the Jordan. Ralph was left somewhat confused by the prayer meeting, for he was convinced of the high level of sharing, prayer, and "lived theology" that he found there, but his university-trained mind was offended by the naïve approach to Scripture and the idea of a direct communication with God.

Of the four Catholics who had attended the first meeting, only Ralph returned the following week (January 20?), bringing with him Patrick Bourgeois, another professor on the faculty of theology. The prayer and discussion at this meeting centered on the Letter to the Romans. At the end, the two men asked to receive the "baptism in the Holy Spirit." One group prayed over Ralph and imposed hands on him; another group did the same for Patrick.

They simply asked me to make an act of faith for the power of the Spirit to work in me. I prayed in tongues rather quickly. It was not a particularly soaring or spectacular thing at all. I felt a certain peace—and at least a little prayerful—and truthfully, rather curious as to where all this would lead.[3]

In the next week Ralph imposed hands on two other Duquesne colleagues. They had the same experience: an interior welling up of the Spirit, and a renewal without any revolutionary upheaval.

On February 18–19 about thirty students and professors gathered for a weekend at Duquesne University. On Saturday evening, at the time set aside for a birthday party celebration, the rhythm of things suddenly speeded up. Paul Grey and Maryanne Springle, an engaged couple, had heard about baptism in the Holy Spirit and now asked Ralph Keifer to pray with them that they might receive it. The little group went upstairs to do their praying; no one else was aware of what was going on. Paul and Maryanne experienced the same conversation and thanked God "in tongues."

At this very same time, another student, Patti Gallagher, had gone to the chapel to pray. She told me the story at New Orleans on June 21, 1974.

We were all tired from our day of prayer and reflection, and somewhat distraught. No one was very eager about setting up the birthday party for that evening. The Lord was at work in us, but we were not aware of it.

I wanted to shake off the feeling of apathy and to get something going, so I went to the chapel to see if any of the other students were there. I went in and knelt down, and began to tremble; I felt the presence of the Lord. I became afraid, yet I wanted nothing so much as to stay there and pray. But I said to myself: "We've done enough praying today. It's time to celebrate our brother's birthday."

One of the students in the chapel said to me: "Patti, I don't understand it. Something's happening that we didn't plan." I answered: "I just want to pray." Then I improvised: "Lord, I don't know what you are asking, but I am ready."

Then I could feel God's love for me; I experienced it. I was prostrate on the ground, overwhelmed by the "foolishness" of this love. I knew no theology, I had never gone to Catholic schools, but as I lay prostrate there I understood Augustine's words: "Lord, you made us for yourself; only in you will we find peace." I realized that the others in the chapel were having the same experience.

Some of the students spoke in tongues, others did not. Patti received this gift a few days later.

## 2. SPREAD

Ralph Keifer telephoned the news to the University of Notre Dame, where at the beginning of the month he had begun his search.

A similar event took place at Notre Dame on the weekend of March 4–5; on Monday, March 13; and then elsewhere. It was like a series of independent explosions, rather than a spreading out from a center, because other people in other places were engaged in the same search for God.

In the fall of 1974 Edward O'Connor, professor of theology at Notre Dame, jotted down his first impressions:

> Even for a priest who has seen some surprising things in the course of his ministry, it is not easy to take it in stride when a friend, a former student, tells you he has received the gift of tongues.
>
> Things moved rapidly. Other students received the same gift. By March 14 I was almost the only one in the group who had not received it.

From this point on the movement spread by leaps and bounds, as is evident from the attendance figures for the annual meetings at the University of Notre Dame:

| | |
|---|---|
| 1967: | 90 |
| 1968: | 100 plus |
| 1969: | 450 |
| 1970: | 1,300 |
| 1971: | 4,500 |
| 1972: | 11,000 |
| 1973: | 25,000 |
| 1974: | 30,000 |

What proportion of the whole do these figures represent? A little less than 10 per cent of the charismatics in the United States. The percentage can only be approximate, because there are no statistics; the movement is concerned with life, not with records, in the spirit of the Bible where the prophets blame the kings of Israel for having a census made. If you treat God's gifts as a form of wealth and try to keep an account of them, are you not turning away from God himself, and from men as well?

A lot of crosschecking gives grounds for thinking that the Catholic Neo-Pentecostal movement has somewhere from 2 million to 4 million participants throughout the world as of May 1975. Two hundred thousand copies of the pamphlet *Pointing the Way* (an aid in preparing for the outpouring of the Spirit) have been distributed in English alone during the past four years. The international yearbook, which is intended to facilitate contact among groups, confirms us in thinking that the membership is doubling every year; the yearbook contained about 1,100 addresses in 1973, and 2,050 in 1974. But the yearbook lists are obviously quite incomplete. For example, forty groups, which form a single parish in an area that has no mail service and no such thing as an address (Khali), are not mentioned in the list, and this is not an isolated case.

The charismatic renewal has become a tidal wave in Puerto Rico, where whole parishes are involved in it; the warm and friendly style of this people is very congenial to the movement. A spontaneous meeting in Quebec in June 1974 brought together over 8,000 people.

The beginnings of the movement in France date from the end of 1971[4]; since the end of 1973 there is no important city in France that does not have one or more groups. The Emmanuel group in Paris quickly acquired 600 members and, like a hive that is too full, twice had to send out colonies. At Lyons the movement began with the visit of an American to Fourvière and the visit of two young Jesuits (Fathers Laurent Fabre and B. Lepesant) to America. In this city the movement developed and reached maturity under more propitious conditions than in Paris; in an atmosphere of tranquillity roots were sunk deep.

According to a recent statistic, 7 per cent of the 47 million Catholics in the United States (therefore more than 3 million) have been in contact with the movement. This would suggest from 1 million to 2 million convinced participants.

In Rome there are seven prayer groups. Three of these speak Italian, the others use French, German, Spanish, and English (this last is not listed in the yearbook). The Holy See has been favorably inclined toward the movement, even if in a discreet way.

## 3. WHAT SHOULD THE MOVEMENT BE CALLED?

We must return to the matter of vocabulary or nomenclature, for it can cause difficulty in a book geared to giving information.

1. Initially people spoke of the "Catholic Pentecostal movement," a name that provided the title for Edward O'Connor's first article in the summer of 1967.[5]

But "Pentecostal" is also the name of an organized Church in the United States. It could therefore cause confusion or imply competition, and it made Catholics uneasy. The report submitted to the National Conference of American Bishops (November 14, 1969) devoted the longest of its six paragraphs to this point; the name was thereafter dropped, and another adopted—"charismatic"—which the report mentions without voicing any reservations.[6]

2. But the name "charismatic" was likewise challenged. It was said to be an "insufferable abuse" on two counts. First, it would limit the word "charism" to "its narrow sense of an extraordinary phenomenon, such as speaking in tongues, prophesying, or the gift of healing." Second, it would monopolize for a few Christians a name that belongs to the Church as a whole, since according to Vatican II the Church in its entirety is charismatic. Yves Congar concludes: "We are seeing the beginning of a very promising movement. We must find for it a name that is beyond reproach."[7]

3. The French leaders of the movement accepted the criticism and tried to introduce other names: "Renewal in the Spirit" or "Spiritual Renewal." But these names are vague and can be confusing. When I ask people, "What do you think of the spiritual renewal?" or "What do you think of spiritual prayer groups?," one out of every two answers is completely unrelated to the Catholic Pentecostal movement. "Renewal in the Spirit" may, strictly speaking, be a satisfactory name for the movement, but it does not enable us to describe the people who take part in it. "Catholic Pentecostals" is clear. "Charismatics" is ambiguous and aggressive. "Those renewed in the Spirit" or "Christians of the spiritual renewal" is impractical. The word "pneumatic," which the Greek Fathers use to signify

what belongs to or is related to the Holy Spirit, has unfortunately been taken over by the automobile tire industry. As a result, we are left with a great verbal confusion.

The difficulties that have led to the downgrading of any viable descriptive name arise in fact not so much from the words themselves as from the irrational disquiet people feel when confronted by movements of an "enthusiastic" or "charismatic" type (we shall return to this point below in Chapter 6). In these circumstances any name whatsoever that proves evocative and meaningful arouses aggressive objections. We shall try to avoid this emotionally charged atmosphere without, however, failing to take into account people's reactions and the serious reasons behind them. Clarity will require us to use, as the context demands, the various names mentioned above. Frequently we shall be using the name that is clearest and most specific: Catholic Pentecostalism or Catholic Neo-Pentecostal movement. The next chapter will explain the sense of the prefix Neo-.

## The First Four Catholic Neo-Pentecostals
### (January 13–20, 1967)

What are the names of the first four who were "baptized in the Spirit" in January 1967? The Ranaghans mention three of them: Ralph Keifer; his wife, Pat; and Patrick Bourgeois. They omit the name of the fourth: William Storey, professor of history, because Storey left the movement in 1969–70. At the end of the Charismatic Congress held in Rome at Pentecost 1975 (which he had tried in vain to prevent being held by sending reports of his own to the Holy See), Storey publicly announced his break from the movement, and so there is no reason now for concealing his name. Every renewal is marked by tensions and conflicts; we see these even at the very beginnings of Christianity, as reported in the Acts of the Apostles. Paul broke off from Barnabas, who had initiated him into the missionary apostolate (Ac. 16:39). The important thing is that such conflicts are fruitful for the ongoing development of spiritual discernment. It is in this perspective that the Ranaghans dealt with the problem of Storey's defection.

*Chapter 2*

# FROM PENTECOSTALISM TO NEO-PENTECOSTALISM

Since Catholic Pentecostalism drew inspiration from a movement that had begun sixty-seven years before, we must turn back to this earlier movement and its influence and situate it in the series of revivals that had taken place since Wesley's time (1738) in Protestant English-speaking circles.

## 1. ORIGIN OF PENTECOSTALISM

Pentecostalism was born on a memorable day: "The first day of the century," according to the unanimous testimony of the historians. But mnemonics such as this one do not always pay due attention to the original documents, and consequently we find various authors specifying the date in different ways. In Edward D. O'Connor's first account, the day was December 31, 1900.[1] In a later account he corrected this to January 1, 1901.[2] Henri Caffarel, however, makes it "the evening of December 31, 1899, the eve of the new century."[3]

The best-qualified witness is Agnes Ozman, who was the first to have the specifically pentecostal experience of "baptism in the Spirit" and "speaking in tongues." According to her, the event occurred during a vigil, at 11 P.M., January 1, 1901.[4]

It happened in a Topeka, Kansas, house where Charles Parham, Methodist pastor, had established a Bible school. He and his students were deeply impressed by the contrast between the gloominess of the present-day Church and the vibrant life of the early Church as described in the Acts of the Apostles: a bracing, joyous, energetic life that was permeated by the breath of the Spirit. How account for the disappearance of those charisms in which the first Christians saw the manifestation of the Spirit, especially the gift of tongues of which Acts speaks? It was not a satisfactory answer to say that these were temporary, exceptional gifts meant only for the period when the Church was being founded, or, to switch to St. John Chrysostom's image, that they were "gifts for the period of engagement" and lost their meaning once the marriage was under way. The Bible, after all, gives no hint that the gifts were to be temporary, while Church history shows them being given again at moments when Christianity was really vital, and especially at times of change.

At this point in his study and reflection Pastor Charles Parham held a prayer vigil on New Year's Eve (December 31, 1900). The next day one of the students, Agnes Ozman (later Mrs. LaBerge) felt impelled to ask the pastor to lay his hands on her head, as described in the New Testament, so that she might receive the gift of the Spirit. The pastor hesitated, then agreed.

"It was as though rivers of living water were proceeding from my inmost being," she said later on.[5] The words echoing in her memory here were those of John 7:38: "Let the man come and drink who believes in me. As scripture says: From his breast shall flow fountains of living water." The evangelist then comments on these words of Jesus: "He was speaking of the Spirit which those who believed in him were to receive" (Jn. 7:39).

Agnes began to speak in strange tongues, and the next day, she tells us, a Bohemian recognized his mother tongue in the words she herself could not understand.

On the following days other members of the Bible school had the same experience.

According to a rigid dialectic, the Churches in which Pentecostalism first appeared rejected it. Despite opposition from the Church of England, Wesley had become the founder of a new confession: Methodism. Now Pentecostalism was in turn rejected by Methodism, within which it had come into existence, and it had to make its own way outside its mother Church. It developed along two different lines.

One group organized itself into a Church that was modeled after the other Churches, and therefore had its own institutions, a theology, a written liturgy, schools, and seminaries.

Other groups preserved a greater fidelity to the original experience and remained informal. They spread chiefly by word of mouth and often among the poor and illiterate, whose experience they shared, especially in Latin America and Africa. Their whole approach matched in many respects the style of the Gospel, the very name of which means the Good News that is preached to the poor.

> Their [the Pentecostalists'] oral liturgy allows the unschooled to participate as equals in the roles of evangelists, singers, and prophets. Even without a theory of group process, they have been able to recognize the natural leaders of the poor community as key figures in the communications network.[6]

> Or else the Pentecostal movement can become a truly proletarian Church, not only providing the disadvantaged with an opportunity to express their sufferings in biblical language, but also giving them a hope which can crystallize in a theology for and by the poor, in a post-literary liturgy, in a non-bourgeois social ethic, and in a political program.[7]

Since the beginning of the century, Pentecostalism has shown greater vitality than any other Christian movement, and now has from twelve million to fifteen million followers; of these two million live in the United States, grouped into thirty-five different denominations.[8] In Latin America they make up the largest religious group after Catholicism. In Scandinavia they are the most closely united body outside the established Churches. In Italy two thirds of all Protestants are Pentecostalists. And so forth.

After having long had the reputation for being aggressive and going to extremes, they have corrected many of their excesses and, unlike the sects (Adventists, Jehovah's Witnesses, etc.), they now participate in the ecumenical dialogue. David du Plessis, a Pentecostalist, was an observer at the Second Vatican Council. In addition, a dialogue between Catholics and Pentecostalists was begun officially in 1972. In June 1973 the second meeting was held at Rome, at the headquarters of the Secretariat for Christian Unity;

the conclusions signed by both parties show a good measure of agreement between them.[9]

## 2. NEO-PENTECOSTALISM

Neo-Pentecostalism is the reappearance of the same experience within the more traditional Christian confessions: the Episcopalian (in California, since 1958), the Lutheran (in the United States, 1962), the Presbyterian, and the Catholic (1967).

Two things are characteristic of this renaissance. The first is that it began *within* each of these Churches in response to the Church's needs and aspirations. The second is that the new Pentecostal groups have remained faithful to their respective Churches.

In March 1967, after the first outpouring of the Holy Spirit at Notre Dame and its manifestation in glossolalia, an old missionary asked some of those involved: "Now that you have received the Holy Spirit, when do you plan to leave the Catholic Church?" Those he questioned were amazed at his reaction, since the only important effect of their experience was that they felt themselves better Catholics for it. Edward O'Connor insisted on this last point in his 1967 article:

> In the Protestant world, the Pentecostal movement has often led people to separate from their parent churches and found new ones. The Catholic Pentecostal movement has manifested no such tendencies: On the contrary, it has greatly deepened the attachment of its members to the Church. They have a livelier appreciation and heightened reverence for the Church's institutions. They welcome the presence of priests at their meetings as an assurance against doing anything which would be incompatible with the teaching or practice of the Church. They do not regard their prayer meetings as a substitute for the liturgy; in fact, many of the leaders of the movement have also been enthusiastic promotors of the liturgy.[10]

The new wave of Pentecostalism promises to be a third ecumenical force in the Christian world by the very fact that it is not an *institution* competing with other institutions, yet does not share the rejection of or contempt for institutions that is so widespread in our day. It may well be able to work from within for the revitalization of Christianity in its entirety (institutions included).

The concord between the charismatic movement and ecclesiastical institutions even takes paradoxical forms. While the confessions most opposed to institutionalization (Evangelical, Methodist, Baptist) have remained pretty much closed to Pentecostalism,[11] this last has flourished in the most highly institutionalized Churches: Episcopal, Lutheran, Presbyterian. It has undergone its most rapid expansion and been given its warmest welcome in the Roman Catholic Church, that is, in the most monolithic of Churches and the one that might have been expected to be most allergic to Pentecostalism. It is also in that body that the pentecostals are most ardently and deeply attached to their Church.

Outsiders are amazed at this phenomenon, and David Wilkerson predicted in 1973 that it would not last.[12] It is nonetheless a fact that Neo-Pentecostalism has thus far met with no official opposition in Catholicism. On the contrary, it has shown itself to be a new source of strength for the Church at a time when rebellion and protest are in full swing and disturbing all the Churches.[13]

## 3. How Do the Bishops and the Pope React?

The late Bishop Alexander Zaleski of Lansing, Michigan, was assigned by the National Conference of Catholic Bishops to look into the movement. On November 14, 1969, he issued a favorable report and gave the following reasons for his judgment:

> There are many indications that this participation [in the Pentecostal movement] leads to a better understanding of the role the Christian plays in the Church. Many have experienced progress in their spiritual life. They are attracted to the reading of the Scriptures and a deeper understanding of their faith.[14]

The report also emphasized the renewal of Catholic devotions in some of the groups, especially devotion to the Real Presence and to the rosary. It thus confirmed what Edward O'Connor had been saying in 1967. The only recommendation the bishop made was that the Church be on guard against possible deviations, especially the substitution of religious experience for doctrine.

Later on, the Theological Commission of the English Episcopate issued a report that was likewise favorable, and Archbishop Dwyer, chairman of the commission, authorized its publication.[15]

At their meeting of April 14–18, 1975, the eighty-eight Canadian bishops approved of the renewal, while noting its dangers. But "no movement has ever been without its difficulties" I was told in July 1974 by two bishops in charge of these matters.

A number of bishops have acquired personal experience of the charismatic renewal. Chief among them is Cardinal Suenens,[16] who chaired the international congresses at Notre Dame in 1973 and 1974, and, with Cardinal Roy, the first congress at Quebec (eight thousand people in June 1974). In addition to numerous interviews on the charismatic movement, Suenens has published a pastoral letter on the subject (1973)[17] and, more recently, a book.[18]

The leaders of the charismatic movement in thirty-four countries met at Grottaferrata (near Rome), October 9–13, 1973. On this occasion Pope Paul VI received thirteen representatives of the movement in an audience on October 10. He told them that the movement was a source of joy for him and urged upon them a vigilant discernment of spirits.[19]

Two months later (December 21, 1973), addressing the College of Cardinals, the Pope said:

> The fresh breath of the Spirit . . . has come to awaken latent energies within the Church, to stir up dormant charisms, and to infuse a sense of vitality and joy. It is that sense of vitality and joy which makes the Church youthful and relevant in every age, and prompts her to joyously proclaim her eternal message to each new epoch.[20]

We may generalize and say that the Pope's theological reflections on the Holy Spirit, as voiced on various occasions, show a surprising likeness to those of the charismatic movement (the more important passages from his addresses will be given below). Confirmation of this harmony came at the International Congress in Rome at Pentecost 1975. The charismatics made a deep impression on all by the quality of their unbroken prayer during the long waits in the Basilica of St. Peter, before the Pontiff's Mass on Pentecost, and before the audience on the next day. The prayer was characterized by prophesying, singing, and a very low-keyed speaking in tongues.

In his address to the participants in the Congress, the Pope said that he saw in the movement "an opportunity for the Church," but added that a sustained effort at discernment was required in order to profit by the opportunity. Speaking extempore in Italian at the end of the audience, he applied the word "charismatic" to the movement for the first time.

## Pertinent Texts of Pope Paul VI

Audience of November 29, 1972 (*Osservatore Romano*, November 30, 1972): The Church "needs the Holy Spirit . . . who is the source of her charisms and her songs. . . . The Church needs to experience the praying voice of the Holy Spirit rising, like tears, out of her inmost being. For the Holy Spirit acts in our stead, praying in us and for us 'with groanings which cannot be expressed in speech,' as St. Paul teaches us. The Spirit expresses what we ought to say, for, when left to ourselves, we do not know how to pray as we ought."

Audience of May 23, 1973 (*Osservatore Romano*, May 24, 1973): "We ask you to think of the proclamation of the Holy Year as inspired by the Holy Spirit. . . . We must all open ourselves to the mysterious inspiration of the Holy Spirit, an inspiration that has now become identifiable to some extent. It is no accident that the Holy Year will be beginning on Pentecost in the local Churches, for all believers are being invited to set out on a new and authentically 'pneumatic,' that is, charismatic, journey . . . toward the new goals of Christian history."

Audience of June 6, 1973 (*Osservatore Romano*, June 7, 1973): "The Christology and especially the ecclesiology of the Council must be supplemented by a new study of and devotion to the Holy Spirit. This is an indispensable complement to the teaching offered us by the Council."

Audience of October 10, 1973 (*Osservatore Romano*, October 11, 1973). The translation in *New Covenant* 3, No. 5 (November 1973), p. 5, gives the Pope's extempore words of welcome to the representatives from the Grottaferrata meeting: "We are very interested in what you are doing. We have heard so much about what is happening among you. And we rejoice. We have many questions to ask you but there is no time." The following words, which the Pope read, appeared in *Osservatore Romano*: "We rejoice with you, dear friends, at the renewal of the spiritual life manifested in the Church today, in different forms and in various environments. Certain common notes appear in this renewal: the taste for deep prayer, personal and in groups, a return to contemplation and an emphasizing of praise of God, the desire to devote oneself completely to Christ, a great availability for the calls of the Holy Spirit, more assiduous reading of Scripture, generous brotherly devotion, the will to make a contribution to the service of the Church. In all that, we can recognize the mysterious and discreet work of the Spirit, who is the soul of the Church."

Address to the College of Cardinals, December 21, 1973: cited above (cf. note 20).

Audience of October 16, 1974 (*Osservatore Romano*, October 17, 1974): "It is absolutely necessary that the miracle of Pentecost continue throughout the history of the Church and the world. The gift of the Spirit must continue to be given in its two forms. This means, first, that the Spirit is given for the sanctification of men. This is the basic and indispensable gift, since by it man becomes an object of God's love (grace here 'makes pleasing' [*gratum faciens*], as the theologians put it). Second, the Spirit enriches men with special prerogatives we call 'charisms' (or graces 'given without merit' [*gratis datae*]), that are ordered to the good of the neighbor and especially to the good of the community of believers (cf. St. Thomas Aquinas, *Summa Theologiae* I–II, q. 3, a. 4). There is much talk of charisms today; it is a complex and sensitive subject. We can only desire a new outpouring not only of grace but of the charisms that are still being given to the Church of God in our day (cf. Cardinal Suenens' recent book *A New Pentecost?*)." At this point the Pope laid aside his prepared address and spoke extempore for several minutes on the subject of charisms.

# Chapter 3

---

# "BAPTISM IN THE SPIRIT"
# AND
# "CHARISMS"

The Pentecostal movement is characterized by a spiritual experience the specific traits of which are easily recognizable amid the great variety of persons and circumstances.

The experience usually presupposes that the subject desires it and prays for it and that the group intercedes for the individual, often while informally laying hands on him or her. The experience has two parts. One is an interior transformation, which is called "baptism in the Spirit" or "the outpouring of the Spirit." The other is external and has a sign value: namely, the *charisms*, that is, the exercise of the *gifts* of the Spirit in the service of the Church.

Both components of the total experience have been challenged. Some people fear that the baptism in the Spirit is being opposed to sacramental baptism, and the charisms to ecclesiastical authority. These, then, are the key points; we must try to approach them objectively and shed some light on them.

## 1. "BAPTISM IN THE SPIRIT" OR "OUTPOURING OF THE SPIRIT"?

Since we are dealing here with phenomena of concrete experience, we must listen first to those who have had the experience, whether in the early Christian community or in our own day.

## DESCRIPTION

We have already heard the testimony of Agnes Ozman, the first to have the experience in modern times. According to her, "it was as though rivers of living water were proceeding from my inmost being." There are the very words Jesus used in promising the Spirit, as recorded in St. John's Gospel (7:38; cf. 4:14).

According to one of the first three Pittsburgh pioneers, "it was just like I was being plunged down into a great sea of water, only the water was God, the water was the Holy Spirit."[1] Here the image is reversed: The water does not flow within the believer, but instead the believer is immersed in the water. But these are only two sides of one and the same symbol, and are quite in harmony with one another since water forms both an internal and an external environment for living creatures.

In a similar way, St. Paul can invert the basic formulas expressing inclusion: We are in Christ, and Christ is in us; we are in the Spirit (Rm. 8:9), and the Spirit dwells in us (Rm. 8:9, 11; 1 Co. 3:6; 6:19; 1 Tm. 1:14). Both formulas occur together in Romans 8:9: "Your interests . . . are in the spiritual, since the Spirit of God has made his home in you." The fact that the inclusion works both ways simply shows the limitations of the spatial image as such; the image must be interpreted in terms of presence and immanence, not of container and contained. (Note that physical life can be regarded as originating in the biosphere but also as springing up from within.)

To the Christian who has received the sacrament of baptism, "baptism in the Spirit" does not bring anything objectively new but simply a renewal in the way he lives the faith that he has already accepted. This point is emphasized by the Pittsburgh charismatic whom we quoted just above:

All in all it is not a new experience. It is not a revolutionary experience because it reaffirmed all the things which I'd been trying to hold on to for years and to affirm for so many years: my appreciation of Scripture, my appreciation of the eucharist, my appreciation of praying and working with other people. The difference is that it seems to me that everything is easier and more spontaneous and comes from within. . . . A much more spontaneous welling up of these aspirations and this power from within. . . . More power in a word than there ever was before.

And this has lasted and endured. It can be lessened or weakened by lack of faith because I am sure that God doesn't work despite us. We have to cooperate with him and let him act, let him have his own way because there is nothing automatic, nothing mechanical, nothing magical, nothing superstitious about it. It is still the old-fashioned Christian life which was first taught to me when I was a child, and yet it has a certain new dimension, a new strength and a new power and interiority which it did not have before, for which I thank him with my whole heart.[2]

Ralph Keifer, the first Catholic who was baptized in the Spirit, saw his experience as a repetition of what he had read in the New Testament: "This [speaking in tongues] seemed to be more in line with what I had come to expect of New Testament Christianity."[3]

More recent testimonies express the same ideas we find voiced by the American witnesses, despite the great variety of ways in which the ideas are formulated, depending on persons, cultures, and circumstances. As one example out of many, we may quote the account given by Brigitte Gauthier:

In my experience the "outpouring of the Spirit" was a vital encounter with the Lord. Despite the group around me I was conscious only of the Lord and myself, and the Lord was waiting for me to give myself completely to him. I wept as I yielded to him, and I understood that all things exist through him and that my whole life could be under his guidance if I accepted him. The experience really meant a new start for me. . . . It gave me an ardent desire to meet him in personal prayer, to *praise* him and not just be always *asking* him for things. He made me see that the Spirit prays in me and asks only that I be docile to him. The Lord also opened up for me the world of communal prayer, the prayer of Christ's body united to his Spirit.[4]

## ANALYSIS

It is impossible to analyze this gift "without seeming either banal or academic because they [its effects] are nothing other than what Christianity has always preached and promised."[5] Descriptions therefore tend to lay an artificial emphasis on anything that seems unusual, or else they become strings of commonplaces. Commonplaces, however, do not sit well with people in an age that is in reaction against the abuse of words.

The most important thing for the reader of the next few pages is that he should try to see how in the testimonies of the charismatics, words have ceased to be trite and have recovered their original vitality. We shall proceed, as far as possible, from the superficial elements of the experience to the more profound.

To begin with, the experience is *not ecstatic* or even extraordinary. There are numerous testimonies to this effect, for example, this one from a young wife: "The Holy Spirit did not bring about any spectacular change in our life; he simply transformed everything."[6]

The outpouring of the Spirit does indeed usually leave a deep, often emotional impression, sometimes to the point of causing tears. But that is not the essential thing. Far more important, as many testify, is the serenity and peace the experience brings. In other words, the emotional element is only an epiphenomenon of a deeper change.

There is a new sense of the presence of God, who makes himself felt even outside the field of clear consciousness. Inhibitions disappear, energies are liberated, dissociations are eliminated, and an inner harmony is restored. It is in this area especially that the surprisingly widespread "charism of healing" operates, that is, it is much concerned with the recovery of psychological and physical balance, due to a new personal and social integration of the individual. But the healing, be it noted, is accomplished by and for God.

All this is, in fact, regarded by the charismatics as a manifestation of the "power of God." "Power," a word that occurs frequently in the testimonies of the charismatics, is a recurring word in the New Testament; the Greek for it is *dynamis*. In modern English, of course, "power" tends to be an ambivalent word, since it may easily have worldly overtones of possessiveness and domination. We might say, therefore, that the person feels within him the "strength" or the "dynamic energy" of the Spirit (cf. Lk. 4:14; Ac. 1:8; 6:8; etc.).

This strength and light manifest themselves in many ways. We might mention, first, a new attraction to *prayer*, especially prayer of praise and thanksgiving. It is a prayer in which the entire person, including the emotive and motive powers, is involved.

The body spontaneously takes part in this prayer, the hands, for example, opening and then lifting. Charismatic groups have rediscovered the prayer posture of the first Christians as it may still be seen on the walls of the catacombs, the posture that the liturgy still prescribes for the priest at Mass and that becomes so awkward if it is not animated by an interior attitude. The charismatics (like many other people today) have also rediscovered the various kinds of prostrations that were practiced until quite recently in the liturgy: prostration full-length on the ground; the profound bow made while kneeling, in which the body draws itself together, and from which it will then rise like the seed that has been sown in the earth. These various postures are not imposed from without nor regulated like movements in a ballet. They proceed rather from within, according to circumstances and the dispositions of the individual. They help to make the body an integral part of prayer, and this is important for Western man, who has become so much the victim of dissociation.

We may add that while the disciplines practiced in the Eastern religions begin with the learning of bodily postures in order thereby to foster prayer, in the charismatic movement the spirit leads and the body follows.

A further point with regard to prayer is that personal prayer and communal prayer, which Christians have tended often to put into separate categories, are brought into harmony and feed one another.

A second manifestation is that the taste for and the understanding of Scripture are deepened. Thus Joseph Fichter's sociological study showed that all charismatics read the Bible more than they did before.[7]

One college student, after receiving the "baptism of the Holy Spirit," as it is sometimes called (Ac. 1:5), experienced such a keen desire to read the Bible that he spent two hours a day at it for the following week, and has continued to read an hour a day for the two months that have since elapsed. A woman who —after a period of great anguish—had been filled by the Holy Spirit with great peace of soul tells how she sat down to read the Bible the next morning as soon as her husband and children had left for work and for school. It had long been her habit to read one chapter every day, but this day she continued right on reading until it was time to prepare supper.[8]

This taste for Scripture extends to liturgical prayer, as this recent French testimony (personal communication) shows: "I had never understood the psalms even though I had been reciting them daily in my breviary for fifty years. Now they are full of transparent meaning for me."

A third manifestation is a new love of the sacraments, including penance. During the charismatic meeting at Laval University in Quebec in June 1974, attended by eight thousand people, the confessionals were busy all night long. Those attending wanted a personal confession, which implied, for them, counsel and spiritual healing. Several hundred priests worked ceaselessly to provide this service, some of them not leaving the confessional throughout the night.

The Fichter survey found that a large majority receive communion more regularly than before, visit the Blessed Sacrament more regularly, etc.[9]

Fourth, the charismatics experience a new vitality in their "love of neighbor," to use a phrase that has unfortunately grown trite for many. A religious involved in the movement told me:

> People are renewed in their relations with others; prejudices vanish, and so does diffidence. They acquire the ability to deal anew with matters over which men dispute; this applies to the "ecumenical" sphere, in the broad sense of the term "ecumenical." For example, there is a radical conquest of antisemitism.

In short, the capacity for friendship, acceptance, and service is widened and deepened. Edward O'Connor had observed this back in 1967,[10] and the communities I have visited bear him out. They inspire one to say of them what was said of the early Christians: "See how they love one another!" It is this deep sense of sharing that has given rise to communities in which resources are pooled and all members take part in the projects.

We must mention here something that visitors find striking. It is that charismatics embrace as brothers and sisters, ignoring all barriers of race or sex. But it is an orderly show of affection, the kind to be seen in a healthy family that is well able to distinguish between eroticism and affection (whereas both the emotionally rigid person and the neurotic tend to confuse the two). Once again, what we have here is the resurgence of an ancient practice that had become codified, stylized, and hieraticized in the kiss of peace which, until the Council, was the prerogative of the clergy. But such a gesture is meaningful only when it is the manifestation of authentic brotherhood.

Lives change when the great event of the Spirit's outpouring occurs, and men bear witness to the change. At Cap Rouge I listened to the story of a former drug addict, a happy, bearded fellow whose evangelical manner of life would remind you of Francis of Assisi and his first companions. His is by no means an isolated case.

The experience has even led to domestic reconciliations. At one of the Notre Dame congresses someone told me: "We had already begun divorce proceedings. But then we found each other again." A new ability to love makes reunion possible when egotism had caused separation.

Nor is the love in question a love only for other charismatics. All the authentic groups have overcome the temptation to live in an ivory tower; the love they practice is the *agapē* of Scripture, the love that acknowledges no limits but is open to all. For this reason, charismatic groups do much to serve those whom society rejects: thieves, alcoholics, drug addicts; in this they imitate David Wilkerson, one of the movement's inspiring figures.

At the beginning of Lent 1973, a group in Paris under the leadership of B. M. Le Braz "received" in prayer "an urgent invitation from the Spirit," similar to those attested in the Acts of the Apostles (for example, 13:2), bidding them: "Go and share the graces you have received with the very poor."[11] Thereupon the members of the group spontaneously went to contact the attic dwellers of the Latin Quarter: the old and the young who were hidden away up there so that those on the other floors might not have their peace of conscience disturbed.

## SHOULD WE SPEAK OF "BAPTISM IN THE SPIRIT?"

"Baptism in the Spirit" was the formula that Ralph Keifer spontaneously used right from the beginning, during the famous weekend at Duquesne University in February 1967. He used it "seriously, yet with a bright smile on his face," says Karen Sefcik, who was there.[12] The formula "baptism in the Spirit" (not "baptism of the Spirit"), which has been used in classical Pentecostalism, is based on Scripture. The first example there is the words of John the Baptist: "I baptize you in water. . . . he will baptize you in the Holy Spirit." The saying is found in all four Gospels, but in slightly different forms.

Mark 1:8 has the dative case here; a literal translation would be "with water . . . with holy spirit," or, as some would prefer, "by means of water . . . by means of holy spirit" (the nouns having no definite article before them). Matthew 3:11, Luke 3:16, and John 1:33 have the Greek preposition *en* ("in"): "in water . . . in holy spirit." Mark's formula makes the Spirit the *agent;* that of the other evangelists makes him the *divine milieu* in which Christians are immersed.

Matthew and Luke add: "and in fire"; the clause is found in a very old manuscript tradition.[13] "Fire" contrasts, of course, with "water," but a complementarity is intended. In the biblical tradition water is the primordial element and the source of life (Gn. 1:1). Fire, on the other hand, is the eschatological element.

Given the general significance of water, *baptism* and *birth* become synonymous. Epiphanius of Salamis says: "The Lord came to beget you from Spirit and water."[14] To be baptized, then, means to be reborn of water and the Spirit (Jn. 3:5; cf. 1 Jn. 1:5; 5:8; and Jn. 19:30–34). Images and poetic symbols must be understood in terms not only of the material things they directly denote but also of the existential realities they signify.

According to Acts 1:5, Jesus repeats the promise of baptism in the Spirit that John had earlier made: "John baptised *with* water but you, not many days from now, will be baptised with [literally: *in*] the Holy Spirit." Luke identifies this "baptism" with the event on Pentecost, where fire is the operative sign. On this occasion, tongues of fire symbolize the action of the Spirit who anoints the disciples—men and women alike—as they wait in the upper room. The transformation that takes place in these individuals finds its first expression in an outburst of praise of God. Baptism in the Spirit is thus inseparable from the charisms and specifically from praise of God "in foreign tongues." To this last point we shall return in the next chapter.

The same favor is bestowed upon Cornelius, a pagan military officer, and on his whole household. When Peter hears them "speaking strange tongues and proclaiming the greatness of God," he realizes that Pentecost has been repeated here: "Could anyone refuse the water of baptism to these people, now they have received the Holy Spirit just as much as we have?" (Ac. 10:46–47). Later on, when justifying his conduct, he insists again on the sameness of the gift:

> I had scarcely begun to speak when the Holy Spirit came down on them *in the same way as it came on us* at the beginning, and I remembered that the Lord has said, "John baptised with water, but you will be *baptised* with [literally: *in*] *the Holy Spirit*." I realised then that God was giving them *the identical thing he gave to us* when we believed in the Lord Jesus Christ; and who was I to stand in God's way? (Ac. 11:15–17).

### OBJECTIONS

There has been a deal of criticism of the expression "baptism in the Spirit." The charismatics, for their part, have heard the objections with the receptivity and humility that are characteristic of them. Thus Simon Tugwell, one of the movement's theologians, goes so far as to say: " 'Baptism in the Spirit' " is a term "which is, unfortunately, in my opinion, unacceptable in the last analysis, being exegetically unsound, theologically confusing, and very risky pastorally."[15]

The following are the principal objections on which this and similar judgments are based:

1. The six New Testament texts use the *verb* "*baptize*" and not

the *noun "baptism."* The latter may suggest that "baptism in the Spirit" means "the action of immersing in the Spirit."

2. This use of the word "baptism" is ambiguous. It may very well compete with, downgrade, and obscure the proper sense of "baptism" as meaning the first of the seven sacraments. There is danger of forgetting that there is only one baptism (Ep. 4:5). Francis Sullivan agrees with Tugwell's overall judgment for the very important reason that "whether they [the charismatics] explicitly draw this conclusion or not, their use of this biblical term ["baptism in the Spirit"] implies the corollary that most Christians have not been 'baptized in the Holy Spirit.' "[16]

### EXAMINATION OF OBJECTIONS

These arguments seem impressive to many and must therefore be examined if we are to proceed in an orderly fashion.

1. The first is in fact trifling and may even seem laughable when we recall how readily the traditional language of the Church and its theology has turned everything into a "substance."

2. The second argument reflects a praiseworthy concern not to cause confusion with regard to the sacrament of baptism. It must be said, however, that Scripture and tradition show no scruples in this regard and no desire to reserve the word "baptism" for such strictly univocal use. The New Testament in fact uses the word to signify three stages in the history of salvation and of God's gifts to men.

There is, first, the baptism with water for the sake of conversion, which John the Baptist administers in order to prepare for the coming kingdom. Second, there is the passion and death of Jesus, which he himself speaks of as a baptism wherewith he must be baptized (Mk. 10:38–39; 12:50; cf. Rm. 6:3–4). At a third stage there is baptism in the Spirit, which signifies either Christian initiation in its entirety (1 Co. 12:13; cf. Jn. 3:5; 1 Jn. 1:5; 5:8) or the most striking aspect of the Spirit's manifestation (Ac. 11:16; 19:2).

These three stages correspond to three successive moments in the communication of sacramental grace: sign, reality-sign, and grace-reality (these three terms are meant as translations of the Latin words *sacramentum, res et sacramentum,* and *res,* to which we shall return later in our discussion).

From the twelfth century until fairly recently it was customary to describe religious life as a "second baptism." The meaning was that those who adopted this way of life corresponded fully to the demands inherent in their sacramental baptism. Such a use of "baptism" comes close to that we now find in the charismatic movement.

The older catechisms also spoke of a "baptism of blood" (the martyrs were "baptized" in their own blood) and a "baptism of desire," by which was meant the catechumen's desire of baptism, a desire by reason of which he was already justified and in communion with God before receiving sacramental baptism.

It may not seem worth devoting further discussion to the phrase "baptism in the Spirit," inasmuch as Catholic Neo-Pentecostalists now avoid it in principle (at least in France) and are attempting to give currency instead to "outpouring of the Spirit" and similar expressions that are not suspect.

Even so, we cannot stop here, but must pursue the matter. There are several reasons for doing so. The first is to gain clarity on the point. The second is that the phrase "baptism in the Spirit" will not simply disappear, but on the contrary will continue to be widely used.[17] The third is that the whole discussion needs to be properly channeled; it has tended to fasten on words while losing sight of the realities involved. The objections to "baptism in the Spirit" on the grounds that it is a substitute for or supplement to sacramental baptism, or even a kind of "superbaptism," have disturbed some charismatics, but their response has been to look for justification at the verbal level, to the detriment of the ecumenical spirit.

For example, the attempt has been made to justify Catholic Pentecostalism by systematically contrasting it with classical Pentecostalism; in the process, the latter becomes a scapegoat on whose back all errors are laid. In fact, however, the Pentecostalists have far greater respect for the sacrament of baptism than Catholics realize. For proof of this, we need only turn to their official writers. Ernest S. Williams, for example, who was for twenty years superintendent general of the Assemblies of God, states quite clearly in his *Systematic Theology* that the Holy Spirit is present in the Christian who has not been "baptized in the Spirit" and that this latter formula refers to a limited experience that is not necessary for salvation, even though God wishes all to have it.[18]

Any real disagreement with classical Pentecostalism concerns nuances that it is not within the scope of this book to discuss. At bottom there are divergent pastoral approaches; of these we shall speak later on. The point we must emphasize here is that it would be unjust as well as unecumenical to represent non-Catholic Pentecostalists as guilty of all the errors the Catholic Pentecostalists claim to be avoiding.

## THE BASIC PROBLEMS

Exegetes and theologians have called attention to some more basic problems. The Calvinist exegete, James D. G. Dunn, for example, has given us a penetrating analysis of the biblical side of the question. He reaches two rather blunt conclusions, one opposed to classic Pentecostal theology, the other to classic Catholic theology.

In Dunn's view, *baptism in the Spirit* was originally the chief element in conversion-initiation, so that only those who had received this baptism could be called Christians. St. Paul says plainly that "unless you possessed the Spirit of Christ you would not belong to him" (Rm. 8:9). This is so because the manifestation of the Spirit is the sign of entry into the messianic age.

*Water baptism*, on the other hand, does not refer, in the New Testament, to our sacrament of baptism. It is neither "a channel of grace" nor a source of "spiritual blessings," but is simply a preparatory rite implying acceptance by the Church and, on the neophyte's part, at most an expression of faith and conversion.[19]

Dunn offers three main arguments to ground his conclusion with regard to water baptism. First, the New Testament sometimes uses "baptism" and "baptize" in a *metaphorical* sense (Mk. 10:38; Lk. 12:50). Second, it *contrasts* water baptism and baptism with the Spirit (Ac. 1:5; 11:16). Third, it sees them as two *different* things. Baptism in the Spirit is received *after* water baptism by the Samaritans (Ac. 8:15–17) and also, in a sense, by the disciples of John whom Paul discovered at Ephesus (Ac. 19:3–6). On the other hand, it *precedes* water baptism for the centurion Cornelius (Ac. 10:44–46; 11:15–16).

Catholic scholars writing more recently have generally accepted Dunn's first conclusion, that the reception of the Spirit is part of Christian initiation, as may be seen, for example, from Paul's reaction to those "disciples" who had not received the Holy Spirit (Ac. 19:1–7).[20]

These scholars reject, however, Dunn's second conclusion, in which he dissociates sacramental water baptism and baptism in the Spirit. Their position is that water baptism is a complete initiation and bestows the Spirit, and that, in accordance with established teaching, we must not confuse the basic rite of water baptism with the secondary and specialized phenomenon of baptism in the Spirit. All these writers link baptism in the Spirit with water baptism, although their descriptions of the relationship vary slightly. Some speak of a "*release* of the Spirit" in the soul where he has dwelt since baptism (S. Clark; K. McDonnell); others of an "*actualization* of the gifts already received in potency" through baptism (K. and D. Ranaghan; S. Clark), or of the "*manifestation*" of baptism (S. Tugwell), or of a "reviviscence" of the gift of the Spirit received in baptism and confirmation (H. Caffarel), or of an upsurge of docility to the grace given in baptism and confirmation (D. J. Gelpi).[21]

There is a shared concern behind all these explanations, and it is entirely laudable. It is the desire not to separate but to link the outpouring of the Spirit with sacramental baptism, and to insist that the grace given by baptism in the Spirit is not a different sacramental grace. We must also say, however, that this praiseworthy desire not to separate baptism in water and baptism in the Spirit has led to an unnuanced identification of the two.

We must be careful here not to try to harmonize the formulas of the Bible with the formulas of Scholastic theology. The two languages reflect divergent perspectives and conceptualizations; any attempt to treat them as identical can only be highly artificial. Some theologians, for example, identify baptism in the Spirit with confirmation, the traditional sacrament of the Holy Spirit, while others identify it with baptism, which already bestows the Holy Spirit and does so without reserve. But it is not permissible thus simplistically to equate the formulas of the Bible with much later formulas that attempt to explicate the language of Scripture within the framework of a sacramental theology that is quite different in inspiration from that of the New Testament.

We should therefore be suspicious of abstract theories that only blur our vision of reality. The following three points ought to be kept clearly in mind.

1. The rich but undifferentiated treasure of New Testament formulations should not be hastily assimilated to the later formulas of sacramental theology. To give but a single example: What are we

to make, in Scholastic terms, of the practice of "being baptized for the dead," to which Paul refers in 1 Co. 15:29?

*Baptize* and *baptism*, in the New Testament, carry a heavy freight of symbolism and signify a dynamic element in the history of salvation. There is the baptism of Jesus in the *water* of the Jordan; this baptism is the prototype of the later sacramental rite. There is his baptism in *death* (Mk. 10:38; Lk. 12:50); this baptism is the prototype of our radical transformation through burial and resurrection with Jesus Christ (Rm. 6:3-4). Finally, there is the eschatological baptism in the *Spirit*, whom Jesus gives to men through his death (Jn. 19:30; 20:22), when his own work is done, so that the Spirit may bring that work to fruition until the return of Jesus at the end. But what Jesus thus gives us at the end of his earthly career is already present from the beginning of his public life, since he then turned his immersion in the waters of the Jordan into the prototype of baptism in the Spirit (Mt. 3:11). This symbolic theology has depths we often do not suspect, and it can be explicitated and applied in many ways.

2. The rite of Christian initiation has taken quite varied forms in the course of the centuries, and the divergent usages have affected the theology of the rite. For example, there has been an evolution of the sign of baptism (immersion, pouring of water, sprinkling) and even of the accompanying formula (baptism in the name of the Lord Jesus, as in Ac. 2:38; 19:6; etc., or in the name of the Trinity, as in Mt. 28:19).

There has been, however, another and far more important evolution. Originally, Christian initiation meant (as it still means in the East) the conferring of the three sacraments of baptism, confirmation, and the Eucharist. There came a time, however, when confirmation and the Eucharist were put off until later. The separation of the three caused confirmation to be regarded as effecting the pneumatic or "Spirit-ual" aspect of initiation, but this development proved embarrassing for theologians. How can it be said that confirmation is "the sacrament of the Holy Spirit" when the Spirit has already been given in baptism and cannot have been given only partially?

In the attempt to meet this difficulty, many theories of confirmation have been elaborated: It confers an "adult faith" or a "militant" faith; it confirms the commitments made in baptism; it gives the mission and power to bear witness (cf. Ac. 1:8). The best (overall) explanation is one that relates baptism and confirmation to Easter and Pentecost, respectively. But even this explanation in the light of salvation history is far from providing a clear solution to all problems.

The conclusion we draw from all this is that the ambiguities people fear when they hear Catholic Neo-Pentecostalists talking of "baptism in the Spirit" are not as great as those present in contemporary sacramental theology. Why? Because the charismatic movement is using the language of Scripture itself and pointing to a problem that is not a problem of sacramental theology as such.

The important thing here is to concentrate our attention on God's plan, which has been implemented in quite different ways and forms by the Eastern and Western Churches over the centuries, somewhat as various vital functions are exercised by different organs in the course of biological evolution.

3. It is important to approach this whole question in a less theoretical fashion, and with our attention focused on the realities of Christian experience, which are too often hidden from view by theological superstructures.

We must realize the difference, even the contrast, between the situation in the New Testament and our own situation. The early Church was necessarily a Church of converts, men and women who accepted baptism out of personal conviction. In the course of time, however, the Church gradually moved to its present situation, in which the vast majority of baptisms are conferred upon those who are unaware of it (young children). In 1971, 92 per cent of Catholic baptisms were administered to children under seven years of age. This meant over 16 million such baptisms, as opposed to 1.3 million administered to those over seven years of age (most of the latter in Africa); if we look only at Europe, there were over 4 million infant baptisms, as compared with 24,227 baptisms of persons over seven (the latter amounting to less than 1 per cent of the total number of baptisms).

Theologians have worked out a justification for this practice of infant baptism. In the process they have tended more and more to equate baptism received by one unaware of it and baptism received from personal conviction. This means that until quite recently they played down the importance of faith and placed their whole emphasis on the "objective" effect of the sacramental rite, an effect that is independent of the free will of the person who consciously receives the sacrament. Theologians developed an ontology of the objective grace of baptism and paid no attention to the experience of the recipient.

Pursuing this line of thought, the theologians even exalted the marvelous presence of God in the pure and spotless soul of the baptized infant. From their point of view, the awakening of free will necessarily meant decadence. The ideal was death in the cradle! This notion was, of course, a consoling one in times when the rate of infant mortality was high, but it was also one-sided and played down Christian life in the interests of a formalism that is alien to the Gospel.

What made this practice acceptable and theologically coherent was the fact that in Christendom faith was effectively transmitted by parents, by the Church, and even by society at large, since the latter was in some measure Christian and still possessed a sacral quality. The practice could also be justified by appeal to the Apostles and the occasions when they baptized a whole household in which the head of the house was converted (Ac. 10:47; 16:33).

A new and more radical change has, however, recently occurred: Christendom has ceased to exist. Most Christians today live in a secularized world in which the faith is no longer transmitted as in the past and very many of those baptized as infants never become aware of their baptismal commitments.

The problem today, therefore, is this: What does baptism really mean in a Church in which the majority of the 680 million baptized Catholics on the books are not instructed in their faith or do not profess it or do not live it? We need think only of the catechetical situation in Latin America with its shortage of priests, or of the situation in France, which has a highly developed catechesis but in which, according to the studies of sociologists, 20 per cent of the baptized Catholics do not believe in the divinity of Jesus Christ, much less in the Resurrection. In the past, such failures in faith would have led to excommunication, but today these unbelieving Christians simply go on having their children baptized! The degeneration is continuing, and we must ask ourselves what it can mean to have "received the Spirit" when these words have no verifiable meaning at the level of awareness and life and human existence and when the environing world stimulates the baptized person to materialism rather than to faith.

The state of the baptized child may be compared to that of a child in its mother's womb. The latter does not breathe as yet, but it will breathe once it is born; if it doesn't, it will have been born dead. In the modern Church, children baptized before they know of it are no longer supported by the maternal womb of a Christian environment, since society is secularized and the family dechristianized. Faith and spiritual life are not necessarily awakened when the child becomes a conscious, autonomous being. When an analogous failure occurs at the moment of physical birth, those present use emergency methods to try to get the child breathing. Similarly, it is essential to get the breath of the Spirit going in the baptized if they are to live spiritually.

The Church did not, of course, need Pentecostalism to make her aware of this basic problem. We may even maintain that the awareness of the problem has always been the dominant motive behind Christian pastoral efforts. It was because of this problem that the Church transformed the rite of initiation by deferring first communion and confirmation until "the age of reason." The two sacraments thus became an opportunity for a fresh initiation, an effort to make the recipient aware of his Christianity and to evoke a commitment from him. Later, when the age for first communion was lowered from twelve to seven, the Church in France instituted the "solemn communion" at a later age, as a way of meeting the pastoral need. The whole purpose of these various moves was to enable those who had received baptism as infants to come into genuine contact with God by awakening faith and love in their hearts.

Ever since patristic times, the collective penance of Advent and Lent has had the same purpose in view. Easter week became a time for baptismal renewal. Later on, parish missions were instituted for the periodic revitalizing of the Catholics' faith.

"Baptism in the Spirit" meets the same pastoral need. It flourishes at a time when traditional means have proved inadequate or in need of supplementing. In this regard, Pentecostalism has drawn its inspiration from the experience and language of the early Church, which found itself in an analogous situation, since the first Christians lived and were vitalized by the Spirit in a non-Christian environment. There is also this difference, however: The environment of the early Church was pagan, and that meant religious; the modern Church exists in a secular, that is, atheistic world. The difference means a radically new problem.

Given our situation, we must be on guard against a theology that is really an ideology that hides reality from us. We must not let ourselves become like a man who refuses to look out his window but instead pulls down the blinds and paints a beautiful, idealized landscape on the inner side so that he can feast his eyes on it. Our real concern here must not be to develop a theology of baptism in the Spirit but to grasp the pastoral and theological meaning of this baptism as an experienced reality.

## PASTORAL SIGNIFICANCE

In the United States, baptism in the Spirit is often called an "experience."[22] In American usage, the word does not mean "a process of experimentation" (a meaning it might convey to a Frenchman), but rather "awareness of what is going on" (in this case, interiorly). The word should be used with some caution, however, inasmuch as it might tend to make baptism in the Spirit something sensible. Divine gifts of the sensible order may in fact be withdrawn for our good, at least temporarily, so that we may be forced to encounter God in the night of faith or trial.[23]

We may say, in less elegant but more accurate terms, that the purpose of baptism in the Spirit is to actualize, in an effective, dynamic, and constructive (that is, "edifying") way, the call to which the individual committed himself in baptism. The important thing, therefore, is not feelings but action: Love of God is exercised; it is not buried and reduced to the condition of the grains of wheat found two thousand years later in Egyptian tombs. For a long time it was said that these grains could germinate even now. This was untrue, however, for the long stay in the tomb had killed the life in the grain.

The Neo-Pentecostal movement is concerned with what has traditionally been called "conversion," by which is meant a "second conversion," that is, the act by which a Christian effectively turns to the living God. We can only be struck by the similarity between the conversion of Pascal and the conversion of modern charismatics (apart from the literary quality of the accounts the latter give!). In both cases there is a light-filled, warm, life-giving encounter with God; in both the recipients may be moved to tears (Pascal's "tears of joy," and the tears many charismatics say they shed).

### THEOLOGICAL SIGNIFICANCE

Is it possible, however, for the renewed experience of "baptism in the Spirit" to find a place and a meaning in traditional Catholic theology? Many people today are obsessed by this question.

Before attempting to answer it, we must be aware of certain limitations that have to be taken into account. For one thing, classical Catholic theology has dealt loosely with the Scriptures; as a result, some highly traditional interpretations of the Bible make no sense by modern exegetical standards. Above all, however, we must bear in mind that it would be artificial to harmonize the various theological traditions, no one of which exhausts the riches of God's gift. Harmonization here would simply be concordism.

The Pentecostalist theology of baptism reflects the effort to break away from formalism and from situations marked by decadence and thus in many respects unacceptable. The break takes the form of a return to the early practice of baptism by immersion, given to adults who show that they have truly been converted. The theology of baptism in the Spirit must be judged in the light of this vital project.

At the same time, however, it must be said that the experience of baptism in the Spirit, which is so rooted in biblical tradition, does indeed have a place in the most classical type of Catholic theology, and that no little light is shed on the experience by such a theology. There are several ways in which baptism in the Spirit can be related to the theological tradition.

### I

We may interpret it (with F. A. Sullivan) in the light of St. Thomas Aquinas' theology of the divine missions. St. Thomas asks: What are the consequences of "an invisible sending [of a divine Person] . . . with respect to an advance in virtue or an increase in grace?"[24] His answer:

Such an invisible sending is especially to be seen in that kind of increase of grace whereby a person moves forward into some new act or some new state of grace: as, for example, when a person moves forward into the grace of working miracles, or of prophecy, or out of the burning love of God offers his life as a martyr, or renounces all his possessions, or undertakes some other such heroic act.[25]

This sending implies, Sullivan adds, "a real *innovatio* of that person's relationship with the indwelling Spirit. Therefore it has to mean a more intimate and 'experiential' knowledge of God as present in the soul, a knowledge that 'breaks out' into more ardent love (cf. *Summa* I, q. 43, a. 5, ad 2)."[26]

This interpretation of the relation to the Spirit has the advantage that it accounts both for "baptism in the Spirit" and for the charisms, as well as for the vital link between these two aspects of the outpouring of the Spirit. However, "baptism in the Spirit" is implicitly sacramental in its vocabulary and therefore should be more specifically related to the theology of the sacraments. It may be related to the latter in two ways.

# II

It is possible to situate "baptism in the Spirit" first of all by relating it to the distinction between *opus operatum* and *opus operantis*. *Opus operatum* ("the work done") is the objective action embodied in the sacramental rite, independently of the recipient's faith. *Opus operantis* ("the action of the doer") is the action of the recipient in receiving the sacrament with faith and thereby profiting from it.

"Baptism of the Spirit" belongs on the side of the *opus operantis*, since its purpose is that sacramental baptism, so often *ineffective*, should become *effective;* that the sacrament that was as it were stillborn should become a sacrament of life; that the sign of condemnation (cf. 1 Co. 11:29) should become a sign of salvation.

The classical theology of the *opus operatum* has the advantage of emphasizing the irreversibility of the sacramental act. The person who has been baptized or married or ordained, even if he received the sacrament while in a state of serious sin, is irreversibly baptized, married, or ordained. It also highlights God's transcendence and fidelity and his sovereign action.

Yet the distinction is fearfully ambiguous and becomes false to the extent that the *opus operatum* (God's infallible action) becomes dissociated from its necessary correlative, the *opus operantis* or faith-inspired reception.

1. When a one-sided emphasis is put on the *opus operatum* in order to elaborate an ontology of God's gift that prescinds from the manner in which the subject receives it, the sacrament that is holy and effective is sometimes treated as being on the same level as the sacrament that is sacrilegious and ineffective. The sacrament is thus made to resemble a bit of magic. This is contrary to the Gospel, which teaches us that baptism brings a judgment with it. This is implied in the biblical image of fire that is associated with baptism (cf. Mt. 3:11; Lk. 3:15) and in the fact that the unworthy reception of the sacrament condemns the sinner (1 Co. 11:29). We will be judged on the basis of our lives, not of the sacramental formula; that is the meaning of the passage on judgment in Matthew 25.

2. Theologians object that if we dissociate and contrast the *opus operatum* and the *opus operantis*, we will mislead people into thinking that the fruit of the sacrament is man's doing (his *opus*) and not God's, which it really is. Such an objection is based on a misunderstanding that is not to be found in the main Scholastic tradition. The objectors fail to realize that the subject's action (*opus operantis*), his receptivity to God's gift, is itself entirely the work of God, in whom "we live, and move, and exist" (Ac. 17:28).

Evidently, then, classical teaching and catechesis contain ambiguities far more serious than any that may lurk in the biblical expression "baptism in the Spirit." Of course, all theological language is ambiguous. The important thing, today as in the past, is to avoid being victimized by the ambiguities; this is done by constantly referring to the realities of Christian experience, of which the Gospel is constantly reminding us.

# III

The experience of baptism in the Spirit can be interpreted at a still deeper level by relating it to some far more notable and more ancient theological categories. I am referring to three successive moments found in every sacrament (these in turn are related to the three phases in the history of salvation: the figures of what was to come; the fulfillment of these in Christ; and the fulfillment of them in believers, by the power of the Spirit).

The three moments bear Latin names: *sacramentum*, the sacramental sign or external rite; *res et sacramentum*, the effect which is also a sign, the effect that is independent of the recipient's dispositions and that also points to the final effect; and the *res*, or ultimate effect, that is, the sharing in divine life that is the purpose of the sacrament.

If we apply this distinction to baptism in the Spirit, we must say that baptism in the Spirit is the *res*, or ultimate effect, aimed at in the sacrament. And yet such a pigeonholing would itself be ambiguous. We may say, therefore, with greater accuracy, that the function and purpose of baptism in the Spirit is the effective accomplishment in a Christian's life of what baptism called for but to some extent did not accomplish.

According to the best classical theology, the *res* or "reality" or ultimate effect of the sacrament is something existential. It lies beyond the external rite (the sacramental sign) and beyond the irreversible incorporation into Christ's body, the Church (this incorporation is the effect that is also a sign). The ultimate effect is the love made possible by grace; in other words, it is the divine life that the Spirit pours out upon us, the communion with God that he initiates.

We must keep this fact before our minds. It will enable us to put our finger on the vital connection between baptism in the Spirit (or the outpouring of the Spirit) and the charisms, which are the second characteristic mark of the Pentecostal experience.

## 2. CHARISMS

### A. DESCRIPTION

The charisms are so closely connected, both in the Acts of the Apostles and in our own day, with the fundamental experience of the outpouring of the Spirit, and they have acquired such importance, that the movement as a whole is generally called simply the "charismatic" movement. One disadvantage of the name is that it seems to imply a monopoly of charisms, as Father Congar has pointed out.[27]

Here, once again, we must start with what really happens; that is, we must begin with the charisms as they are manifested in Pentecostal groups and especially at their prayer meetings.

## LEADERS

A leader who has no strict authority at his disposal gets the prayer meeting under way and sees to it that it progresses in an orderly fashion. He is chosen because he has a gift for this sort of thing and because the community recognizes the gift. Such leadership corresponds to the function of "presiding," of which Romans 12:8 speaks (cf. 1 Th. 5:12; 1 Tm. 3:4–5).

Need we worry that this charismatic function may derogate from the official ministry of priests and bishops? According to a fanciful description given me before I visited the Ann Arbor community, the latter was directed by "overseers" and "elders," titles that recalled the *episcopoi* and *presbyteroi* of the New Testament. The offices of overseer and elder were originally polyvalent and quite undefined, and not identifiable with what our modern bishops and priests actually do; nonetheless, the very titles roused fears that a charismatic hierarchy was being established, in competition with the official hierarchy. In point of fact, however, the Ann Arbor community does not use the title of "overseer," but speaks rather of "co-ordinators," "elders" (in the simple sense of "older"), and "servants."

It is nothing new for laypeople to preside over the common prayer and indeed over the whole life of groups. That has always been the situation in communities of religious women, of religious men who are not clerics, and of others. In the charismatic groups, moreover, responsibilities are carried out in an especially humble, communal, and nondirective style, in obedience to the norms of and the ministers responsible for the local parish and diocese. At Mass the priest clearly exercises the presidency that is his.

## PROPHETS

During a prayer meeting, some individuals speak in order to communicate to the others the interior lights God has given them. These inspirations often take form during the reading of Scripture or while others are speaking, and those who receive them have a sense that God wishes them to communicate these to the group at large. They express their thoughts at times in a style analogous to that of the Hebrew prophets when they would speak to Israel and end with the formula: "Thus says the Lord your God." The charismatic prophets, however, make no claim to be adding anything to revelation that is now complete. This, then, is what is meant by the charism of prophecy, a Greek word that means, literally, a "speaking in the name of . . ."[28]

The prophecies are generally short and often beautiful. Only rarely, however, have I jotted one down; here is one from Ann Arbor: "My children, yield to my love. You are wheat, and I wish to make bread of you so that others may be fed." The prophet makes the community aware of the living presence of God. Like the Old Testament prophet, he reminds the community of the covenant.

## TEACHING

At some meetings, time is set aside for those who have the charism of teaching and of giving their hearers a deeper understanding of some point of faith. Such teaching is given in a lively but more didactic fashion. At a meeting on June 19, 1974, at Ann Arbor, a good ten minutes was allotted to such an exposition, with the others present simply listening.

## DISCERNMENT

After each meeting, those who are recognized as having the charism of discernment gather to review the meeting and draw conclusions, so as to improve the next meeting. At the annual International Congress, discernment is based on a systematic consultation of the participants.[29]

## CHARISMS INDEFINITE IN NUMBER

Many other charisms (witnessing, for example) are exercised during a prayer meeting, and these meetings are not the only context in which charisms are exercised. Each individual, according to his capacity and the graces he has received, serves all ranks in very varied ways. At Ann Arbor, where about forty households are federated in a great community of over eight hundred people, I saw how impossible it would be to draw up a complete list of the charisms exercised, that is, of the many services rendered, daily or from time to time, in each household, and each specialized workshop, at the level of the two subcommunities, of the total community, of the parish, and of the city. Such services include service of the poor and the socially needy. All these services reflect the gifts and aptitudes, natural and supernatural, of the various individuals involved. They can, therefore, be legitimately called "charisms."

The large range of such charisms corresponds to what we are told in the New Testament, where we find eight lists of charisms, four in which the word "charism" is used (1 Co. 12:4–10, 28–31; Rm. 12:6–8; 1 P. 4:10) and four in which it is not used (1 Co. 14:6, 13; 14:26; Ep. 4:11; Mk. 16:17–18). The eight lists, in which twenty-four gifts are listed, are not simply repetitions one of the other, even though certain more important gifts, notably apostolate and prophecy, do occur in several lists.

## B. A REBIRTH

The rebirth of the "charisms" (a word long forgotten, and often suspected where remembered) is in keeping with the teaching of the Second Vatican Council, where the question was raised. Cardinal Ruffini tried to give it an honorable burial by claiming that these gifts, though mentioned in Scripture, belonged exclusively to the Church's past history. An address of Cardinal Suenens, however, presented the true doctrine based on Scripture and tradition. In consequence, the Council did justice to the charisms in its ground-laying *Dogmatic Constitution on the Church* (Nos. 4, 7, 12), its *Decree on the Apostolate of the Laity* (No. 3), and its *Decree on the Missionary Activity of the Church* (Nos. 4, 23).

The rebirth of the charisms did not take place, however, through an application of conciliar texts or even of the New Testament, nor was it the result of archaeological restoration. It came about, as in the early Church, because the Spirit was at work and because there was a need: the Spirit being the source of the charisms, and the organic needs of the Church being their determining purpose.

At the same time, the rebirth is in keeping with the reality we read of in the New Testament. So true is this that the New Testament texts shed a real light on the actual practice of Catholic Neo-Pentecostals, and vice versa. We have had constant evidence of this in the course of our investigation.

There is a partial identity between the charisms of the early Church and those of our own day, although the modalities may differ because the needs differ. Especially notable is the revival of prophecy, teaching, and discernment; healings, speaking in tongues, and interpretation (we shall be returning to these three below, in Chapters 4 and 5); and the works of mercy and charity.

## C. DEFINITION[30]

How are we to define the charisms? The Council was quite tentative in its approach and in fact ended up using the word in different ways. The *Dogmatic Constitution on the Church*, in No. 7, contrasts two types of gifts—hierarchic and charismatic—and seems to think of the latter as being preternatural. But in No. 12 it speaks of the charismatic gifts as "special graces" by which the Holy Spirit makes the faithful of every rank "fit and ready to undertake the various tasks or offices advantageous for the renewal and upbuilding of the Church, according to the words of the Apostle: 'The manifestation of the Spirit is given to everyone for profit' (1 Co. 12:7)."[31] In one of his articles, Edward O'Connor distinguishes two further senses of the word.[32]

Let us stick to the essential point. It is clear that the word "charism," which is derived from the Greek word *charis*, meaning "grace," signifies a freely given gift. Theological (and even biblical) usage distinguishes between sanctifying grace (*charis*), as the basic and essential gift, and the charisms (*charismata*), which relate to special functions. The charisms are freely given to a further degree, in that they are not part of the one necessary gift of grace, but are diverse gifts betowed upon various members for the building up of the Church.

### PURPOSE

Classical theology usually claimed that the charisms, as thus defined, did *not* have for their purpose *the good of the subject possessing them, but the good of others.* A careful reading of 1 Corinthians 12–14, however, suggests that we at least modify this claim. If the purpose of the charisms is edification (in a more than superficial sense: to edify means to build up), then some charisms are meant for the personal edification of the one who exercises them.

This is true, for example, of speaking in tongues, since, as St. Paul says, "The one with the gift of tongues talks for his own benefit" (1 Co. 14:4), in contrast to prophecy, which is "for the benefit of the community" (ibid.). Paul heightens this contrast to the point of suggesting that speaking in tongues is useless and disappointing to the community (1 Co. 14:6–11), while it may even be harmful to the unbeliever by making him think the community is a community of madmen (1 Co. 14:23).

The charism of celibacy has appeared at Ann Arbor (as it had at Taizé), and there is reason to think that, while this gift may be edifying to the community at large, it has a constructive value first and foremost for the person who lives it according to the Gospel. The witness and availability that spring from celibacy are really what "edifies" the community as a whole.

This flexible definition, freely given gift of the Spirit, meant for edification, seems to us quite adequate, and we will spare the reader any elaborate discussion of the various other definitions proposed.

### CHARACTERISTICS

The charisms can be described as follows:

1. They are *attributed to the Holy Spirit* by St. Paul (1 Co. 12:4, 7, 8), by the Acts of the Apostles, and by Vatican Council II (*Dogmatic Constitution on the Church*, Nos. 4, 7, 12, 21, 32), and are the *effective manifestation of his dynamic presence in the Church*, at the service of Christ's body and its mission in the world.

2. The charisms are *freely given*, and this in two senses: The Spirit is free to give them or not give them, and they are freely accepted, desired, or requested by those who receive them (cf. 1 Co. 12:31; 1 Tm. 3:1). Their gratuitous character is also shown in the generosity and creativity their exercise entails.

3. The charisms *relate to the whole of human reality*—individual

and collective, body and psyche—according to needs and commitments.

4. They do *not constitute a uniform and well-defined species, nor even a closed series*. We must therefore take with a grain of salt the widespread claim that the range of charisms has become much narrower since the time of the early Church. Not some but all of the charisms are to be exercised today, from A to Z.

But we should not be fooled by the "A to Z" image. The charisms do not constitute a pre-established set of gifts that was as it were programed into the computer on the first Pentecost. We must emphasize rather that the series is open-ended, that there is an unlimited number of tasks that Christian creativity can invent in response to an unlimited number of needs, and that new times call for new responses (to use the language of Jürgen Moltmann or even simply of Henri Bergson). The charisms are, so to speak, the cutting edge of the Church's eschatological advance. We must distrust a static or archaeological outlook in this area.

5. Charisms are not special prerogatives of the early Church but permanent gifts. They are the essential wellspring of the Church's life. This insight of Johann Adam Möhler, who renewed ecclesiology on the basis of the charisms, at the beginning of the nineteenth century, has today become common teaching.

6. *Nor are charisms the privilege of certain individuals*. According to St. Paul and Vatican II, each and every Christian is to exercise his charism or charisms.

7. Charisms should *not* be defined as *extraordinary gifts*, and it would be misleading and unhealthy to single out those that seem extraordinary, or those exceptional cases in which the exercise of charisms seems to involve the miraculous. To do so would be to risk emphasizing the accidental at the expense of the essential, the essential being the exercise of ordinary gifts within the normal framework of faith, hope, and charity.

8. The exercise of charisms often takes the form of a permanent ministry. The Church acknowledges and consecrates certain ministries in a solemn fashion, through the imposition of hands. The ministries in question are those that guarantee the structure and unity of the Church, the celebration of the Eucharist, and the exercise of authority. All charisms, including those attached to a ministry, come from one and the same Spirit; his normal procedure is to

assure from within both the organic unity of the Church and the division of labor undertaken by the Church.

## D. CHARISMS AND INSTITUTION

The theologians of the charismatic movement insist that there is no conflict between charisms and institution, but that, where men allow him to do so, God normally works through both. This is a point that cannot be overemphasized.

The theology of the divine missions clarifies and confirms the principle just stated. The invisible sending of the Spirit who gives the charisms, and the visible sending of Christ who establishes the institutional ministries are both the Father's work. It is he who sends both Son and Spirit to accomplish one and the same work. The Spirit's mission is to "remind" men (Jn. 14:26) of what Christ taught through his word and his whole human existence, and to make that teaching a reality in men's lives. He is not sent to establish a further institution but to make real, to actualize, vitalize, and spread the institution Christ founded when he was on earth. The charisms are thus meant to be a source of vitality for the ministries that are an organic part of Christ's body, the Church. The *gifts* that God gives are implemented through the *charisms* and find institutional expression in *ministries*. St. Paul suggests this kind of interrelationship when he emphasizes the trinal unity of the three aspects: There is a diversity of spiritual *gifts* (*charismata*), but always the same *Spirit*; there is a diversity of *ministries*, but always the same *Lord*; there is a diversity of *works*, but the same *God* works in all of them (1 Co. 12:5–6).

Yet it is frequently claimed that institution and charisms are opposed. Is the claim ungrounded or even malicious? No. It arises from the fact that the harmony that exists *in principle* is often broken *in reality*, because men are sinners and history is woven of ups and downs. To the extent that the ecclesiastical institution has taken the form of closed hierarchical and juridical structures, and to the extent that it has been organized not on the basis of the charisms but by the appointment of clerics who monopolize possessions, knowledge, power, and initiative in the Church, the growth of the charisms has been stunted. They have been distrusted and therefore excluded or made peripheral or neutralized.

The historian could draw up a long list of the corpses, often difficult now to identify, that the institutional Church has thus left strewn by the wayside of history. Only by exercising great care was Francis of Assisi able to pull through, against the established rules and with the personal help of the Pope. The same goes for Canon Cardijn, founder of the Young Catholic Workers. Both of these men (and the work they set in motion) had to pay a heavy price.

We shall return to the historical aspect of the problem in Chapter 6, where we shall see that the charismatic movement has had an exceptional career. This is because its balance, its openness, its emphasis on study and reflection, and its obedience have greatly facilitated its welcome by a Church that is herself more open, now that the Council has taken place and she finds herself humbled and confused.

## 3. CHARITY

It is important that we get beyond the many objections and the often oversubtle discussions to the essential, which is always simple both in sound theology and in life.

The difficulties raised against baptism in the Spirit and against the charisms may be summed up as follows: Baptism in the Spirit derogates from sacramental baptism, and the charisms from institutional authority. The objection is evidently the same in both cases, and the same fear is at its root.

The answer to the objections has often been theoretical and simplistic, rejecting any possibility of opposition between the movement and the Church. It is impossible that there should be any opposition between the water baptism that Christ instituted and the existential fulfillment of that baptism that the Acts of the Apostles calls "baptism in the Spirit." Similarly, it is impossible that there should be any opposition between charisms and institution, since the same God and Father is the origin both of the visible sending of the Son and of the invisible sending of the Spirit.

The answer is valid in theory but not always in practice. As a result we find both the official Church and the charismatic movement obsessively preoccupied with these points. It is important, therefore, that we not focus solely on statements of principle while refusing to look at the reality.

To reject baptism in the Spirit on the grounds of the supposed objection would lead, logically, to putting ineffective or even sacrilegious baptisms on the same footing as those that are a source of the divine life God wishes us to have. It would also be to assimilate the night of ignorance and sin to John of the Cross's night of the soul and senses.

To reject charisms would be to overlook the tension that normally exists between the free upsurge of the Spirit's initiatives and the permanent work of order, unity, and authority. The tension is not resolved by denying it!

The concrete resolution of these conflicts is to be found in the fact that the Church is an ultimately viable enterprise only because of charity, that is, the divine life that God instills into men's hearts, or what the Scriptures call *Agapē*. Even Peter's ministry is founded on love (cf. Jn. 21:15–17). The tensions inherent in the Church's structure cannot be resolved if love is lacking. Charity alone can overcome the frictions created by a type of government that is sometimes said to be "simultaneously democratic, aristocratic, and monarchic," or, more accurately, that is based on the *unity* of the people, the *collegiality* of the bishops, and the assurance of *supreme authority* given to the successor of Peter. Charity alone can render fruitful the tensions inherent in the free upsurge of the charisms.

At a deeper level, *charity* is the source both of the interior renewal that *baptism in the Spirit* represents and of the *charisms* that build up the Church. St. Paul tells us of this unity in 1 Corinthians 13, when he speaks of love as *the inspiration and substance of the charisms.*

This, then, is the essential point. Originally, indeed, I thought of this book as ending here. And yet the book would not achieve its purpose if we did not discuss two unusual charisms that have drawn so much attention that they make people forget the more important things, and that also raise a number of problems. I am referring to speaking in tongues and to healing. Only after gaining some clarity on these two matters will we be in a position to explain the nature of the charismatic movement and to assess its future.

# A Word About the Laying On of Hands

The laying on of hands is a common practice of charismatic groups. Usually it is an act of the whole group, is done at the individual's request, and is accompanied by common prayer for the individual's need. He may be seeking an outpouring of the Spirit, a grace of light or strength for the apostolate or in some difficult situation, a healing, and so on. The laying on of hands is a concrete, sensible expression of solidarity, this last being highly esteemed in the charismatic movement.

Are we to regard the action as an ambivalent imitation of the gesture used in some sacraments: confirmation (to symbolize and call for the outpouring of the Spirit), ordination of priests and bishops, and penance (where it symbolizes the reconciliation of sinners)?

Not at all. Scripture itself shows that the action can have many meanings. In the New Testament we see the laying on of hands used in the official ordination of those in charge of a community (1 Tm. 4:14; cf. 5:22; 2 Tm. 1:6) or of the "seven" who are assigned to handle material needs (Ac. 6:6) and in calling down the gift of the Spirit on the newly baptized (Ac. 8:17–19; 19:1–8; cf. Heb. 6:2 and Ac. 1:5). But it is also used in sending someone on a mission (Ac. 13:3; cf. 14:26) and especially in healing (Ac. 9:12, 17; 28:8–10; cf. 5:2, 16; 14:3; 19:11), a practice that is very old and is used by Jesus himself (Mt. 9:18; Mk. 6:5; 7:32; 8:23–25; Lk. 4:10; 13:13), who bids his disciples do the same (Mk. 16:18). In Acts 9:12 Ananias, who seems to be a layman, lays hands on Saul of Tarsus to give him back his sight.

Finally, the laying on of hands can also be a simple gesture of blessing, as in Matthew 18:15. In summary, this ancient and deeply meaningful gesture can be used for many purposes.

As a matter of fact, the laying on of hands was a widely used and traditional gesture until quite recently. "Not too long ago, the parents of Christian families used to impose hands on their children at important moments in the life of faith, such as the eve of first communion or entry into religious life."[33] The new rite of baptism provides once again for the laying of hands on the baptized by their godparents or even by everyone present.

There is, then, no problem with the practice as used by Catholic pentecostals, especially since the action, though linked to fraternal prayer, is not sacramental but relates to any need of Christian life.

## Chapter 4

# SPEAKING IN TONGUES

*Do not suppress the gift of tongues*
*(1 Co. 14:39)*

What most intrigues many people about Pentecostalism is tongue speaking (or glossolalia, the technical term we shall use henceforth), that is, extemporaneous speaking in a language that is not the speaker's native tongue nor any that he or she has ever learned.[1] Edward O'Connor describes the phenomenon as follows:

> It is a mode of prayer, not a means of communication. The one who speaks in tongues addresses God, not his fellowmen. What he says is ordinarily not understood either by those around him or even by himself. If someone happens to be present who knows the language used, he will be able to understand it, of course; but that is quite accidental. . . . The subject is perfectly calm and in full command of his senses; he is aware of what he is doing and of what goes on around him. Frequently he is engaged in a normal, rational conversation immediately before and after the speaking in tongues.[2]

## 1. An Absorbing Question

Catholic Pentecostalists deplore the excessive emphasis on glossolalia in discussions of their movement. "Drop the subject," they say; "it's secondary, and really just the overflow of God's interior gift. Mere curiosity will distort the truth about it. Moreover, it is only one charism among many that are more important: prophecy, discernment, and so forth." That is the kind of answer I have received from all the charismatics I've questioned on the matter.

Arnold Bittlinger moves in the same direction when he urges the following two objective considerations:

1. Among the hundreds of charismatic prayer meetings I have attended since 1962 I cannot recall even one in which glossolalia was the subject either of a teaching session or of biblical study. Charismatics simply mention this gift as part of the complete list and lay no special emphasis on it.

2. The practice of glossolalia is given minimal attention at a charismatic meeting. In a meeting of about two hours no more than two minutes is usually given over to speaking in tongues. I have even attended meetings in which there was no tongue speaking at all. . . .

The charismatic movement is not a tongue-speaking movement.[3]

Yet the phenomenon of tongue speaking inevitably draws attention. The reason for this is not simply its unusual and spectacular nature, but the interests and concerns it stimulates.

Tongue speaking is an experience, an activity, even a spiritual technique, that seems more amazing than zen or yoga, and it raises a question that seems to fascinate many: Can a person speak a foreign language without having learned it? Moreover: Can religion provide a way of scaling linguistic barriers and avoiding the humiliating and scarifying experience of the traveler who finds himself to be an infant (in the etymological sense: one who cannot speak) and, in some countries, an illiterate as well (in countries like China and Japan, which use a different alphabet)?

Glossolalia reverses the story of Babel. The dream of an anti-Babel lies behind the Jewish traditions on the Sinai revelation and the account of the Christian Pentecost in Acts 2:1–13, which, via those traditions, evokes Genesis 11:1–9.

Deep within us there is a nostalgia for a primal language that belongs to a lost paradise and to a golden age of childhood, whether the individual's or mankind's. We dream, too, of a universal language that would unite all peoples, and an angelic language that could express the ineffable God.

Over against these ancestral myths, so dear to Jung, stands the science of linguistics. Linguistics has become the most popular and also the most rigorous of the sciences of man, the pioneering discipline that elaborated the methods of structuralism and thus revitalized so many other disciplines. People think of glossolalia as defying linguistics, but tongue speaking can also be recorded and studied; in fact, scientists have already begun to inquire into it.

It is not mere curiosity or sensationalism, therefore, that causes us to spend time here on glossolalia. On the contrary, glossolalia is a tangled skein, and we must make the effort to unravel it.

We do so with some apprehension. This chapter will not escape the reviewer's usual stock criticism: "The author has devoted more space to the gift of tongues than to baptism in the Spirit or to the Holy Spirit himself," etc. And yet the number of pages devoted to a point evidently depends not on its importance but on its difficulty, complexity, or novelty. Glossolalia bears all of these marks. It takes but a moment to indicate the traditional ground that the charismatic movement shares with the rest of the Church. It takes time to become informed in areas of uncertainty, discussion, and confusion.

If any further justification for the length of this chapter is needed, we may add that despite numerous minimizing declarations, the phenomenon of glossolalia does in fact occupy a considerable place in the charismatic movement, for the following reasons. First, this gift renews an experience that is well attested in the New Testament (Ac. 2:4–11; 10:46; 11:15; 19:6; 1 Co. 12–14; Mk. 16:17); by so doing, it has revitalized one area of scriptural exegesis. Second, glossolalia was, for the first wave of Pentecostalism (in 1900), the specific test for whether the outpouring of the Spirit had occurred; some today share this conviction.

The third reason is that although Catholic Neo-Pentecostalism insists that this charism is subordinate, accessory, and secondary, the charism is nonetheless the most widespread of all. One leader of the movement in France assured me that 80 per cent of the charismatics there speak in tongues. Everywhere else those speaking in tongues seem to be in the majority, except in Canada (where one of the most important leaders does not have this gift) and in some groups that distrust the unusual (the *Feu Nouveau* [*New Fire*] groups).

In most prayer meetings some time (usually quite brief) is spent in a *collective* speaking in tongues, a practice that can appeal for justification to what happened on the first Pentecost (Ac. 2:4). Moreover, the formation of charismatics involves asking for and practicing this gift.

Finally, I heard one of the early leaders of the movement say: "I do not challenge the statement that glossolalia is unnecessary and secondary . . . but I cannot help thinking that without it something is missing." The speaker was an intelligent woman of realistic good sense. During an evening I spent at her home she showed herself an effective mother (of three young children) and housewife. What she had said of glossolalia was spoken in the same tone of voice as her comment at table that "they advise a salt-free diet, but soup without salt is not good soup."

It might be observed that the great movements of spiritual renewal have often emphasized things that seemed arbitrary and specific, even physical at times: the gift of tears, fasting, the breathing techniques of the hesychasts, the yoga and zen postures that Christians are using today in order to attain contemplative enlightenment. These varied practices are, however, catalysts or at least humble means of opening spiritual paths that have been blocked by the barriers, inhibitions, and defenses that various temperaments and cultures erect.

## 2. What does "Glossolalia" Mean?

The first step is to be clear on the precise meaning of the word, especially in the New Testament, where the expression "to speak in tongues" occurs twenty times to refer to the phenomenon with which we are concerned.

The technical term *glossolalia* is neither biblical nor patristic. It is a late coinage from two words. *Glōssa* means "tongue" in both the anatomical and the linguistic sense: the fleshy organ attached to the floor of the mouth, and a system of oral communication. *Lalein* means "to speak," a verb that occurs 299 times in the New Testament (apart from compounds). The New Testament links the two words in the following two ways. First, *glōssais lalein:* "to speak in tongues," as in 1 Corinthians 12:30; 14:5, 6, 23, 29; Acts 2:4 (speak in foreign tongues); 2:11 (speak in our own tongues); 10:26; 19:6. Note also Paul's phrase in 1 Corinthians 13:1: "to speak in the tongues of men and angels." The second combination is *glōssēi lalein:* "to speak in a tongue," as in 1 Corinthians 14:2, 4, 13, 15, 27.

The Apostle Paul also has the following expression, which gets to the heart of the matter: "to pray in a tongue" (*proseuchesthai glōssei*, 1 Co. 14:13). Equivalent expressions are: to pray by the Spirit (*tōi pneumati*, 1 Co. 14:15); to sing psalms by the Spirit (ibid.); to bless by the Spirit (1 Co. 14:16); and to speak to God (1 Co. 14:2). And compare Ephesians 5:19: be filled with the Spirit and speak to one another in psalms and hymns and spiritual songs (*ōdais pneumatikais*).

In these expressions, "spirit" denotes the nonrational wellspring of the psychism, as distinguished from reason (*nous*, in Greek); "hymns" and "songs" imply chanting of some kind.

Paul also uses less formal expressions: to give thanks with beauty (*eucharistein kalōs*, 1 Co. 14:17), or simply "thanksgiving" in 1 Corinthians 14:16; to speak "countless words in a tongue" (*murious logous en glōssei*, 1 Co. 14:19).

In some of these varied expressions the word "tongue" alone, without an accompanying verb, means the gifts of tongues, as in 1 Corinthians 12:10 (*genē glōssōn*, "types of tongues"); 13:8; 14:22, 26.

The conclusion to be drawn from this varied evidence is that glossolalia is an ambiguous word, as indeed are each of its component parts.

## LALEIN

The verb *lalein* can signify any utterance of sound, whether or not it be intelligent and/or intelligible. This is clear from the list of meanings given in Bailly's Greek dictionary,[4] where we find the following: I. Inarticulate sounds. 1: Cries of animals, as apes . . . dogs, cicadas (Theocritus 5:34), and birds (Moschus 3:47). 2. Emit sounds with flute, trumpet, harp. II. To babble or chatter, as opposed to *legein*: to say something (Plato *Euthydemus* 287: "You speak much but you give no answer").

Similarly, the noun *lalia* means first of all a babbling or chattering, and only secondarily (by extension) a word. The intelligible word was designated by *logos*.

Nonetheless, Scripture does put *lalein* to use. God speaks (*lalein*); his word here is not the *logos* of wisdom (cf. 1 Co. 2:1, 4), but his addressing himself to man.[5]

## GLŌSSA

*Glōssa* is likewise ambiguous, since it can mean "language" in a very broad sense, that is, any kind of utterance (presumably intended for communication), as when we speak of the "languages of animals." Or it can mean "language" in the narrower sense of phonemes constructed into words and arranged according to a grammar.

## 3. The Types of Tongue Speaking

If the expressions used to designate glossolalia are fluid and ambiguous, it is because the phenomenon itself is protean. Its forms vary greatly since each speaker creates his own tongue, according to his native resources and the inspiration he receives. The major categories, however, are these:

### COLLECTIVE GLOSSOLALIA

The most widespread form of glossolalia today is collective; it can even become a mass occurrence, as at the Notre Dame meeting of June 1974, which thirty thousand people attended; at one point a harmonious murmuring arose from the whole assembly; there was nothing harsh or cacophonous about it, and at moments it was quite beautiful.

Such a phenomenon usually occurs at a time when prayer is more intense and seems to be poised between silence and speech. The ordinary words of shared thanksgiving—*Amen* or *Alleluja*—are no longer adequate, and one or another of those present begins to utter, half aloud, sounds that are more or less articulated and fall into a chant pattern; others gradually pick it up, always calmly and in a moderate tone. Nothing is prearranged, and each individual expresses himself as he wishes. You would expect cacophony, but what you hear is a soothing, attractive melody that soon stops after a short decrescendo.

If you ask the participants about this harmony, they tend to give one of two answers. Either the Holy Spirit is there as an invisible leader of the orchestra, or each participant attunes himself to the others, like a jazz combo improvising. The two explanations are not mutually exclusive.

In such collective glossolalia, however, what we have is less a "speaking" than a chant or lyric modulation in praise of the "marvels of God" (Ac. 2:11), even though one or another of the many participants may be expressing himself in a more distinct way.

### INDIVIDUAL GLOSSOLALIA

Sometimes one individual speaks in tongues and the others listen in silence. On such occasions it is easier to observe what is going on.

The speaker calmly utters a rhythmic sequence of distinct, articulated, structured sounds (or syllables) that possess a degree of coherence and phonetic clarity. "A genuine speaking is neither a stammering nor sighing nor simple exclamations of joy nor a mumbling of gibberish."[6] This is acceptable, but we must add that neither does a collective speaking mean simply—at least for many of the participants—an emotional babbling of thanksgiving, mixed with the Hebrew liturgical words *Amen* and *Alleluja*. Bittlinger would probably say that the people who do pray in this "nonspeaking" way are associating themselves with the glossolalia but are not themselves, in the proper sense, speaking in tongues.

Speaking in tongues does not mean trances or delirium. If such occur, they represent a pathological form of the phenomenon, as David du Plessis, one of the most qualified representatives of a classical Pentecostalism, has clearly stated:

> I consider it heretical to maintain that spasmodic movements, dancing, shaking, collapses, handclapping, cries, and similar things are manifestations of the Holy Spirit. No, these are purely human reactions to the experience of the Spirit's power, and often they are more a hindrance than a help toward openness to the Spirit's authentic manifestations.[7]

There are different degrees of structuration in glossolalia. Some speakers always speak the same kind of tongue, others speak several different ones. Moreover, the form can develop.

Glossolalia is not an ecstatic phenomenon, despite a tenacious persuasion to this effect. To say that it is is contrary both to the New Testament and to experience. The speaker remains in full possession of his senses. He feels inspired, he even feels the indwelling Spirit, but he does not feel possessed. He can speak or not, continue or stop, as he wishes; he is always able to put an end to his speaking if he sees that someone else wants to speak or that the common prayer has taken a different turn.

The speaker deliberately uses his speech organs, even when at times (especially on the occasion of his first experience) the words come unexpectedly and, as it were, imperiously to his lips. Sometimes, the speaker must stumble and grope in his effort to get the words out. Those who wish to acquire the gift are advised to exercise tongue and voice in order to induce the charism. In one fashion or another, speakers acquire mastery of the phenomenon once it has become habitual. I asked one of the French leaders of the movement: "When you speak, are you yielding to force, to an irresistible impulse?" His answer: "No, I speak freely. Ever since I received the gift, it has been at my disposal to use according to the inspiration of the moment and the needs of the community."

## INTERPRETATION

The speaker in tongues does not understand what he is saying. Consequently, if he is speaking in a group, there must be someone to interpret his words, according to the advice of St. Paul in 1 Corinthians 14:27.

Interpretation is not translation. Should there happen to be someone present who recognizes the words and phrases of a language he knows, he might translate them but would not be said to be interpreting. Interpretation is itself a gift and complements the gift of tongues; it consists in an intuitive understanding of the meaning.

The interpretation may be notably shorter or longer than the speaking in tongues. Sometimes a person who is going to talk after a tongue speaker is asked whether he is going to exercise the gift of interpretation or is simply picking up the theme of the shared prayer.

The first time I heard tongue speaking (at the University of Dayton in 1971), the leader, a Marianist brother, asked if anyone had received the gift of interpretation. The young lady who had initiated the meeting began to speak after a period of silence. What she did was to read on in the passage of St. Paul that had served as the starting point for prayer. Some of those present thought she was interpreting. Did she herself think so? At least she was helping to keep the shared prayer moving forward in a coherent way.

## 4. WHAT TONGUES?

### THE INDIFFERENCE OF THE TONGUE SPEAKERS

What tongues are spoken? Ask a tongue speaker and you may well be surprised at how little interested he is in the question. In a letter, Edward O'Connor observed: "The people who have the gift are not interested in proving anything whatsoever about it. They are happily content simply to use it" (June 1973).

"But," I asked the French charismatic leader quoted a page or two back, "aren't you even curious enough to tape your speaking in tongues and have someone possibly identify it?" "I don't think it worth my while to take the trouble. I just accept the gift as it comes and for the fruits it brings, and otherwise I'm not curious about it."

This speaker feels that the language he uses is "organic" and stable. He has some background for judging, since he has university training and currently speaks at least two languages.

Linguistic researchers have had to give up on asking, "What language do you speak [when 'speaking in tongues']?," since the question always elicited the same answer: "I don't know." The researchers therefore fell back on a vaguer formula: "To what language is your speaking related?" According to Bittlinger, of eighty-five tongue speakers who were asked this question, thirty-eight had no opinion, while forty-eight suspected a relationship with one or another of the following languages: Chinese, Polynesian, Japanese, Spanish, Italian, French, Latin, Greek, African, Hebrew, Arabic, Aramaic, Scandinavian, Slavic, and Indian.[8]

William J. Samarin, professor of linguistics at the University of Toronto, has made the most complete study thus far of tongue speaking in Pentecostalism as a whole, and has come up with similar results. A total of 27 per cent of those questioned are not convinced that their "tongue" or *glōssa* is a language. To the question "What languages have your tongues resembled?," 50 per cent (43 of 85) said they did not know or gave no clear answer, while most of the remaining 50 per cent (29 respondents, to be exact) thought chiefly of one or another oriental language. Some named several languages (consequently there are more than 42 choices in the following list). The languages listed were: Romance, 24 (Spanish, 12; Italian, 6; French, 3; Latin, 3); African, 8; Semitic, 8 (Hebrew, 3; Arabic, 1; Aramaic, 2); Greek, 3; German, 4; Indian (Western Hemisphere), 4; etc.[9]

Samarin illustrates the arbitrary and unreliable character of these identifications by reminding the reader of Edgar Allan Poe's story "The Murders in the Rue Morgue." The unseen murderer's outcry sounds like Spanish to a Frenchman, French to an Irishman, German to an Englishman, English to a Spaniard, and Russian to an Italian. When the murderer is finally captured, "he" turns out to be an orangutan![10]

One point that these statistics do not sufficiently emphasize is the conviction of the tongue speakers that their language is not inferior to usual languages. In fact, since it is a gift from God and a means of addressing him, it is superior rather than inferior to the others.

It is because of its source and purpose that glossolalia is sometimes described as "speaking with the tongues of angels," in a Pauline phrase (1 Co. 13:1) that Samarin finds intriguing. Some tongue speakers, as we have indicated, think their inspired language to be as coherent as the languages men use for communicating with one another, but they have never attempted to prove this point by analyzing their *glōssa*. Despite the lack of any proof, the opinion is widespread in Pentecostalism and in Neo-Pentecostalism that the tongues spoken are genuine languages.

## FOREIGN LANGUAGES?

The traditional view of the Fathers of the Church and the theologians from the fifth century on was that the tongues were foreign languages. In their view, which was independent of experience or experiment, the only reasonable interpretation and the only interpretation worthy of God was that the "tongues" of which Paul and Acts speak were foreign languages and intended for the spreading of the Gospel among the peoples of the world. This was the meaning given to Acts 2:4: "They . . . began to speak foreign languages" (cf. Is. 28:11–22, cited in 1 Co. 14:21).

Charles Parham, a pioneer of Pentecostalism, simply accepted this widespread view when he judged that the rebirth of glossolalia would dispense missionaries from having to study foreign languages. He maintained this opinion until his death, against all objections.[11]

Repeated failures to verify the languages have discredited this functional interpretation of glossolalia. There are those who still maintain that St. Vincent Ferrer and St. Francis Xavier and various Protestant missionaries preached in languages they had not learned.[12] But the grounds for the statement are very weak as far as St. Vincent Ferrer is concerned,[13] while historical criticism has fatally undermined the legend for St. Francis Xavier.[14]

Stories continue, however, to go around in charismatic circles about foreign languages. A chance visitor to this, that, or the other prayer meeting was greatly surprised to hear a tongue speaker uttering words in his, the visitor's, native language; on the spot, he gave a translation (not an interpretation).

Such stories called for investigation, and so I asked about them in most of the interviews I conducted. I always insisted, however, that they tell me only of cases they had personally witnessed; stories people hear from others always get exaggerated and embellished in the process of repeating them. I received positive answers from a few serious witnesses.

Several told me that at Aix, in August 1973, a participant who was a Spaniard by birth came to a tongue speaker after the meeting and told him: "You were speaking Basque!" Then he repeated the essential points in what the tongue speaker had said, and they fitted right into the flow of the shared prayer.

In southeastern France, on September 10, 1972, one of the participants heard, during a glossolalia, "a greeting in Arabic, pronounced perfectly."

Patricia Gallagher told me that in February 1967 she heard one of the first students to receive baptism in the Spirit and the gift of tongues speaking perfectly correct French. Miss Gallagher herself was just finishing her university studies in French.

B. M. le Braz, a Capuchin, tells the following story:

At a meeting of charismatic group leaders on January 5, 1973, I heard a young lady give a message in a language she did not know, but which I did. It was Hebrew, and I translated it for the group: "Brothers and sisters, wisdom has been given to you. From now on, make that wisdom yield fruits of grace and holiness."[15]

One of the chief leaders of the charismatic movement in Quebec, Father Regimbal, has authorized the publication of the following interview. He said that the first time he himself spoke in tongues,

while I was speaking, I saw two persons there deeply moved and becoming deathly pale; I did not understand why. A few moments later they came up to me and asked: "Father, did you ever live in Greece?" "No," I told them. "I've never been near Greece and do not speak Greek." "But how can that be? You were not only speaking Greek just now, but the dialect of the village we come from!"

The two men were Orthodox priests dressed as laymen. They immediately recognized the prayer I had uttered in a language that was unknown to me; the prayer had been part of the Orthodox Greek liturgy in the last century but had later been eliminated. The two priests had studied at the same seminary at Athens and had been particularly struck by this Trinitarian doxology, which had come up in their course on the history of the liturgy. They could not understand hearing it on my lips and in the very dialect of their own native village!

As a result of this experience, the two Orthodox parishes of St. George and of the Holy Trinity in Phoenix, Arizona, became completely charismatic parishes. I had a similar experience in another prayer group with which I met every week. . . . I had begun to sing in a language that was completely unknown to me, using a very oriental-sounding melodic pattern that I had never learned. . . . One man present, about fifty-seven or fifty-eight years old and a stranger to me, began to weep copiously and to tremble all over. Shortly after, he came to me and asked whether I had been a student in Jerusalem.

"No," I answered, "I've never been outside of North America." "Well, the song you were singing is a Hebrew Christian song from the fourth century, and when I myself was a student in Jerusalem, this was one of the songs used to prove there had been a Christian community in Jerusalem at that time. It's a song about the Prince of Peace, and you used the words and music that I learned five years ago in Jerusalem."

I was dumfounded by all this! The man himself was a Baptist minister from the south. His experience that evening was the starting point for tremendous spiritual progress for him, and for a new stage in his ministry.[16]

## 5. ANTHROPOLOGICAL ANALOGIES AND HYPOTHESES

Before we submit these descriptions and data to analysis from the linguistic, psychological, and religious points of view, it will be well to situate them in anthropological terms. Where does glossolalia fit into the vast spectrum of human language?

### SOME ANALOGIES

1. Some compare glossolalia to the various levels of nonconceptual expression: poetic and artistic expression, the automatic writing of the surrealists, lettrist poems (an aesthetic invention), and the cries and other utterances used in psychotherapy as helps in attaining inner freedom. In short, the comparison is with all the forms of irrational or inspired language.

2. Those who regard *glōssai* as genuine languages use other analogies in attempting an anthropological explanation of the phenomenon.

Men have at times been obsessed by the dream of creating a language that would be in no way inferior to existing languages and in which the speaker would be able to express himself in a completely fulfilling way. The German Romantic writer Justinus Kerner (died 1862) has given a profoundly poetic and novelistic interpretation of this myth in his account of *The Seeress of Prevorst*. The seeress was a young woman, Frederike Hauffe (1805–29), who possessed a very special power of self-expression.

Frederike believed that this language was innate in her; she also thought it resembled the language spoken by men in the time of Jacob and that such a language was latent in every human being. It was extremely sonorous; it was also thoroughly coherent and consistent for the ideas it sought to express, so that those around her gradually learned to understand it somewhat. Frederike often said that she could express her inmost and deepest feelings in this language and that if she wanted to say something in German she first had to translate into her own special language. But the thoughts she voiced in this special language did not come from her head but from her very depths. It was a language not for the reasoning mind but for the interior life, since it came from the wellsprings of the heart.[17]

This mythical discourse shares certain traits and aspirations with glossolalia. It is an inner language that arises from "the heart," not from "the head," or, as St. Paul would put it, from the *pneuma* (breath of inspiration) and not from the *logos* (mind, reason) (cf. 1 Co. 14:14–16). It is regarded as an ancient, even archaic language (glossolalia seems to rise out of the archaic depths of the unconscious).

It would seem, then, that man, as a being capable of linguistic expression, can create or re-create languages in the proper sense of this term.

## SOME EXPLANATIONS

The probability of our last statement may be shown by a comparison. When a newborn child is thrown into the water, he proves to have excellent amphibian reflexes, especially those that close the breathing passages while he is under water. These reflexes, inherited from our distant aquatic ancestors, are lost, however, if the child is not put at a very early age into the conditions that cause the instincts to operate. Later on, fear, inhibitions, and consciousness will neutralize the reflexes. But the reflexes can nonetheless be regained and re-educated. Why, then, should not the innate reflexes possessed by the inventors of language long ago come to life again in glossolalia? Why should the charismatics not be inventing or reinventing genuine languages?

Every human being has the native capacity of forming sounds and grasping relationships. We may even claim, with linguist Noam Chomsky, that every language has a predicative structure: subject, verb, predicate; this means that speaking is always a process of attributing some quality to a thing, no matter who the speaker is or what the language is.

Against this background, two types of explanation have been offered of the innateness of language, that is, of the linguistic propensity inherent in the mental, bodily, and vocal capacities of man.

1. According to Karl Bühler,[18] the child gradually draws upon the wealth of sounds that reside (by heredity?) in each man and puts together the elements of the language spoken by those around him; but the process involves a good deal of groping and presents the child with real possibilities that go beyond what is done in the language he must learn. The unexploited sounds do not disappear but are accessible to the adult once he has achieved a degree of interior freedom (such as we find in the poet, for example).

2. According to Morton T. Kelsey, a disciple of Jung, glossolalia is a manifestation of the collective unconscious.[19] Jacques Lacan claims that "the unconscious has a linguistic structure." It might be easily inferred from this that man can create or re-create authentic languages. Since all languages are the creation of man, why can't an individual man re-create existing languages or create others that are just as good?

But all these hypotheses are either myths or rough guesses. When it comes to language, the real answer must be given by linguistics.

# 6. The Linguistic Viewpoint

## A CHALLENGE

Arnold Bittlinger issued a challenge to the linguistic science experts. He printed these two phonetic transcriptions, one of a glossolalia, the other of a foreign language:

> *méyana linimibo, noliloubé*
> *méyana linimibo, noliloubé*
> *séhouyanangou séfo, séfo agolamémo*
> *méyana li nimibo, noliloubé . . .*

> *yamana kita siyanayasi*
> *yamana kita siyanayasi*
> *anakiana tiyasonaya*
> *anakiyotana siyanayasi . . .*

His challenge: Can you tell me which is which, using only internal criteria?[20]

He proposed a second test: four transcriptions of a charismatic glossolalia, a foreign language, a lettrist poem, and a language invented as a pastime. Here they are:

> *oiai laéla aia sisialou, ensoudio trésa, soudio mischnoumi ja lon stouaz, brorr schjatt, ojazo tsigoulou . . .*

> *zizka drou vishindramanta, koyantré sizhindri, pilisindri kézan, troupala yindri palosou, zandré kéla santrou . . .*

> *tyrini zanyma timi, ny rytyni trassima thama, mamitiri rari taynyma, rintymi nama . . .*

> *omili douchou svaty, raé nasim hostem byti, jjenz jisiv darich bohaty, némeskejknam prijit . . .*

Which of the four is the glossolalia? the foreign language? the lettrist poem? the language invented as a diversion? "You try to distinguish them!" No one to whom I submitted the texts could give an answer, and it was only from Bittlinger himself that I found that in both sets of samples the second item was the glossolalia. But experts have cautioned me: Just because you can't distinguish them right off does not mean there are no differences among the entries; it means only that it would take time to say which is which.

## AN EXPERT'S FINDING

One expert, William J. Samarin, did take up the problem raised by Bittlinger. For a number of years, Samarin systematically recorded and studied examples of glossolalia in Italy, Holland, Jamaica, Canada, and the United States. His book on the subject, published in 1973, concluded that the *glōssai* of the tongue speakers do not show the traits of a genuine language. From the linguistic viewpoint, the *glōssai* are very rudimentary, lacking a grammar and other typical linguistic structures and giving little evidence of distinct "words."[21] Moreover, the frequency of vowels or consonants corresponds to that which characterizes the native language of the tongue speaker. For example, *glōssai* of Americans show that 52 per cent of all the consonants are accounted for by *t, k, s, y*, and *p;* consonants made with the tip of the tongue represent 56.7 per cent of all consonants occurring at the beginning of a syllable—but that is exactly the per cent of such alveolar sounds in English, according to one tabulation.[22]

The analysis of tape-recorded samples always yields the same result: The samples prove to be "strings of syllables, made up of sounds taken from among all those that the speaker knows, put together more or less haphazardly."[23] In short, a *glōssa* is "like language" in some ways, but it "is fundamentally *not* language."[24]

The innate predispositions of which we spoke above do not suffice, therefore, to create the coherent system we call a language, with its lexicon of words and especially its rules for lexical combination that are in fact complex and strict norms for selection. The formation of any language has a long history behind it, and the speaking of any language demands strict adherence to rules.

In addition, it makes no sense, from a linguistic viewpoint, to say that a "speaker" can express himself in a language whose meaning he does not understand. Spontaneous psychological mechanisms are not an adequate means of suddenly reinventing a language hitherto unknown to the speaker. This fact compels us to the conclusion recently expressed by Cardinal Suenens, that if a charismatic discourses in a coherent way in a language he does not know, his feat belongs "to the order of miracle."[25]

Let us consider this hypothesis of a miracle.

## 7. Is the Miraculous Excluded?

Charismatics do not agree on the answer to this question. Some consider glossolalia to be an ordinary charism; their own daily experience and their repugnance to the thought of God acting as a magician force them to deny anything properly miraculous. Our own reflections thus far lead us to agree that, despite appearances, a miracle in the area of tongue speaking would be no less extraordinary than the spontaneous regrowth of an amputated leg. We know, however, that even Lourdes has not seen anything so extraordinary as this, despite the fact that, as embryology shows, every individual human being has an innate capacity for forming the limbs he needs.

What we are doing here is not "to forbid God to perform a miracle in this matter"! We are simply facing up to two undeniable data, one of principle, the other of fact. The principle: From the linguistic standpoint, it is a contradiction and an impossibility for anyone to reinvent a language he has not learned and to speak it correctly while remaining ignorant of its meaning. The fact: None of the tape recordings made on so many different occasions has ever shown anyone speaking a language (in the proper sense of the term) that he had not learned. People claim it happens, but there is no proof.

We have no intention of denying the seriousness and good faith of the witnesses and their testimonies. It is simply that, until there is some strict proof of a miracle having occurred, we are justified in falling back on one or another natural explanation of the alleged facts. It is possible that the speaker may have dredged up memories of a language he heard as an infant from his nurse (the type of thing that hypnotized patients have done); if the "unknown language" consists only of a few isolated words, this explanation affords no difficulty at all. It is possible, above all, that on the basis of a relatively small number of sounds, the hearers may have read a meaning into the glossolalia. From what is objectively a quite inadequate type of expression, a hearer can grasp a speaker's meaning, especially when the two parties are closely united and have an intense desire to communicate with one another (a mother and her child, for example).

At the end of his life, only the secretaries of the paralyzed Cardinal Suhard could interpret what he was trying to say, and even they had great difficulty. I myself heard him say the same phrase ten times over to me; I finally understood it only with the help of the context of the conversation, his gestures, and his extraordinarily lively gaze.

I also remember the case of a priest who landed in England in 1945, wearing a soutane and knowing about twenty words of English. He managed to communicate for hours with some people who took an interest in this unusual-looking person with his gestures and warm personality. It would be a mistake, however, to think that he "spoke English" or was even making any progress in it. Nonetheless he did communicate, at least enough to get directions for his further journey.

Incidents of this kind are quite numerous. A Parisian guitarist who is an accomplished mimic enjoys singing in an American or a Spanish flamenco style, though he knows neither English nor Spanish. Occasionally a listener will tell him: "You were singing in the Portuguese dialect of such-and-such an area!" The listener had caught a few syllables that reminded him of a word he knew.

This is what happened in the case of a tongue speaking that seemed to be in Greek and in fact contained a couple of Greek words or, more accurately, Greek roots. Bittlinger cites the words, but insists that the speaker was in fact not speaking Greek or any known Greek dialect: "*hippo gerosto niparos—borastin farmai—o fastos sourgor borinos—épongos ménati—o déripangito borin—ariston ékrampos—sénoté hupanos nostin—hupen hippo boros.*"

Bittlinger does not say where he heard this or who told him about it. The thing I found striking was the similarity of the opening words to those of a short bit of (Irvingite) glossolalia that E. Lombard recorded in a 1910 book. Both examples begin with the same five syllables (of which the first two resemble the Greek word for "horse"): "*Hippo-gerosto hippos booros senoote,*" etc.[26]

What frequently happens, as I can attest from personal observation, is that one or two words of a tongue speaking will resemble roots in an existent language. The hearer who speaks the language hears the one or two words (*hippos* and *ariston*, which in Greek mean "horse" and "best," respectively) and says: "Why, he's speaking Greek!" At one meeting I attended, the word "miriam" was used by a tongue speaker, and someone present said: "He is speaking Hebrew and talking about the Blessed Virgin." Mary then became the theme for the next part of the prayer meeting.

There are, then, natural explanations of tongue speakings that seem to involve foreign languages that the speaker does not know. But some serious Pentecostalists maintain the miraculous infusion of unknown languages. They do so, however, with definite restrictions. The first is that such a miracle is extremely rare. One highly respected classical Pentecostalist told me he had come across only two indisputable cases of miracle in his long years of experience. The second restriction is that if a miracle does occur, it is never clear-cut. But "that is always the case with authentic miracles," another Pentecostalist told me, "and that is also how the Holy Spirit acts."

We would be wise to leave this an open question, especially since thus far there has not really been sufficient methodical observation of the facts or adequate linguistic analysis. There exists no scientific classification of the various types of speech characterized as glossolalia and of analogous forms found in art and psychotherapy. The characteristic structures of all these need to be better defined, and the precise differences among them need to be pinpointed.

In any event, xenoglossia (the speaking of a foreign language) is not essential to glossolalia. In addition, to the tongue speaker, his charism is not a proof or argument for anything, nor is it a privilege. It is simply a gift meant to be fruitful. But fruitful in what way? That is the important thing, and to it we must now turn.

## 8. Glossolalia from the Psychological Viewpoint

Glossolalia, when taped and studied, does not seem to be a true language, and the linguistics people set little value on it. Psychologists, however, do think it important, especially on two counts.

The first is that the glossolalist speaks out, that is, he overcomes internal inhibitions and social pressures. The importance of this aspect of the phenomenon has been remarked many times since May 1968.

The second is that even if glossolalia is not a language, that is, a system of phonemes that are articulated into words and grammatically organized, thus enabling men to communicate with each other, it nonetheless does have a certain value simply as an utterance, that is, a mode of expression that makes use of the speech organs. But in what does this value consist?

Speaking quite generically, we would have to say that glossolalia has its value inasmuch as it is part of a wide range of possibilities for human expression; these possibilities are not only vocal but also plastic and kinetic (the dance, for example). Again, no scientific classification exists of these various modes of expression, but the

most evident characteristics of glossolalia can be pinpointed. To list
them is to indicate how glossolalia can be a valuable kind of human
utterance.

To begin with, glossolalia is a spontaneous, preconceptual utterance and possesses the freshness proper to any return to the roots
and wellsprings. From this point of view, it can be compared to the
more or less ephemeral or fragmentary languages children invent
when they play. It has been noted that child tongue speakers show a
high degree of spontaneity.[27]

Glossolalia is, further, a disinterested utterance, quite different
from ordinary language, which is conventional and utilitarian. From
this point of view, it can be compared to artistic expression in music
and poetry. It has been seen as analogous to the automatic writing
of the surrealists and the poems of the lettrists, that is, phonetic
compositions without any intelligible words or phrases. (But we
must remember here that tongue speaking is inspired by a movement toward God.)

Tongue speaking, finally, has an aesthetic aspect, analogous to
that of the arts and poetry. All are types of expression that bypass
reason and convention, and draw instead upon a source that, for
want of a better name, we call "inspiration" (musical, poetic,
other). No comparative structural study of these various forms has as
yet been made.

On all these counts—speaking out, spontaneous, disinterested, aesthetic utterance—glossolalia can be a means of liberation from psychological repressions, blocks, and alienations. Some kinds of psychotherapy makes use of similar means. Jung has interpreted
glossolalia as an upsurge into consciousness of the contents of the
deepest levels of the collective unconscious and, consequently, as a
help to personality integration. Morton Kelsey has studied what
Jung has to say, and concludes:

> Those [of Jung's followers] with whom I have talked have
> evinced an interest in the experience [of glossolalia]. Three of
> them have each commented that one or more patients had had
> experiences of tongues which had led them to integrate their
> lives. Without these experiences they believed that these people
> would never have been able to come to psychological maturity.
> The experience of speaking in tongues opened them up to the
> unconscious and to fuller, though more difficult, life.[28]

British psychiatrist William Sargant thinks that tongue speaking can have effects similar to those of shock treatment. In both cases, a block is removed and the individual becomes capable of acting in new ways.[29]

## 9. GLOSSOLALIA FROM THE RELIGIOUS VIEWPOINT

Although Samarin, as we have seen, reaches negative conclusions from the linguistic standpoint, he finds nevertheless that glossolalia is very important as "a linguistic symbol of the sacred."[30] In fact, glossolalia has a number of religious functions; these may be viewed as prolongations of the psychological function we have just been examining.

1. Glossolalia is a form of spontaneous prayer, and spontaneity is a major goal of the liturgical movement as it endeavors to overcome the formalism of the past.

2. It has an aesthetic and specifically a musical function as an inspiration for sacred music. After hearing simple peasants of the Ardèche region singing in tongues (around 1930), Pastor Brémond compared their melodies with the finest of Gregorian chant and suggested as a hypothesis that the sung liturgy developed out of the music created on Pentecost, when the first Christians spoke in tongues of "the marvels of God" (Ac. 2:11). G. Rubach develops the hypothesis as follows:

> Glossolalia in the Eastern Church, as a primitive form of music, was the germ or even the first form of sung liturgical prayer. We must think of this early music as very simple and even primitive by comparison with our present musical development. Yet it possessed the essentials of all music: rhythm, movement, and a harmonious flow of sounds in a state of grace. In the almost unearthly harmony of ancient Church melodies and in Gregorian chant we hear an echo from the glossolalic depths.[31]

Whatever we may think of this hypothesis, it is true enough that the charismatic movement has produced an original repertory of melodies in which the shared yearnings of the group find warm, simple expression. The movement's musical creativity is dependent on the special qualities of collective singing in tongues, and draws upon the same inspiration as the latter.

Paul was sensitive to this aspect of glossolalia, for, though he downgraded the phenomenon, he did acknowledge its beauty. He says (in a literal translation): "You give thanks beautifully, but the other gets no profit from it [because it is unintelligible to him]." (1 Co. 14:17).

3. We said that glossolalia has a liberating effect. From the religious point of view, it liberates man from inhibitions in regard to men and to God, that is, from human respect and from fear of approaching the God whom no words can describe. As a result, interior energies, both mystical and apostolic, are released. This is a fact of daily experience.

Bittlinger insists that this unblocking helps the individual become aware of his sinfulness.[32] It strengthens the action of grace and facilitates intercessory prayer, which is often inhibited by the fact that "we cannot choose words in order to pray properly" (Rm. 8:26).

4. Tongue speaking is emancipated from the limiting conditions of ordinary language with its earthy quality and its corruption by usage and lies. Frederike Hauffe, the seeress of Prevorst, thought of herself as speaking a language that was "pure." From the religious point of view, tongue speaking is an act analogous to putting on liturgical robes and performing rituals foreign to everyday life. A person thereby rises above the profane.

In this respect, glossolalia is comparable to the language of initiates, a language therefore reserved to the priestly class and not understood by the people. In Catholicism, Latin has been this kind of sacred language, set over against ordinary language. Cardinal Ottaviani gave a brilliant defense of this position at the beginning of Vatican II. The nostalgia for Latin that is to be found in some Catholic circles is largely due to Latin having been this kind of sacred language in the past. It is not accidental that tongue speaking developed in Catholicism once Latin had disappeared.

5. Tongue speaking is also a (modest and peaceful) challenge to the limitations and platitudinous character of everyday language. It represents an escape, a nonviolent release. As a form of prayer, glossolalia is a means of escaping the limitations, poverty, and conventions of the new official liturgy, which has drawn fire from both

right and left (though it must be remembered that we are in a transitional phase).

At a deeper level, glossolalia reverses the ordinary religious process in which men move, often unsuccessfully, from language to life. It is an effort, along quite feasible lines, to revitalize prayer starting from life as itself an outpouring of praise. Words are often powerless to create life; life, on the other hand, has the ability to renew language as an exteriorization of the gift of grace in man's heart.

6. Glossolalia is also a private "language." Couples or groups sometimes try to create, or make use of, a language that will be a haven for them, a place inaccessible to others. In some parts of France, dialects (Breton, Alsatian, Flemish, Provençal) are spontaneously used to keep private matters from outsiders.

In the charismatic movement, tongue speaking creates a very personal bond of intimacy with God, while the gift of interpretation guards against the danger of individualism and esotericism.

7. As a preconceptual type of utterance, glossolalia meets the need for an ineffable language that attempts to reach God through discourse of the apophatic (negative, or "beyond language") kind or, in a more positive way, by imitating "the tongues of angels," in Paul's phrase (1 Co. 13:1). From this point of view, glossolalia may rightly be said to be a nonlanguage.[33]

As preconceptual utterance, glossolalia is also comparable to the interior speech that the Old Testament prophets and psalmists describe as "pouring out the heart" (Lm. 2:19; Ps. 42:5; 62:9). This outpouring of the heart is represented as a victory for the persecuted, a conquest of suffering and darkness (Lm. 2:19; cf. Ps. 42:4).

The tears that Lamentations 2:11 mentions in this context show the bond that exists between the gift of tongues and the gift of tears.[34] The two gifts have analogous functions, since tears too are an ineffable language. Tears do away with interior tensions and inhibitions, and thus liberate. As a matter of fact, the gift of tears was widespread during the period when the gift of tongues had almost disappeared.[35] The charismatics to whom I suggested the analogy accepted it immediately. Some of them had experienced both gifts, although the gift of tears has a modest place today, while the gift of tongues is honored, unlike in the past.

St. Paul recognizes the nonrational character of glossolalia, for he regards it as the language of the *pneuma* (a "breath" or inspiration coming from the heart), as opposed to the language of the *nous* (the intellect). Paul emphasizes the opposition in 1 Corinthians 14:13–19.

With glossolalia here belongs what the Eastern monks call the prayer of sighs or spontaneous, half-voiced groans (which, however, are a means of establishing conceptual contact with God).

What we have here, then, is what Karl Barth calls "an attempt to express the inexpressible."[36] Speaking in "other tongues" (a literal translation of the phrase in Ac. 2:4) is a way of achieving union with the Wholly Other.

8. Glossolalia is also a speaking of "new languages," as Christ promised in Mark 16:17. These languages give expression to the "new Man" of whom Paul speaks, that is, the man in whom God has instilled a "new heart" and a "new spirit" in the words of Ezekiel (36:26) that are often repeated in the New Testament.

Those who find this new language welling up within them think of it mystically as archaic, primitive, and coming from God, but also as the language of the future. In symbolic language, future and past fuse. We see the same golden age as existing at the beginning and at the end of time, as earthly paradise and as heavenly paradise. Tongue speaking thus reawakens a feeling both for the origins of things and for eschatology. Rudolf Bohren writes:

> It is a language of freedom. . . . He who speaks it exists in tomorrow's world. Tomorrow becomes today, and the jubilant speaker experiences the beauty which some day will redeem the world. . . . I would therefore call tongue-speaking the sabbath of language, a sabbath made for man.[37]

Glossolalia is therefore an activity meant to edify, that is, build up, as St. Paul insists in 1 Corinthians 14:4. And this is precisely the result that is most evident in those with long experience of the gift: a development, in depth, of the spiritual person; an overcoming of many difficulties; an accessibility to the interior movements of the Spirit.

## 10. RETURN TO THE SOURCES

One of the most interesting things about the gift of tongues is that it repeats an experience of the first community. The fact is well attested in the New Testament, but the gift seems to have been quickly lost.


TRADITION

Irenaeus of Lyons tells us that tongue speaking was still known at the end of the second century: "We hear of many brothers in the Church who possess prophetic charisms and, with the Spirit's help, speak in tongues of all kinds."[38]

Did tongue speaking come into discredit because the Montanists practiced it (or so the sources seem to say)? St. John Chrysostom, at any rate, has no knowledge of it as something current, and openly admits he is puzzled by Chapters 12–14 of 1 Corinthians: "The whole passage is very obscure. . . . The obscurity is due to our ignorance of something that was common then but does not exist in our day."[39]

Once the historians of the Church reach the third century, they have no more glossolalic phenomena to record; the same is true of the many dictionary articles on the subject. I have consulted the Bollandist archives that cover so many centuries; even these supply almost nothing.

Even the passage from Irenaeus is so isolated that scholars have tried to read a different meaning into *glōssai* ("tongues"). And, as a matter of fact, while the word can mean "foreign tongues," it can also signify any exotic or affected expression. Aristotle, for example, contrasts the "ordinary" (*kyrion*) word, that is, in general use in a country, with the "strange word" (*glōssa*) used elsewhere.[40]

The poverty of documentation on glossolalia in the past is due partly to a lack of interest in it, but partly also to shame and fear. Tongue speaking has been discredited because of the Montanists, and the only place given to it in Church life was as a sign of diabolic possession, back in the time of the witch-hunts. This interpretation started during the Montanist disputes; we find the first trace of it in St. Jerome's *Life of Hilarion*,[41] and it is still mentioned as a sign of possession in the *Roman Ritual*.[42]

The disparagement of the gift of tongues led, as we pointed out, to the development of the gift of tears. It should be noted, however, that to cry without shedding tears was regarded as another sign of diabolic possession; the totally arid individual must be possessed.

We may ask, nonetheless, whether glossolalia did not in fact survive, as something private, secret, and sporadic. Scholars are beginning to put together texts and other indications that such was the case, although these initial dossiers are not critical enough to be the bases for any valid conclusions. The stories are usually secondhand, the texts ambiguous, the evidence disillusioning.

When unsubstantiated cases (St. Francis Xavier, the Curé of Ars, and others) have been eliminated, and despite all the questions that remain unanswered, we have the feeling that monasticism, Eastern and Western, indeed had some experience of tongue speaking. We believe, moreover, that tongue speaking began to come back into its own, not at the beginning of the twentieth century, but in the pietist circles of seventeenth- and eighteenth-century Protestantism.

Isolated instances had been recorded in the earlier Catholic mystical tradition: St. Hildegard of Bingen (d. 1179), David of Augsburg, O.F.M. (d. 1280), and Hendrik Herp, O.F.M., better known as Harphius (d. 1477).[43] But we shall dwell for a moment on an example from the Catholic tradition at a later period. In his *Spiritual Journal*, St. Ignatius Loyola makes daily mention, during the period May 11–22, 1544, to *loquela*, or "speech," that came to him in prayer. Here are the first and last of these entries.

> Sunday [May 11th].—Tears before Mass and during it an abundance of them, and continued, together with the interior *loquela* during the Mass. It seems to me that it was given miraculously, as I had asked for it that same day, because in the whole week, I sometimes found the external *loquela*, and sometimes I did not, and the interior less, although last Saturday I was a little more purified.

And on Thursday, May 22:

> Many tears before Mass in my room and in the chapel. In the greater part of the Mass, no tears, but much *loquela*, but I fell into some doubt about the relish and sweetness of the *loquela* for fear it might be from the evil spirit, thus causing the ceasing of the spiritual consolation of tears. Going on a little further, I thought that I took too much delight in the tone of the *loquela*, attending to the sound, without paying so much attention to the meaning of the words and of the *loquela;* and this with many tears, thinking that I was being taught how to pro-

ceed, with the hope of always finding further instruction as time went on.[44]

As was noted by the Jesuit who called these texts to my attention, the *loquela* of which St. Ignatius speaks is a gift he asks for; moreover, the *loquela* not only has a meaning, it has "sound" and "tone" as well. These latter qualities presumably relate to what Ignatius calls "external *loquela*."

Concerned as he always is with the discernment of spirits, Ignatius fears that the *loquela* may be inspired by the demon on such days as it is not accompanied by tears (tears, in his view, being an important sign of authenticity). He also worries about paying more attention to the sound of this speech than to its meaning—a problem analogous to the one St. Paul takes up in 1 Corinthians 14.

Experience of the contemporary charismatic movement is beginning to attract observers' attention to texts hitherto more or less ignored, like those of St. Ignatius, but even more to texts in the Bible that for a long time were obscure because the charism of glossolalia was no longer given in the Church. Exegetes and others had been reduced to interpreting the New Testament texts in terms of abstract and artificial theories or in the light of other facts that are more or less pathological in character. Thus psychiatrists spoke of "tongue speaking by people out of their senses," and one exegete was reminded of "the holy madness often found in ancient cults."[45]

Shrewder exegetes, however, had occasionally gone beyond the accepted clichés and noted that glossolalia is not xenolalia; that it is not an ecstatic state; and that it was not a means of spreading the Gospel, since, according to tradition, Peter used interpreters and Paul did not understand the Lycaonian tongue (Ac. 14:11–14).[46]

Parallels and explanations were also sought at times in Old Testament texts such as Numbers 11:25–29; 1 Samuel 5:6, 10, 13; 9:20–24; and 1 Kings 22:10. But these texts were really not to the point, since they depict states of ecstasy or even delirium, at least in the popular interpretation, which was evidently ironic and critical (and which the Bible echoes).

The Jewish tradition could probably supply some interesting material. According to a tradition concerning Exodus 20:18 and the feast of Weeks or Pentecost, the voice of God as he promulgated the Law on Sinai was heard by all the nations of the earth and thus spoke as many languages as there were people. Chapter 2 of the Acts of the Apostles alludes to this tradition.[47]

According to the *Testament of Job*, a Jewish-Christian composition, the three daughters of Job began to sing just before their father's death: One imitated "the hymnology of the angels," another "the dialect of the archons," and the third "the dialect of the cherubim," each as she chose "in her ecstasy."[48]

All of this, however, sheds no great light on the New Testament texts.


### EXEGESIS AND EXPERIENCE

Today is a different matter. The resurgence of glossolalia has indeed shed light on this obscure point in exegesis. To those who experience glossolalia or at least witness it, the texts become clear; they speak of what we know well. It is important, therefore, that we compare contemporary experience with what the New Testament has to say in texts that occur chiefly in two writings: Acts 2:4, 6, 7, 11; 10:46; 19:6; and 1 Corinthians 12:10, 30; 13:1, 8; 14:2–40.[49]


### THE ACTS OF THE APOSTLES (CA. A.D. 80–90)

Tongue speaking is mentioned in three passages of Acts, each time in connection with the outpouring of the Spirit, of which tongue speaking seems to be the clearest sign.

The first occurrence is on Pentecost:

> They were all filled with the Holy Spirit, and began to speak foreign languages as the Spirit gave them the gift of speech. . . . All assembled, each one bewildered to hear these men speaking his own languages. They were amazed and astonished. "Surely," they said, "all these men speaking are Galileans? How does it happen that each of us hears them in his own native language? Parthians, Medes, and Elamites . . . we hear them preaching in our language about the marvels of God (Ac. 2:4–11).

The general significance of the event is clear: The coming of the Holy Spirit reverses what happened at the Tower of Babel. But the way it is described is disconcerting for anyone attempting to reconstruct what actually happened, for the language is the symbolic language of the epic.

In this first text, unlike the others, say many exegetes, we really have not a speaking in tongues but a hearing in tongues. The first Christians emerge from the upper room and speak their own language, but in this Galilean speech the pilgrims to Jerusalem hear their own various languages. To lend emphasis to the account, verses 9–11 list the many peoples present (not all of whom, in fact, speak different languages).

Such an interpretation is contradicted, however, by the first verse we quoted: "They . . . began to speak foreign languages as the Spirit gave them the power of speech" (2:4). A literal translation of "gave them the power of speech" would be "gave them to utter." The Greek word for "utter," *apophtheggesthai*, means to speak plainly, and especially to speak seriously and solemnly. The word is appropriate here when the subject is "the marvels of God" (2:11).

According to this verse, then, the Spirit's gift is a gift of speech, a point emphasized by the use of two different verbs for "speak." Even though the following verses interpret the event rather as a miracle of hearing, the final verses (12–13) make it clear once again that a miracle of speech has occurred—something that certain people in the audience cannot accept.

On the other hand, how could a large crowd (verse 41 speaks of "about three thousand") hear distinctly a hundred or so people (cf. Ac. 1:14–15) who were all speaking at once (2:4)?

The whole account becomes more intelligible if we relate it to our contemporary experience of tongue speaking. The 120 disciples, now inspired by the Spirit, emerge from the upper room. Their tongue speaking is a collective glossolalic prayer. The impressive musical harmony of this praying arouses the enthusiasm of a crowd of Eastern pilgrims, and the enthusiasm spreads rapidly through the crowd. Despite the language barrier, the pilgrims recognize an inspired celebration of "the marvels of God," as they assert in 2:11.

Some confirmation of this interpretation is afforded by the fact that some in the crowd are perplexed or outright ironic and even sardonic: "They have been drinking too much new wine" (2:13).[50]

It is to this group of opponents that Peter addresses himself first. He alone speaks, and he directs his words not to the cosmopolitan crowd but only to the "men of Judaea" and "Jerusalem" (2:14; in verse 22 he addresses a wider audience: "men of Israel"). In the language shared by Jews he explains the charismatic manifestation of the Spirit. The glossolalia is finished; a new kind of discourse, addressed to a different type of audience, begins.

A second case of glossolalia is quite explicitly mentioned in Chapter 10 of Acts. The Holy Spirit comes down on (literally: falls upon) the very pagans Peter is hesitant about baptizing, and he comes even before these pagans have received baptism in the name of Jesus (10:47). "Jewish believers who had accompanied Peter were all astonished that the gift of the Holy Spirit should be poured out on the pagans too" (10:45). What was it that had provoked this astonishment? They knew the Spirit was given, *"since* they could hear them speaking strange languages and proclaiming the greatness of God" (10:46).

These last words show that here as on Pentecost the glossolalia was a prayer of praise. Peter's own words also show that he identified the gift received by the pagans with the gift given on Pentecost: "They have received the Holy Spirit just as much as we have" (10:47); "God was giving them the identical thing he gave to us" (11:17).[51]

The same phenomenon occurs a third time among John the Baptist's disciples at Ephesus. These people had not even heard there was a Holy Spirit. But when Paul had them baptized and then laid his hands on them, "the Holy Spirit came down on them, and they began to speak with tongues and to prophesy. There were about twelve of these men" (Ac. 19:7).

## THE CHURCH OF CORINTH (CA. A.D. 50)

It is quite possible to question the precise historical value of the Acts of the Apostles, since the book was written more than fifty years after the event and in a style influenced by epic and even by apologetics. The First Letter to the Corinthians was written a good thirty years earlier, around A.D. 50. Moreover, in it Paul is dealing with glossolalia as a present fact that is causing abuses, and he wants to restore a proper order. Far from being an apologist for this charism, his aim is to signal abuses of it. It is hard to imagine, therefore, a more unimpeachable testimony to the fact that twenty years after Pentecost, tongue speaking was still a daily occurrence in the life of the Church, at least at Corinth.

Paul's first mention of this gift comes at the end of a list of the charisms "in which the Spirit is given to each person for a good purpose" (12:7): "Another [may receive] the gift of tongues and another the ability to interpret them" (12:10). He emphasizes the fact that glossolalia is only one gift among others, and the need of relating it organically to the service of Christ's body.

He ends this chapter with a series of questions that leads to a second listing of charisms. Here again, glossolalia and its correlative gift of interpretation come last: "Do all speak strange languages, and all interpret them?" (12:30).

In Chapter 13, verse 2, Paul begins another list, with the purpose of showing their contingent character and subordinating them to the one absolutely necessary gift of charity, which is far better than any other gift, is all-important, and is within the reach of all (12:31; 13:3, 13). In this list the order is reversed: Paul begins with the gift of tongues because he is moving from the lesser gifts to the greater. "If I have all the eloquence of men or of angels, but speak without love, I am simply a gong booming or a cymbal clashing" (13:2). Paul's irony comes through here not only in the images used but also in the very sound of the Greek words, which imitate gongs and cymbals: *gegona khalkos ēkhōn ē kumbalon alalazon.*

In Chapter 14 Paul sets out to show the great importance of prophecy in comparison with the other charisms: "You must want love more than anything else; but still hope for the spiritual gifts as well, especially prophecy" (14:1). He goes on then to contrast this gift, which is the most useful, with the gift of tongues, which is the least useful.

> Anybody with the gift of tongues speaks to God, but not to other people; because nobody understands him when he talks in the spirit about mysterious things. On the other hand, the man who prophesies does talk to other people, to their improvement, their encouragement, and their consolation. . . . While I should like you all to have the gift of tongues, I would much rather you could prophesy (14:2–5).

As he goes on in this chapter, Paul will wax very ironic about glossolalia, but he begins by acknowledging it and even wishing it for all, in principle. His preference for prophecy is based on the very purpose of the charisms, which is to build up ("edify") the Church. "The one with the gift of tongues talks for his own benefit [literally: builds up himself], but the man who prophesies does so for the benefit of the community [literally: builds up the community]. While I should like you all to have the gift of tongues, I would much rather you could prophesy, since the man who prophesies is of greater importance than the man with the gift of tongues, unless of course the latter offers an interpretation so that the church may get some benefit" (14:4–5). Paul is here contrasting a purely personal edification, which is a fitting purpose for private prayer, and the edification of the Church, that is, the entire community, which is the purpose of prophecy.

Paul now goes into the limitations of glossolalia: It is incomprehensible, unintelligible. Knowing that the Corinthians liked to hear him speak, he asks them to reflect on how disappointed they would be if on his next visit he had only glossolalia to offer them. "Now suppose, my dear brothers, I am someone with the gift of tongues, and I come to visit you, what use shall I be if all my talking reveals nothing new, and neither inspires you nor instructs you?" (14:6).

The irony intensifies as Paul compares glossolalia to a flute or harp that emits only noise, for lack of a skilled player, then to a bugler who substitutes his own tunes for the sounds whose meaning the soldiers recognize: "If no one can be sure which call the trumpet has sounded,[52] who will be ready for the attack? It is the same with you: if your tongue does not produce intelligible speech, how can anyone know what you are saying? You will be talking to the air" (14:8–9).

The irony becomes extreme in verse 10, at least if we follow *The Jerusalem Bible* in its French form, where verse 10 reads: "There are God knows how many different intelligible languages in the world, and nothing lacks its intelligible language." In any case, the next verse is sarcastic: "But if I am ignorant of what the sounds mean, I am a savage to the man who is speaking, and he is a savage to me." "Savage" or, literally, "barbarian," was the name given to someone who did not understand Greek.

If only this passage (14:2–12) of 1 Corinthians had survived, we would be forced to think that Paul had simply condemned glossolalia. In fact, however, he goes on to urge, in a positive way, that the gift of tongues not be separated from the accompanying gift of interpretation: "That is why anybody who has the gift of tongues must pray for the power of interpreting them" (14:13). Later on, in 14:27, Paul is thinking of two different persons having the two different gifts, but here his wish is that the person who speaks in tongues should also do the interpreting. He justifies this by a penetrating observation: "For if I use this gift in my prayers, my *spirit* (*pneuma*) may be praying but my *mind* (*nous*) is left barren. What is the answer to that? Surely I should pray not only with the *spirit* but with the *mind* as well? And sing praises not only with the *spirit* but with the *mind* as well?" (14:14–15).

In this passage *pneuma* signifies the spirit of man, that level of the soul at which inspiration is given and that has an affinity for the gift of the Holy Spirit (*Pneuma*). Jewish-Hellenistic circles were familiar with the connection between *pneuma* and *logos* (the intelligible word that proceeds from mind or *nous*). For Philo, *logos* indicates the intelligible structure that is externally perceived, while *pneuma* is the life or breath that is perceived internally.[53] The *logos*, therefore, is intelligible and can be apprehended; the *pneuma* cannot be apprehended (no one knows whence it comes or whither it goes). The *pneuma*, though nonrational, is neither inferior to nor contrary to reason, for it enables man to share in the interiority of God himself. This is why Paul does value the gift of tongues (despite abuses of it). He simply wishes that it not be dissociated from the intelligible or noetic dimension (supplied by interpretation), because the goal is always edification: "Any uninitiated person will never be able to say Amen to your thanksgiving, if you only bless God with the spirit, for he will have no idea what you are saying. However well you make your thanksgiving, the other gets no benefit from it" (14:16–17).

Evidently, then, in the port town of Corinth, where so many Christians had to be polyglots in some measure, tongue speaking was not intelligible. This is a sign that it was a matter of an ineffable language rather than specific languages.

Thomas Aquinas, whose exegesis followed the general lines we have been following here, thought himself obliged to interpret the next verses as though tongue speaking were a matter of speaking foreign tongues. He was led astray by traditional mistranslations and especially by the Vulgate's mistranslation of verse 18. The Vulgate makes Paul say: "I speak the languages of all of you." The proper translation is: "I thank God that I have a greater gift of tongues than all of you, but when I am in the presence of the community I would rather say five words that mean something than ten thousand words in a tongue" (14:18–19).[54]

The remainder of the chapter has been a stumbling block for the exegetes. Paul there argues that glossolalia is "meant to be a sign not for believers but for unbelievers," whereas "prophecy is a sign not for unbelievers but for believers" (14:22). Paul probably says this with the idea that believers are interested in the meaning of the words, while unbelievers are more impressed by the unusual and miraculous.

The next verses, however, contradict this first statement, for now it is prophecy that is presented as a sign that edifies unbelievers, while they would regard tongue speaking simply as a sign of madness:

> So that any uninitiated people or unbelievers, coming into a meeting of the whole church where everybody was speaking in tongues, would say you were all mad; but if you were all prophesying and an unbeliever or uninitiated person came in, he would find himself analyzed and judged by everyone present; he would find his secret thoughts laid bare, and then fall on his face and worship God, declaring that *God is among you indeed* (14:23–25).

The seeming incoherence of thought (for which explanations as subtle as they are varied have been offered) is perhaps due simply to the fact that in piling up dialectical arguments to downgrade the gift of tongues, Paul allows it value only from the viewpoint of unbelievers, but then adds that, since unbelievers too are really interested in meaning, even they will regard this gift as ridiculous and without value. Paul's diatribe thus causes him, as on other occasions, to write in a superficially illogical way.

In 14:21 Paul quotes Isaiah 28:11–12, an oracle in which God threatens Israel that he will henceforth speak to her in strange languages and through the mouths of foreigners. Thus Paul is even willing to regard glossolalia as a punishment! This is the high point of the whole passage as far as severity and subtle reproach are concerned.

Paul now ends his stream of ironic criticism and turns to practical conclusions.

So, my dear brothers, what conclusion is to be drawn? At all your meetings, let everybody be ready with a psalm or a sermon or a revelation, or ready to use his gift of tongues or to give an interpretation; but it must always be for the common good. If there are people present with the gift of tongues, let only two or three, at the most, be allowed to use it, and only one at a time, and there must be someone to interpret. If there is no interpreter present, they must keep quiet in church and speak only to themselves and to God (14:26–28).

How can Paul give such orders? Because "prophets can always control their prophetic spirits, since God is not a God of disorder but of peace" (14:32). Our contemporary experience confirms that of the Apostle.

After a digression on women, Paul ends by telling his readers not to suppress the gift of tongues: "And so, my dear brothers, by all means be ambitious to prophesy, do not suppress the gift of tongues, but let everything be done with propriety and in order" (14:39–40).

## 11. CONCLUSIONS

For the sake of greater clarity, let us briefly indicate the conclusions we have reached in this chapter:

1. Glossolalia is a preconceptual, nonrational language, "another" tongue in which to speak to the Wholly Other God.

2. It is a healthy, liberating, therapeutic psychological phenomenon. Glossolalia is not glossomania (that is, an unhealthy kind of speaking).

3. Nor is glossolalia a xenoglossia (a speaking in foreign languages), except in miraculous instances that would be highly exceptional and have never been scientifically verified. Psychologists allow glossolalia to be language in the sense of a speaking out spontaneously, but linguists do not find in it the characteristics of a genuine language in the sense of a coherent system of communication.

4. Glossolalia, consequently, is not an extraordinary charism, but

an ordinary one, that is, it calls upon the individual's natural resources. It is a reaction against intellectualism and a return to the
freedom of infancy, to the first gropings after self-expression in
words, and to poetic and musical inspiration.

5. It does not in itself require ecstasy. Trance and delirium are
pathological forms of the phenomenon, since "prophets can always
control their prophetic spirits" (1 Co. 14:32). Where such self-con-
trol is lacking, we are dealing with false prophets and false charismatics, for the Spirit of God is a Spirit who liberates and does not
alienate. He who speaks under the impulse of the Spirit is inspired
and has the Spirit within him, but he is not possessed. That is the
point of the humorous slogan we found in a "charismatic" pamphlet: "He smokes his pipe and speaks in tongues."

The tongue speaking of genuine Pentecostalists is under their
control; it is also usually brief (one or two minutes, in my experience). This differentiates it in a significant way from the tongue
speaking of schizophrenics, who cannot control themselves and cannot stop when they wish to.

6. As a charismatic group becomes more mature and its interior
life deepens, tongue speaking becomes less and less prominent.
Thus, at the parish mass in Houston on Sunday, June 23, 1974, I
heard no tongue speaking, although all members of the parish are
charismatics. The liturgy lasted over two hours and was a fulfilling
experience for the large assembly of about a thousand people. No
one felt anything but the liturgy to be necessary. It is only now and
then, on certain Sundays, that tongue speaking occurs; on these occasions it happens, not because anyone regards it as necessary, but
because some of the small groups present consist of beginners.

In the Lutheran Church of the Holy Trinity at San Pedro, California, "over half the members have the gift of tongues," but the
use of the gift has gradually been restricted to "personal prayer."
For four years now, the gift has not been used at charismatic meetings in this parish.[55]

## A historical note on glossolalia

When and how did people speak in tongues, from the third century to the birth of the Pentecostal movement in 1900? The dossiers

hitherto compiled on the subject are more or less disappointing, since they are vague, fragmentary, uncritical, and often second-hand. We may note the following:

Johann Joseph Görres, *La mystique divine, naturelle et diabolique* (Paris, 1861), pp. 451–53. Speaks of glossolalia but gives no references.

E. Lombard, *De la glossolalie chez les premiers chrétiens et phénomènes similaires: Études d'exégèse et de philologie* (Lausanne-Paris, 1910). Well informed on nineteenth-century phenomena.

Karl Richstätter, "Die Glossolalie im Lichte der Mystik," *Scholastik* 11 (1936), pp. 321–45.

Morton T. Kelsey, *Tongue Speaking: An Experiment in Spiritual Experience* (Garden City, N.Y., 1964). Lists incidents (pp. 32–68) and gives a lot of references at the end of the book (p. 252), but few of these have to do formally and certainly with glossolalia, except in the modern period.

Simon Tugwell, *Did You Receive the Spirit?* (New York, 1972), pp. 66–74. Mentions the following cases: St. Ephraem, *Apophthegmata Patrum: Ephraem* 2 (PG 65:168); St. Dominic, in *Nine Ways of Prayer of St. Dominic*, Chap. 6; Augustine Baker, *Confessions* (London, 1922), pp. 101–2; the Curé of Ars, according to Margaret Trouncer, *Saint Jean-Marie Vianney, Curé of Ars* (New York, 1959), p. 201; finally, the xenoglossia (speaking of foreign tongues) attributed to St. Francis Xavier and St. Vincent Ferrer (for these two cases, cf. notes 13 and 14, above).

Arnold Bittlinger, *Glossolalie* (Wetzhausen, 1969). Cites the following names: St. Polycarp (d. 155; but the Acts of his martyrdom say only that he prayed "in spirit," which signifies an inspired prayer but not necessarily a speaking in tongues); St. Anthony the Hermit, according to Marcel Viller, *La spiritualité des premiers siècles chrétiens* (Paris, 1930) (but Anthony is reported to have said only that a monk's prayer is not perfect if he understands what he says while praying); St. Pachomius (292–346), who, according to Görres, op. cit., spoke Latin and Greek, two languages he had never learned; and St. Hildegard of Bingen (d. 1179). Of the latter's *Ignota Lingua*, F. Vernet says ("Hildegarde [Sainte]," *Dictionnaire de théologie catholique* 6:2,470) that it is "a kind of *volapuk*"; P. Franche, *Sainte Hildegarde* (Paris, 1903) suggests that it is "a disguised form of German and Latin, the two languages Hildegarde knew, which are combined at whim or possibly according to a planned way of substituting vowels and diphthongs" (p. 96).

*Conclusion:* While we await a critical dossier, which has now become urgently necessary, we can say the following:

1. There is almost no indisputable evidence of glossolalia from the time of St. Irenaeus to the sixteenth century, and almost no serious suggestion of xenoglossia.

2. Testimonies become consistent beginning in the eighteenth century (the Quakers), but glossolalia never became as common as it is today, when, according to Kelsey, "two million Christians" practice it. There is no proven case of xenoglossia in the modern period.

3. Glossolalia, which tradition regarded chiefly as a sign of diabolical possession, continues to be distrusted. A candidate for the Protestant ministry was rejected in 1960 because it was learned that he spoke in tongues (Bittlinger, op. cit., p. 65, n. 60).

## A historical note on the gift of tears

The religious literature of the seventeenth, eighteenth, and nineteenth centuries speaks so often of tears that modern readers think it must be a figure of speech. In the article "Larmes," *Catholicisme* 6:1, 849–50, M. Théron writes: "Even today a preacher who wishes to strike a solemn note says: 'Repentant sinners, I see your tears wetting the floor of this sacred building.' But no one is really crying, and in fact the hearers have to repress a smile. 'To shed tears' is simply a metaphor for interior repentance."

As a matter of fact, however, it was the immense prestige of the gift of tears, combined with the religious sensibilities of the seventeenth, eighteenth, and nineteenth centuries, that led to such inflated language. The whole subject of the gift of tears is an important and neglected chapter in the history of spirituality.

The Roman Missal that was in use until the recent Council even had a prayer for requesting the gift of tears: "Almighty and merciful God, you made a fountain of living water spring from the rock to slake the thirst of your people. Strike tears of repentance from our hardened hearts, so that we may be capable of bewailing our sins and thus, by your mercy, receive forgiveness of them."

Monastic texts show that the gift of tears was held in high esteem; at times the esteem is expressed in exaggerated ways. Thus one of the desert fathers, Abbot Arsenius, had wrinkles on his chest that were caused by the tears constantly dripping from his eyes, and because he wept so much his eyelids had fallen (*Apophthegmata Patrum: Arsenius* 41–42; *PG* 65:105–7). The *Cistercian Menology* for May 18 says that Pierre Le Borgne had lost the sight of one eye because he wept so much for his own sins and those of others. How very highly esteemed the gift of tears was we may see from the case of Blessed Daniel (*Cistercian Menology*, Aug. 11): "He heard the Lord say to him in a vision: 'Ask whatever you want and you will receive it.' He answered: 'Your grace is enough for me. I desire only the gift of tears whenever I think of your passion.'"

In his *Spiritual Journal*, St. Ignatius notes each day the presence or absence of tears: *con lagrimas . . . sin ellas*. The formulas occur so often that they are gradually shortened to *con* and *sin*.

St. Teresa of Avila puts the gift of tears in its proper place, as St. Paul had the gift of tongues. "Tears, though good, are not invariably signs of perfection" (*The Way of Perfection*, trans. E. Allison Peers [New York, 1946; Doubleday Image Books, 1964], Chap. 17, p. 126).

> Note also that distress of this kind is apt to be caused by weak health, especially in emotional people, who weep for the slightest thing; again and again they will think they are weeping for reasons that have to do with God but this will not be so in reality. It may even be the case . . . that some humour has been oppressing the heart, and that it is this, rather than their love of God, which has excited their tears. . . . Do not let us suppose that if we weep a great deal we have done everything that matters [*Interior Castle*, tr. E. Allison Peers (New York, 1944; Doubleday Image Books, 1961), Sixth Mansions, Chap. 6, pp. 166–67]

The very restrictions the saint felt obliged to point out tell us indirectly of the high esteem her readers had for the gift.

In the period when the gift of tears was prestigious, people spoke of it a good deal; the word went from mouth to mouth. Today, no one speaks of it, for it only makes people smile—even the author of the theological article we quoted at the beginning of this note. René Schwob had the gift of tears (especially after Communion), and only his closest friends knew about it. Today, no one would know.

# Toward a Typology

The name "glossolalia" or "tongue speaking" is really a rather broad and vague name that covers a large variety of phenomena. A typology is needed both in order to prevent confusion and in order to establish criteria for discernment. Each of the disciplines that are pertinent—linguistics, psychology (and sociology), religion, and even aesthetics—requires its own appropriate typology.

1. Linguistics. Emile Lombard offered a provisional classification in his article "Essai d'une classification des phénomènes de glossolalie," *Archives de psychologie* 7 (1907), pp. 1–51. The results were incorporated into his book *De la glossolalie . . .* (Lausanne and Paris, 1910), pp. 25–42.

Lombard's material consists chiefly of phenomena observed in the nineteenth and early twentieth centuries, some of which had already been studied by linguists (for example, the studies of Hélène Smith's "Martian language" by V. Henry and T. Flournoy in 1901 and 1902). Lombard's dossier contains chiefly *religious* manifestations of recent date, some of these marked by extremism and morbidity (the "little prophets" of the Cévennes, the Irvingites, the Roestar group in Sweden, the Welsh revivalists, etc.). It also includes, however, *literary* testimonies (for example, Albert Le Baron, man of letters and observer of his own psychological automatisms; he was studied by William James) and *mediumistic* or somnambulistic phenomena (for example, Frederike Hauffe, "the seeress of Prevorst," 1805–29, studied by Justinus Kerner).

On the basis of this evidence, in which the Pentecostalist movement plays only a minor role, Lombard constructs the following typology:

A. *Inarticulate utterances* and connected phenomena.
B. *Glossolalia*
    Pseudolanguages
    Occasional neologisms
    Systematic formation of neologisms
C. *Xenoglossia*
    Isolated occurrence of foreign words
    Linguistic counterfeits
    Xenoglossia in the proper sense: the gift of tongues

2. Psychology. Kilian McDonnell is at work on a synthesis (limited to Pentecostalist glossolalia) that we hope will provide the basis for a typology, especially by distinguishing pathological forms (those of schizophrenia, for example) from the gift of tongues recognized by Pentecostalism.

3. Religion. Further examination is needed of the two basic forms: glossolalia whose purpose is praise (whether individual glossolalia or group singing in tongues) and the much rarer prophetic glossolalia. There is need, above all, of situating glossolalia proper in relation to other uses for prayer of verbal mechanisms and techniques such as: the "prayer of sighs," practiced by Eastern monks; various types of exclamation and mumbling that serve to support or act as an overflow for mystical contemplation, and perhaps having various functions; the Jesus prayer (constant repetition of the name); etc. Glossolalia would also have to be related to various kinds of spontaneous expression, rough or artistic, sung or spoken. Magdalith sees an analogy between improvised religious hymns and glossolalia.

In Volume 10 of his *Histoire littéraire du sentiment religieux en France* (Paris, 1932), pp. 336–41, Henri Bremond has some interesting observations. At one point he mentions glossolalia: "If the mystics recommend vocal prayer," they do so not simply out of prudence, but because the activity of the fine point of the soul "unsettles the whole organism and . . . tends to manifest itself outwardly in signs. Think, for example, of glossolalia and, at a much later period, certain types of dancing. It might be said that the fine point has its own language, which however inevitably approaches that of the intellect or, better, makes its own the language of the intellect while stripping it of what is specifically intellectual: a stripping which can go so far as to coin words without a meaning. How make this comprehensible to the pure intellectual? How indeed, for is it not incomprehensible by its very definition? When we say 'prayer of silence,' our first thought is that the phrase means a prayer without words. Not so! . . ." (p. 339).

4. Aesthetics. Here, too, a typology is needed. Inspired improvisations are one thing; the surrealists' automatic writing, which brings more rudimentary mechanisms into play, is another, quite different thing; and deliberate compositions like the poems of the lettrists are still another.

## Chapter 5

# HEALINGS

When it comes to healing, medicine has replaced miracles these days. Scientific reason has supplanted the mentality of the primitives, and the very concept of "miracle" is now regarded as belonging to an outmoded idea of God as the "God of the gaps."

These principles are tacitly accepted throughout the Western world today, even in the Church. One sign of the times is that at Lourdes the International Medical Commission has not met since May 3, 1971. Five of the recent cures accepted by the medical authorities have been thrown out of court by the bishops assigned to pass canonical judgment. The chairman of the medical board at Lourdes has been forced to ask: In our day and in the years ahead, can we expect to see cures that are medically inexplicable?[1]

But suddenly, the past few years have seen a revival of cures! "Healings" have multiplied in the charismatic movement, to such an extent that the 1974 international conference at Notre Dame began with a "healing service" at a plenary session of twenty-four thousand people on June 14, 1974.

Does this revival represent a step backward or a return to the sources? Is it illusory or real, ephemeral or here to stay? To answer these questions, we shall begin with the facts and go on to explore their meaning.

# 1. How is the Charism of Healing Exercised?

## OUT INTO THE OPEN

My first impression, as a result of my inquiry into the charismatic movement in France, was that healings played a very secondary role in it and that a discernment of spirits had eliminated a phenomenon more highly regarded in the English-speaking world. I thought, therefore, that I would not have to bother with the gift of healing. People soon set me straight: There are plenty of healings, but we don't go around advertising them. What would be the point of publicity? We simply thank God for them.

The charismatics have as little inclination to look for medical verification of healings as they have to record tongue speaking so as to find out whether or not it involves a foreign language. They live the charisms as part of their encounter with God and their fellow men. The important thing, in their view, is that the Lord is alive today as in the past; that salvation is for the entire man, including his body, and not just for his "soul"; and that what the Gospel preaches with regard to the body's salvation is hope rather than resignation. People spoke to me only in passing of healings, and without any desire to go into details; they were not looking for publicity. They certainly did not want the movement to get polarized in the matter of healings; the important thing about healings is that they should come as the overflow of a deeper, interior restoration.

In all the countries I visited I was told of healings. I was also told that they have occurred since the very beginnings of the movement. Patricia Gallagher Mansfield, for example, told me that healings began right after the famous weekend at Duquesne in February 1967. She herself felt impelled to pray for a woman afflicted with phlebitis, whom she was visiting around that time, and make the sign of the cross on the woman's forehead (she had not yet begun the laying on of hands). The woman recovered rapidly.

Healings can occur spontaneously, apart from any special rite of healing, most often in connection with the prayer of the community and the laying on of the participants' hands. The laying on of hands is intended not simply for healing but also for obtaining the initial outpouring of the Spirit or any help needed in interior or apostolic difficulties. It was seen, however, that various charisms were being exercised through the laying on of hands. These were distinguished, and specialized "healing services" were begun. Workshops were set up for practical and theoretical reflection on healing, and conferences of people from diverse geographical, scientific, and cultural backgrounds were held for the purpose of introducing order into the ministry of healing.

## THE HEALING SERVICE AT NOTRE DAME (JUNE 14, 1974)

The public healing service (or "Large Healing Rally," as the newspapers called it) that was held at the beginning of the eighth international charismatic conference at Notre Dame on June 14, 1974, was not intended as a challenge or provocation. Its purpose was to bring these activities out into the open and thus clarify them. Back in 1971, Edward O'Connor had already said: "The place of faith healing in the Pentecostal movement is so important that one may wonder why only a few paragraphs are being devoted to the subject here."[2]

It was felt within the movement that the whole matter was ripe for open treatment and discussion, and that a certain timidity and preference for secrecy had to be overcome. The healing service was therefore organized by those most responsible for the mature attitude that had developed on the subject: Francis MacNutt, O.P., whose book *Healing* was published for the occasion; Father Michael Scanlon, rector of St. Francis Seminary (Loretto, Pennsylvania), who was interested more especially in the sacrament of penance and interior healing; and Barbara Shlemon, nurse, mother of five children, and teacher at a pastoral institute, who has taken part in healing services for several years.[3]

The healing service on June 14, 1974, began with a long prayer of praise and with the testimonies of three individuals who had been healed earlier. The prayer gradually moved from praise to petition, but the petition itself took the form of thanksgiving in anticipation for healings to be received. Up in the tiers of seats throughout the stadium in which the meeting was held, those present who had received the charism of discerning cures began to announce healings that had just been effected. Barbara Shlemon did so at the microphone on the central platform.

> We praise you, Jesus, because you are healing the many illnesses we have long been asking you to touch, especially the chronic illnesses among us that we have spent so many years treating with medicine and therapies. This is the night on which you have chosen to manifest your glory among us.
>
> We feel your sweet warmth penetrating our hearts, and we praise you, Lord, for being here and for the many healings of cancers that are now taking place in this stadium; people called incurable have been cured by the touch of the Lord Jesus Christ. All you who feel the warmth of the Lord's presence, praise him and thank him for healing you. Yes, praise him and thank him!
>
> There are people here tonight with leukemia who have been instantaneously healed. . . . You had blood tests recently, and they showed the worst. But Jesus is telling you interiorly—and you are well aware of it—that things have changed: that he loves you so greatly, that his arms are about you, that he is giving you a spiritual transfusion of his precious blood.

She continued in this vein while giving details of further healings.

When those present who had been cured were asked to declare themselves and present themselves to the doctors present, those cured were far too many for any serious examination to be conducted.

After the singing and prayers that were meanwhile continuing to deepen the enthusiasm of the participants, Father MacNutt asked those present who had experienced some form of healing (physical or spiritual) to stand up. At this about half the stadium stood up. This is the usual proportion noted at such services.[4] A number of those healed were examined by physicians and gave their testimony the next day. The chief cures were of blindness, deafness, and arthritis. The reports speak of hundreds of spiritual healings and about fifty physical healings.

At the time of this writing, I have been unable as yet to obtain dossiers of these healings; only improvised controls had been exercised, in no way comparable to what is required at Lourdes. However, at Ann Arbor, on June 21, I met a "blind" woman who had been "cured" at Notre Dame on June 14, and whose case had drawn particular attention. I offer it here in some detail, not in order to prove anything, but simply in order to make the whole business more concrete for the reader.

The woman's case caused a stir because everyone had known her as a blind woman who walked about with a white cane and a guide dog. It is a fact that after her return from Notre Dame she walked without cane or dog and that she could see well enough to learn to read (hitherto she had been dependent on Braille). This young woman, who had attended the university (using Braille), had been prematurely born; as she tells it, too much oxygen in the incubator had injured her eyes seriously. She had no vision in one eye and less than 1/10 vision in the other. Her sight improved in two stages, the second beginning on June 14 at Notre Dame. In this second stage, she felt improved enough to live independently and no longer as a blind person dependent on cane and dog and other people. When I met her, she was preparing to see her doctor, and was also reflecting on a change of occupation, since she did not want to make unnecessary use of employment reserved for blind people. Nonetheless, it was clear that her eyes were still seriously defective (one pupil misshapen, etc.).

Was the improvement functional rather than organic? I did not press the young woman on this point, since her answer was: "God is asking me to give thanks, not to measure the improvement of my sight." The important thing, as she sees it, is that she has gotten new hope and has improved to the extent that she can undertake projects hitherto seemingly impossible.

A few days earlier, at the Canadian conference of June 1974, on the campus of Laval University, Quebec, the healing service was held not at a plenary meeting of the conference but at one of the dozen workshops available to the participants. There were doctors present. Just as one of them was beginning to object rather strongly to the whole business, a paralyzed woman who had not walked in six years got up from her wheelchair. She left the workshop on her own feet, visited other workshops, and walked about for the whole evening. Such a cure would probably not be seriously considered at Lourdes, where cases of paralysis are eliminated unless organic lesion and restoration are duly established and properly described.

Nonetheless, we know how difficult it is for a person to walk after his leg has been in a splint even for only a month. It is, therefore, simply astounding that a person with muscles atrophied from six years of complete disuse should suddenly start walking and remain on her feet for an hour or more.

The same kind of thing happened at Lourdes at the beginning of the century, when Gargam got up during the procession of the Blessed Sacrament and walked on his skeletonlike legs (he was a big man who normally weighed about two hundred pounds but at this time weighed only about eighty-eight pounds). He walked about for the rest of that day, and during it took three meals without discomfort, contrary to what we know of people suddenly eating heavily again (he had fasted from solid food for months!). His cure was never officially listed at Lourdes as a "miracle," although he bore convincing public witness to it for the next thirty years.

## A SERVICE AT ANN ARBOR

I shall dwell for a moment on a healing service that seems to me quite typical of the kind of thing that is a daily occurrence in the United States and Canada. This particular service was organized by Doug Gavrilides on Friday evening, June 21, 1974, at the end of a prayer meeting held by one of the two subcommunities at Ann Arbor. The subcommunity in question is made up of groups from the university section of town. The service had been announced in advance and took place in a hall next to the one in which the prayer meeting had been held.

About ten people came forward for healing. There were no seriously ill individuals that evening, but that is perhaps all to the good, since it allows us to describe an average meeting in which nothing outwardly extraordinary happens. The service began with a prayer of praise in which all took part. Then those who wanted the others to pray for them and over them came forward and knelt down. Four of the workshop leaders questioned them briefly and simply, then prayed to God while imposing hands on them. The invocations were of a simple traditional type, but there was also fervent, intense, but unemotional praying in tongues.

Others present then joined the leaders in praying and imposing hands: no one had a monopoly on the right to heal. The leaders struck no theatrical attitudes and did not call attention to themselves. One of them was a young man in blue jeans that were cut short and fringed and all the color washed out of them, the kind of fellow you saw in great numbers during the summer, at Ann Arbor and elsewhere. All were brothers praying for a brother in a spirit of warm friendship; they passed easily from dialogue with the person who sought healing (asking him questions and encouraging him) to prayer. When this part of the service was finished, all gathered in a circle once again for the final prayer, which consisted of fervent, joyous thanksgiving by all.

During my tour, I often heard of recent healings. People spoke of these in a simple, joyful, unemphatic way, as though telling about some family incident; they even joked about the circumstances of the healing.

## 2. WHY THIS SUDDEN CHALLENGE?

When the modern European intellectual hears of religious healing services, he feels as if he were being challenged or deliberately affronted, for he sees such things as evidence of a return to the magical mentality of the primitive.

Why has this therapeutic activity become so widespread in the very country that is the most scientifically advanced in the world? Why has it arisen within Catholicism, which is not at all disposed to move in this direction? These are questions we must try to answer.

The phenomenon of the healing service is itself the result of several converging challenges.

### EXPERIENCE

The first of these challenges is experience. Healings, both physical and moral, are a simple fact that is connected with the interior conversion called "baptism in the Spirit." This sheer fact was the starting point for the services, as we pointed out earlier in this chapter. It was because the fact was there that people in the charismatic movement began holding healing services, workshops, discussion sessions, and producing books on the matter. All has had its origin, not in a reflective decision or act of planning, but in a collective, in-

ternal impulse. The experts in this matter did not create the phenomenon; it was there and they responded to it.

## THE CULTURAL MILIEU

A further challenge was the numerous experiences of healing in
the English-speaking churches that had sprung from the Reforma-
tion. Among them was the Christian Science movement of Mary
Baker Eddy (1821–1910), who scandalized many by her simplistic
radicalism.

Twenty-five years ago, Leslie D. Weatherhead, an Anglican
minister and university chaplain, made this movement the subject of
historical analysis. He tells of the very divergent efforts to explore
this ambiguous area and to discern the role that Christian faith may
possibly have. Catholics who today engage in healing have implicitly accepted the conclusions he reaches in his book: "Leave out
Mrs. Eddy altogether" and "use the Bible as textbook."[5] Christians should see to it that the ultimate goal of healing services is
worship of God. They should try to understand how illness can be
due to distortion of our relation with God and neighbor; stay in
contact with the doctors and not play down the usefulness of therapeutic treatment; discourage any spirit of unhealthy excitement; use
the laying on of hands only as the climax of a lengthy period of
prayer, not as a magical flourish before an audience that is looking
for the sensational; etc.

These experiences of healing, the high repute in which some of
the practitioners stood, and the wisdom of the principles gradually
established, especially in Episcopalian and Presbyterian circles, all
had an influence on the charismatic movement. Francis MacNutt,
for example, tells of attending pastoral sessions on healing in non-
Catholic circles.

The best-known healer of recent years was Kathryn Kuhlman
(now deceased), who held regular healing services in the Presbyterian church of Pittsburgh Downtown, as well as on television and
in any church to which she was invited (she held one at Ann Arbor
on June 1, 1974). Pastor Wohlfahrt has given a lively description of
the weekly service in Pittsburgh.

Crowds of people have been here since 5 A.M. When we ar-
rive at 8.30, the nave, the huge choir, and the balconies are all

filled—2,500 people in all! They have kept a place for us in the
front row . . .

Everything is in proper order. At the appointed time, Kathryn Kuhlman, a tall, slender woman of uncertain age,[6] wearing
a long, flowing, brightly-colored dress . . . hurries to her place.
Applause breaks out, but she immediately asks the assembly to
praise God. The singing begins, its pace determined by her
gestures. After a prayer of thanksgiving, the healings begin.

People come forward: first, the diabetics, in large numbers.
When she touches them, they fall backwards and are caught by
two male assistants, who themselves are touched from time to
time and almost fall, especially if they are tired. Kathryn sends
some individuals to their doctors for analysis. . . . When the
sick person falls backwards, she often says: "What a power!"
But she also repeatedly insists: "It is not Kathryn Kuhlman
who is healing you, but the Lord! Remember: It is the Lord,
and He alone!"

Then the other sick come up, among them two Catholic
Sisters from Canada. She cures one of her deafness, the other of
her bad eyes. The Sisters weep for joy and do not know how
to thank her. Then the people with broken backs are brought
up. Kathryn Kuhlman makes these people bend down again and
again. A man of fifty weeps for joy. Kathryn says to him:
"Don't cry! Isn't this what you wanted?"

The star attraction is undoubtedly the young woman whom
Olivier Brés (a theology student in Paris) and Bernard Chevaley
(pastor of the community at Meux, Oise) have brought in her
wheelchair into the lower church where we had been sent because of the crowd. She has been crying out: "Help me! Help
me!" Now, suddenly, she comes from the back of the church,
walking with uncertain step . . . her husband comes behind,
holding the crutches. She is walking! Kathryn Kuhlman comes
down from her podium and touches the young woman. She
falls. Then Kathryn makes her walk around the whole church
and then kneel down. The assembly breaks out into praise! I
am not ashamed to say that we wept, it was all so extraordinary.

Kathryn Kuhlman calls up the two men who had brought
the young woman, and blesses them. Then she passes down
through the church, touches us and blesses us. I do not fall

down nor am I healed; neither is my neighbor, but we praise God along with the others. Kathryn now moves down the side-aisles; asthmatics and others are cured. She returns to her po-dium and addresses a woman on the dais: "You over there, your breast cancer is cured. Go and see your doctor tomor-row."

It is impossible for me to tell of everything we saw in the church that night. Each time there was a healing, Kathryn asked the sick person what Church he or she belonged to, and urged continued fidelity to it. To a woman who belonged to no Church, she said: "You see how good God is. Do not forget to thank him! Go and join some Church."

Finally, the healings were finished, and Kathryn began her sermon. . . .

"The Lord has done all this, and he can do even greater things. But what he cannot or will not do is take possession of your heart if you are unwilling. Your heart is something you must freely give him! The greatest of all miracles is a human life that has been changed by the Holy Spirit."

At this fervent call, one to two hundred people came for-ward. The service ended at this point; it was 1 P.M.

In this church the last days have begun; evil is loosening its grip on sick mankind. "Know that the kingdom of God has overtaken you" (Lk. 11:20).[7]

How does Kathryn Kuhlman herself view her healing activity? She tells us in her book *I Believe in Miracles*.[8] Here she narrates twenty-one cases of cures that were later tested by doctors, and tells us how she views the whole problem.

She regards medical science as a gift from God, which no one should neglect. She adds, however, with the testimony of great phy-sicians to back her up, that while the doctor attends to the patient, the cure is nonetheless always a gift of God, or, as Huguenot sur-geon Ambroise Paré once expressed it, "I bound up his wounds, but God healed him." In her view, then, healing is the work of the Lord, who is restoring his creature's wholeness.

At the end of her book, Kathryn Kuhlman thanks God in a con-fession of faith that could not be more orthodox and that lays spe-cial emphasis on the Holy Trinity. Pastor Wohlfahrt ended his ac-count of the healing service at Pittsburgh by saying: "These services are not, like many others, demonstrations of mass hysteria. Everything is orderly . . . and calm . . . and even the manifestations of joyous praise remain within bounds."[9]

Kathryn Kuhlman regards herself simply as a catalyst, but also sees her charism as a permanent gift and ministry that God has entrusted to her, to be used in an orderly fashion in accordance with the spirit and principles of St. Paul in his First Letter to the Corinthians.

### SCRIPTURE

Mention of St. Paul brings us to the third factor, which, however, did less to start the healing movement than to confirm it. Francis MacNutt tells of being struck by the fact that in modern Catholicism illness is usually asserted to be a trial sent by God, which we must accept and draw profit from. Yet according to the Gospel, Christ never told the sick any such thing! Instead, he encouraged, stirred up, and praised their faith that God would heal them. No one heard him say: "Accept your illness." What he did say was: "Of course I want to! Be cured!" (Mk. 1:41; cf. Mt. 8:7).

As a matter of fact, says MacNutt, many illnesses are not useful to the patient, especially psychic imbalance and mental illnesses. "God cannot play on a broken violin."[10] Christ did not come to save only man's spirit; he came to save the whole man, for "holiness is wholeness."[11]

Healing indeed plays a large role in the Gospel, where four different verbs are used to express it. One is *therepeuō*, which is used forty-two times in the New Testament (Mt. 16; Mk. 6; Lk. 13; Jn. 1; Ac. 4; Apoc. 2). Another is *iaomai* (*iatros*, "physician," is a noun from the same root), which is used twenty-six times in the New Testament, especially by Luke, who was himself a physician (Lk. 11; Ac. 4; Mt. 4; scattered use in other New Testament books). A third is *katharizo*, which means "purify" (Mt. 8:2, 3; 11:5; Mk. 1:40; Lk. 5:12; 17:14). The fourth verb is *sōzein*, "save," which is often used of "salvation" in the full and transcendent sense, but is also used in the sense of "heal" (notably in Mt. 9:21–22; 14:36; Mk. 5:23, 28; 6:56; Lk. 7:3; 8:36, 48, 50; 17:19; Jn. 11:12; Ac. 4:9; 14:9; Jm. 5:15).

Healing is always attributed to the *dynamis* or power of God, and described as an astonishing event or a miracle (*thauma*, a word from which the noun thaumaturge, or wonder worker, is derived).

Christians too often fail to realize that the Gospel is a Good News of healing, not an exhortation to resignation in illness. Jesus rejects the request for a "sign from heaven" (Mt. 16:1; cf. 12:39), but he never refuses to heal when asked (Mt. 4:23; 8:16; 9:35; Lk. 9:11). Have we not paid too little attention to his teaching on hope, thanksgiving, and the faith that moves mountains?

Matthew even cites the prophecy of Isaiah: "He took our sicknesses away and carried our diseases for us" (53:4) and claims that it was fulfilled when Jesus "cured all who were sick" (Mt. 8:16–17)!

Among the tasks Jesus gives to his apostles on their mission, he includes the healing of the sick (Mt. 10:1, 5; Lk. 9:1, 2). And according to the ending of Mark's Gospel, one of Christ's last instructions to his disciples is that they should heal the sick: "They will lay their hands on the sick, who will recover" (Mk. 16:18).

The Acts of the Apostles in fact narrates the therapeutic activity of Peter, Paul, and the other disciples of Jesus (3:1; 4:9, 10, 14, 22, 30; 5:16; 8:7; 9:17, 18, 34; 14:8–10; 28:8, 9, 27; cf. 10:38). Paul mentions the charism of healing (*iasis*) in 1 Corinthians 12:9, 28, 30, while James (5:14–16) gives orders that prayers and healing rites are to be conducted for the sick, in accordance with the usage of Jesus himself during his public life. James mentions explicitly only the rite of anointing, but we know that the laying on of hands was also in common use at the time; it is attested to in Acts 9:17, where a simple Christian, Ananias, uses it to cure Paul of his blindness.

This whole side of the New Testament has been played down, while a one-sided emphasis has been placed on the exhortation to carry the cross (cf., e.g., 1 Co. 4:10; Col. 1:24) and, more generally, on texts that speak of the redemptive value of suffering (Ga. 4:13; 2 Co. 8–9; 12:7–10). All these passages continue to be valid, of course, but in their proper place. It is noticeable, moreover, that they are couched in very general terms and do not specifically mention the acceptance of illness.

We may ask whether in this area the legitimate concern properly to interpret and demythologize the texts has not ended up throwing the baby out with the bath.

## A CONSTANT TRADITION

When it comes to healing, we are no longer speaking of a remote biblical idea that was forgotten for almost two millennia (as the gift of tongues was). The tradition on healing is rich and unbroken through the centuries, and has quite varied forms.

The rite of anointing the sick became a permanent fixture in the Church. In the Middle Ages it was listed among the seven sacraments[12] and was later formally defined as a sacrament by the Council of Trent.[13] During the first eight centuries of the Church's history, the anointing of the sick was regarded as a rite of healing for all kinds of illness. Only by a distortion that began in the nineteenth century did it become the "sacrament of the dying," with its administration deferred more and more to the last moments of life, when the person was in his death agony or already unconscious.

The tendency to make this anointing "extreme" has now been reversed, and it is reacquiring its proper status as a prayer for healing. The reversal is due simply to a return to the sources and to an experience that has never been totally lacking.[14] Long before Vatican II, those who made bold to administer the sacrament under normal conditions (that is, the sick person was able to receive it with conscious faith) often saw its beneficent effects. Not only did it liberate the person from the anxiety that lying relatives often cause to hang like a pall over the sickbed, not only did it effect a "moral" renewal, often it also had physical effects so great that the sick person was put back on his feet. When I myself have administered this sacrament, I have been struck by its power to pacify, integrate, and restore.

Throughout the history of the Church, healing has been carried on in countless forms: prayer, pilgrimages, the action of wonder workers; never has it been challenged or caused open conflict. Among the countless condemnations issued by Church authorities over the centuries, "there has never been a single censure of healing as such."[15] Even in the period that has been most critical of and reserved toward such healing, Lourdes has stood as a symbol—and a symbol all the more striking, since it was one of the rare refuges of explicit healing activity in the Church.

There are, however, a number of other sanctuaries that are visited by the faithful as places of healing, for example, Notre-Dame des

Victoires in Paris (Miraculous Medal); Pontmain in Brittany; and Notre-Dame d'Issodon. People leave crutches and orthopedic braces behind them at these shrines. The archives of Pontmain, which were destroyed by a fire in the chaplains' house, at the beginning of the century, were quite extensive.

When Charles X was anointed King of France, the people of Rheims recalled that on the day of his anointing the King had power to cure scrofula. According to tradition, the many who presented themselves for healing were in fact cured. In any event, the Church has never objected to this custom. There were other spontaneous resurgences of the charism of healing in the nineteenth century. There was, for example, Léon-Papin Dupont (1797–1876), "the holy man of Tours," who anointed the sick with oil from the lamp that burned before the image of the Holy Face.

In some abbeys, the monks were asked for prayers and cures by the peasants of the surrounding area and, on the basis of a few traditions, improvised a new ministry. This was the case with Dom Jean-Baptiste Auger, abbot of Bellefontaine, who had resigned his office for reasons of health; the time was between the two World Wars. Other monks questioned the merits of so special a ministry, but the pleas of the peasants were so insistent, and the man himself so prudent, that he was not forbidden to engage in an activity regarded as marginal to the life of the monastery.

Was it not better to take over the healing function in this manner? It had hitherto been exercised without any control by the Church (except at Lourdes), and it was surely an improvement to deal properly with it, if only to prevent deviations and distortions. In this area, as in others, the practice of ignoring and shunting aside is dangerous as a pastoral technique; moreover, the reductive method is unhealthy because it smothers the vital forces that are a basis of hope. The wisest course is to accept and discipline energies that otherwise run wild. Those who try to pursue such a course will, like everyone else, make mistakes; but mistakes made in the effort to see are ordinarily less serious than mistakes springing from neglect and rejection.

### THE NEED OF MANKIND

Here we have the fifth operative influence, the fifth challenge that explains the resurgence of the charism of healing: the appeal from mankind which, today as in the past, is confusedly looking for salvation in the midst of the many anxieties springing from the human condition, and sees in healings an encouraging sign that God indeed bestows the gift of salvation.

The desire for such healings has been rejected in the name of scientific progress. Give illness to the doctors, as Christ gave to Caesar what belongs to Caesar.

The principle is a fine one. It has helped to eliminate the unfortunate conflict between the Church and science that had been symbolized by the condemnations of Galileo and a few physicians. But at the same time we can legitimately question the simplistic application the principle has received.

Has this application accomplished what was intended? The point had been to eliminate the traditional therapeutic function of religion as having been a stopgap and to let medical science now do the job. But has the result been that men indeed consult the doctor more than formerly? It is not clear that they do! The Church's loss of conviction concerning, and ultimate abandonment of, its proper function has chiefly profited those who practice a non-medical healing art in every possible form.

How many "healers" are there active today? Their unofficial and sometimes semiclandestine position make any accurate statistics impossible. Their numbers, if we may trust educated guesses, are quite large: forty thousand, according to one source[16]; fifty thousand, according to a researcher[17]; seventy-five thousand, according to Dr. Gladys Medina, or twice as many healers as official medical men. These figures are surely exaggerated, but even according to one of the most modest estimates, that of Maurice Mességué, two thousand to three thousand healers devote full time to this activity, and they accept all comers.

The sick look to these people for what they cannot find in scientific medicine, except by accident, that is, because of something special in one or other physician. This phenomenon has been accentuated by the very development of medicine, especially the use by practitioners of new and untested techniques that sometimes transform the sick person seeking a cure into a guinea pig; then medical science profits rather than the patient. Medical practice in hospitals has become increasingly impersonal; some hospitals are organized on a really inhuman pattern, as has recently been shown by testimony that has excited wide interest. The result? An immense, unsatisfied need, and improvised efforts to meet it.

Christianity, of course, does not have the resources for meeting each and every human need or question. But it should have been more aware of what really does come within its scope, rather than have left so many human beings in the lurch.

The same kind of problem has been posed by the abandonment of spiritual direction, compassionate listening, and the confessional, as the men who should be doing this work have been drawn instead into psychoanalysis or psychotherapy. We have no intention of attacking these disciplines or minimizing their importance. It is regrettable, however, that in the redistribution of efforts required by the rise of these new disciplines, the servants of the Church should too often have simply abandoned their proper function and, because they lacked faith and imagination, should have been unable to redefine and resituate that function.

Contact with a priest or other religious counselor can be beneficial to persons undergoing psychoanalysis, as I have personally been told by a number of people I have tried to help. In such cases I have scrupulously refrained from interfering in any way in the conduct of the psychoanalysis itself. But men in such a situation need more than a simple friendly presence; they also need a basis for hope and a sense of direction as they travel the new paths opened to them.

The temporary failure of the Church in this area is not without its value, inasmuch as it can help us see the great range and number of physical, psychic, and spiritual needs (all inextricably intermingled) that go unmet and thus lead to imbalance in so many people who do not know where they are coming from or where they are going. In their confusion they turn less to the physician and the psychologist than to palmists, astrologers, and occultists of every kind, all of whom claim clear knowledge of the future. Even people who in their everyday lives are rationalists and will have nothing to do with signs and miracles, sometimes turn in this direction when overwhelmed by personal distress. The healers like to boast that among their clients are doctors who have run into problems!

In short, we can say that in this area as in others, there has been a reaction against rationalism and radical secularism. The only healthy resolution of the situation will require prolonged serious reflection by a community that is bent on discernment and guided by a more comprehensive vision of man and his destiny. That is precisely what the Catholic pioneers in the healing movement have been about. They are men of balance, culture, moral stature, and qualified in theology and the human sciences, even if they sometimes simplify excessively or see things too much as black and white. They have set out on a course that many find unacceptable: "As a Harvard graduate with a Ph.D. in theology I am as aware as anyone of problems of credulity and of a prevailing theological climate which questions whether God 'intervenes' or 'interferes' in the universe.[18]

## THE CHALLENGE OF VATICAN I

The Catholic pioneers are really endeavoring to do justice to a point of doctrine taught by Vatican I but upon which doubt had since been increasingly cast: the importance of the external signs of revelation, "especially miracles and prophecies."[19] In opposition to this teaching, people in the past few decades have been increasingly insisting: "We believe, not because of miracles, but despite them."

Professor Mauriac and other doctors used these words at Lourdes in 1958. When the Acts of the Congress held there were about to be published, an envoy of the Holy See asked these Catholic doctors to change a statement so contrary to the teaching of Vatican I. But the conviction thus censured had been spreading and continued to spread because no effort had been made to come to grips with the underlying problems, namely, the requirements implicit in the true postulates of scientific method and the impossibility of accepting a widespreading rationalistic conception of miracles.

The abstract formula defended by the Holy Office has turned out to be, for the charismatic movement, a living, meaningful reality. The Christian is one who believes in the signs God gives, in "the marvels of God" that the contemporary liturgy continues to celebrate, although in terms that mean little because they have no effective basis in men's lives.

The problem raised by the six factors or challenges we have been discussing had inevitably to be faced. Thus an issue of the review *Concilium* had been planned, even the books of MacNutt and Scanlon appeared, in which the problem of healing, as seen in the perspective of the Gospel and Christian tradition, would be handled, with the necessary discernment and care to point out ambiguities.[20]

## 3. SOURCES AND MEANING

It is true enough that in this matter of healing we are faced with something quite ambiguous. The ambiguities are in fact numerous; distinctions must be made between salvation and healing (although the Gospel unhesitatingly uses the former term to describe the latter reality), miracles and healing (we shall come back to this), magic and religion, the physical and the psychic (we know how many attempts to elaborate an intermediate category of the psychosomatic have been attacked by both psychoanalysts and medical men), the domain of the exact sciences (in this case, physicochemical therapy) and the doctor-patient relationship, etc. A long list could be made of ambiguities like these on which not much clarity has yet been achieved.

It is not enough simply to say that healings take place at charismatic meetings; wheelchairs return home empty, their former occupants now walking; these people resume their normal activities, continue to be healthy, and thank God for it. Not only is it not enough simply to make such assertions; it is even dangerous to stop with them. We need to go to a further question: Is the source of these healings itself safe or dangerous? Are those engaged in such healings relapsing into magic or illusion?

As those involved see things and consciously reflect on them, the healings come about in this way. The restoration of an individual's proper relation to God, through prayer, penance, and confession, restores interior balance, and this has psychic and physical effects. At the same time, the interiorly dissociated individual is reintegrated, and this means the elimination of many alienations and inhibitions that may well have had bodily consequences. Finally, the same causes lead to a restoration of human relationships that are so often confused and disturbed. (I myself have heard so many times from people in charismatic communities: "I was on the point of getting divorced; now I'm back with my family, and we're all extremely happy.")

These three aspects of spiritual healing and its repercussions in the human being as a whole are sometimes summed up in the saying "Love heals." It is a motto I have often heard in the course of my investigations. In somewhat fuller terms: When the love taught by the Gospel, the divine love called *agapē*, is truly lived and made effective in a human life, it restores the human being's inner harmony and integrity.

This essential causative factor is being ever more fully appreciated and interiorized in the more mature charismatic communities. At Houston, for example, healings take place without fanfare, as part of daily life in a genuinely fraternal community. At the parish high Mass, my neighbor exchanged a few words with the person in front of him, then turned to me and told me, as though it were a piece of ordinary good news, "She is my mother-in-law; she had a spinal problem, and she has just been cured." And, as a matter of fact, I saw the woman stooping as she worked all afternoon in the garden, but no one said another word about the change in her. Healings are the daily bread of these people.

After spending a few years as a medical missionary, Dr. Bob Eckert, now a member of the Houston parish, started a clinic in one of the poorest sections of the city. The principle that guides his work is this: to give the sick not only the remedies and technical assistance (very up-to-date) they need, but also the friendship and fellowship they all need for survival and healing. The experience of the clinic testifies to the validity of the principle. Here the healing power of *agapē* works harmoniously with medical technology. The clinic is free, with each person giving what he wishes. The staff forms a community and lives on very little; they represent an incredible challenge to the country of the dollar. And yet they are making headway, for similar clinics are being founded elsewhere.

In all of this practice, the basis of which is highly empirical, two points have received little theoretical clarification. The first: What is the nature of the restoration produced by the encounter with God in prayer and more especially in the sacrament, which is the place of encounter with the Savior? The second: How are we to conceive of the interrelationship between what, for lack of better names, we call the moral, and the physical, at the ill-defined point where the biological (physicochemical) and psychological sciences overlap?

At Notre Dame, Francis MacNutt said that the healings effected there in June 1974 were "psychosomatic." This ambiguous and perhaps deceptive word was challenged, but the challenge did not do away with the underlying problem. By any accounting, health and healings have to do with the way in which a man takes possession of himself and mobilizes all the resources he has, of whatever order.

A healing that took place during a prayer meeting in Puerto Rico throws a suggestive light on this complicated area. The priest who presided at the prayer meeting told me of the incident. A lady from a rather well-to-do family was brought to the meeting in her invalid's chair, as someone who had not walked for several years. She returned home on her own feet, after bearing witness to this effect: "I was enjoying my invalid state, because it meant I was served, cared for, protected, and coddled. Tonight I received the strength to reject this situation and to walk again."

We have shown how faith can have a role to play in moral and physical healing. Still unanswered is the question of how God can make use of faith to accomplish what human actions and agencies, left to themselves, cannot do. Here again, God is not forbidden to work a miracle—but when do we have a miracle? And what is a miracle anyway? A difficult problem; we shall return to it shortly.

Shedding light on these problems that arise where several domains of reality meet is a long-range business. The charismatics are aware of the limitations and obscurities, which they try to isolate without going beyond their competence, and with the help of representatives from the various scientific disciplines.

## 4. The Charism at Work

1. Pentecostalist healing services are theocentric—they focus, that is, on Christ, on grace, and on the generosity of God. The prayer is humble, and does no violence to heaven, even though it be persevering. God is regarded as more important than his gifts. In the services I have attended there has been hardly any departure from the pattern of praise and adoration. The prayer for healing often takes the form of anticipated thanksgiving, or of the exercise of the charism of discernment with regard to the healings God wishes to bestow or has just bestowed.

During the service at Notre Dame, for example, the charism of those doing the praying was not the only one being put to use; other people throughout the stadium or at the podium (like Barbara Shlemon) were exercising the charism of discernment. The important thing is that the attitude to God embodied in the exercise of the charism eliminates the temptation to practice magic, that is, to use God as a means of serving man. This is a matter of high importance and cannot be overemphasized.

2. The activity of healing is not regarded as miraculous or extraordinary—on the contrary, for the underlying conviction is that healing is an integral part of the Gospel message and an ordinary part of the whole Christian community's ministry toward its sick members.

Adopting a perspective that is clearly that of the Gospel itself, the charismatics take a comprehensive view of the place of healing within the overall plan of salvation. That plan looks upon healing as both religious and moral, individual and social.

Such an approach to the need of healing in both man and society arises out of a very vivid awareness that is widespread in the United States. In fact, this perspective is so dominant in the culture that we find an echo of it in the speech Richard Nixon gave when he announced his resignation from the presidency.

> As we look to the future, the first essential is to begin healing the wounds of this nation, to put the bitterness and divisions of the recent past behind us and to rediscover those shared ideals that lie at the heart of our strength as a great and as a free people. By taking this action I hope that I will have hastened the start of that process of healing, which is so desperately needed in America.[21]

3. Healing services aim at restoring the *existential* relation of the individual to himself, to God, and to other men. The thing that is formally and specifically improved is the way he accepts his own life and that of others, on the basis of a renewal in the fundamental reference to the transcendent God who is Love.

4. Those who exercise the ministry of healing respect the medical profession and the treatment the individual is receiving. They do not try to alienate the sick from their physicians; on the contrary, when a person has been "healed," the healers bid him go to his doctor to have the cure verified. In the last analysis, the relation of the

healers to the medical profession raises a problem analogous to that raised in the writings of M. Balint, namely, the relation between medical science and the doctor-patient relationship in which the medical practitioner is involved and that plays an important, even indispensable role.[22] We should bear in mind, too, that the doctor-patient relationship is not the only personal relationship the sick person needs if he is to be cured. The family relationship and the religious relationship are also important and must not be left to chance.

To this end, those who exercise a healing ministry within the charismatic movement work in a co-operative effort with the doctors. The former believe that the future belongs to a habitual, organic collaboration between healers and physicians. They are convinced that God, the ultimate author of every cure, can work a cure either through medical means or "directly through prayer."[23]

5. Possessors of the charism of healing do not behave as wonder workers but as men of prayer and as brothers praying for a brother. The ambiguity to be noted here is that those who exercise this ministry note within themselves phenomena of a kind associated with the medium at a spiritualist séance: the feeling that a sick person is present, that he needs healing, that God wishes to heal him. During a prayer meeting, the leader may say (as I heard one leader actually say), "God wishes to heal someone who has trouble with his leg. Can that person make himself known?"

We may wonder about a charism whose function is to discern a need of healing, even before the sick person is aware of it. May such a charism not become a means of group suggestion?

Frequently, the person with the charism of healing feels in his hands a warmth, a slight trembling, the passage, as it were, of some fluid. The two index fingers of Barbara Shlemon tap lightly one against the other as she prays with hands joined. I noticed this at one of the Notre Dame services, when I was only a couple of yards distant from her. Francis MacNutt also notes this kind of phenomenon in his book but does not go into its nature. Barbara does not dwell on it but interprets it as an invitation to continue praying as long as the signal lasts.

Men need symbolic referents of various kinds for their presence to and action upon other men. Presence is an important element in every human relationship. We often speak of an actor's "presence," but there is also the presence of a leader who issues orders, of a doctor, or of a priest, and, of course, the basic presence of each person to himself and to God. These various types of presence are connected with signs, and these signs consequently play an important role in the dialectic of "being there" and "not being there."

6. An important point is that in Catholic Pentecostal groups the healing ministry is exercised by the community, not by isolated individuals. The person who prays and imposes hands does not do so alone. The reason behind this is the desire to highlight the importance not of the individual but of the community, though always, of course, in subordination to God, the source of all healing.

Here the Catholic Pentecostal healers stand in sharp contrast to Kathryn Kuhlman, who adopted an almost theatrical manner, along with her stylish white or multicolored dress. This is not to deny that she had a deep personal awareness of being only an instrument in God's hands. Yet many people who attended her healing service believed more in Kathryn than in God,[24] however pure her own intentions may have been. If this individualistic style were to prevail, it would give rise to serious abuses in more than 90 per cent of the cases.

There is another point to be noted about the communal exercise of the healing ministry. It is that, in the Ann Arbor communities, the teams that exercise the ministry of healing are made up of an equal number of men and women, perhaps in order to avoid giving men or women a monopoly. Two women participated in the service I reported earlier. Of these, one was pregnant and close to term. I had noticed the difficulty she had in seating herself on the wooden benches during the meeting, and I thought she had come to ask for help; instead, she came to exercise her ministry of healing prayer! The other woman was young, with Indian features, and quite beautiful; her beauty, however, owed nothing to artifice, but was the expression of a simple, sincere life. Both women wore inexpensive dresses that did not appear new to me.

In summary: Those who exercise this charism concentrate on God rather than on his benefits; on the sick person, not on the minister; on the healing, not on a miracle; on personal encounter rather than on results; on thanksgiving more than on petition. All this creates an attitude that is proof against any temptation to deal in magic.

## 5. HEALING AND MIRACLES

We began this chapter by contrasting, in rather cavalier fashion, the crisis of miracles at Lourdes and the recent revival of the charism of healing within the charismatic movement. The contrast surely calls for discussion, and we must try to draw some lessons from it.

### THE EVOLUTION AT LOURDES

To begin with, we need a certain amount of historical background. The early history of cures at Lourdes was accompanied by a great wave of popular enthusiasm, but the enthusiasm was not free of confusion, nor did it always distinguish authentic cures from illusory cases. The illusory cases were eliminated first by the effort at classification on the part of the episcopal commission (1858–62)[25] and later by the activity of the bureau in charge of verifying cures. Dr. Boissarie did good work, especially in showing up the role of hysteria in some apparent cures. The end result was a list of cures in which there seemed to be good reason for maintaining that God had intervened.[26]

Two difficulties, however, gradually led to an impasse.

1. The definition of miracle as an exception to the laws of nature belongs to a different culture than the one that reigns in medical science. The postulates underlying scientific research do not allow for such exceptions being made; neither do they permit the researcher to admit that any phenomenon is permanently inexplicable and thus beyond his reach. Thus the very development of science and the acceptance of its increasingly strict demands have caused a crisis as far as the medical verification of cures effected directly by God is concerned.

2. The value attached to a scientific verification of miracles has led to a growing gap between cure and verification. In this situation, to emphasize the importance of scientific verification is to play down the importance of the cure as an event that is humanly and spiritually significant.

There can be no question, of course, of minimizing the importance of controls. These are needed if we are not to be taken in by illusory cures and if we are to be able to say, with Bishop Laurence at Lourdes in 1862, "The finger of God is here."

The trouble is that, given the process of verification as it is carried on today, many cures that the sick experience as a physical and spiritual benefit are cast into outer darkness. Almost no publication of such cures is allowed; the persons concerned are not to speak of them as long as the cures are considered doubtful. Here we have a particular case of emphasizing the juridical at the expense of life. Vatican II pointed out how this phenomenon operates in many areas, and it attempted to reverse the trend; henceforth, law is to be subordinate to life, not life to law, in accordance with the principle enunciated by Jesus himself that "the sabbath is made for man, not man for the sabbath." But such a reversal of perspective is difficult to achieve in a number of areas (the handling of marriage cases, for example).

When it comes to cures, the overshadowing of the event by the requirements of official acknowledgment becomes a source of uneasiness and difficulties for the sick themselves, for the doctors, for the public, and for faith.

•The sick person who comes, full of gratitude, to the medical bureau immediately encounters the impersonality that necessarily marks official procedures. His cure is quickly rejected if it is minor, or if it seems explicable, or if the sickness was not organic, or the organic nature of it was not established by a complete and probative documentation. But even in the very exceptional cases where all the necessary conditions are at hand, the verification of cure will be delayed for the years a complete examination will take.

•The doctor who receives the cured person at the medical bureau is quite aware of how the bureau's procedures distort reality. How is he to reconcile the strict demands of his investigative technique with his concern not to do psychological damage to a person who has found new reason to live and hope, to believe and thank God, even if his case is not one that can be scientifically verified?

•A similar distortion is evident when it comes to informing the public. Thus there is to be no spontaneous broadcasting of the news. "The good news of a cure" must be placed under a bushel or in cold storage if the cure cannot be verified or until it is verified. Jesus did not manage to secure the silence of those he had cured

(Mk. 1:45), but at Lourdes, with a hundred years of experience behind them, they have learned how to command a silence that makes the event a nonevent and neutralizes any influence it might have.

Since the headline "Miracle at Lourdes" is still an alluring one, the journalists whose job it is to get the latest information, "the news," check periodically for any recent occurrence. In their book, a cure, no matter how striking, cannot be "news" five or ten years later; they don't want what they call "mummies" or "dead miracles." The result is periodic tension between the medical bureau and the religious journalists.

As a result of all these considerations, there is now a felt need of revising the whole approach to verification. In the present system, justice is done neither to the sick nor to the doctors nor to faith nor even to God, who is expected to perform in a close to magical fashion.

These difficulties also suggest that we look at the respective aims of scientific verification (which has become the focal point of the whole pastoral effort related to miracles at Lourdes) and of healing (which is the point on which the charismatic movement concentrates). Examination quickly shows the aims to be diametrically opposed in several respects:

1. The charismatic ministry of healing aims at creating the conditions for an encounter with God in which health will be restored. Verification aims at a classification in which any cure will be eliminated whose "unexplainableness" is not strictly proved.

2. The ministry of healing fosters belief, trust, and therefore a certain naïveté. The process of verification fosters the critical spirit and the methodical doubt, and thus a form of disbelief. On the one side, the aim is to have unbounded hope; on the other, it is to admit nothing that is not strictly demonstrated.

3. The ministry of healing aims at stirring gratitude by focusing on God and not stopping at his blessings. Verification is concerned with the cure itself, that is, with objective medical facts, and the intention is to achieve an official proof that cannot be gainsaid by unbeliever any more than by believer.

We need only take these two attitudes and translate them into terms of human relationships and we will see how very much opposed they really are. On the one hand, there is the attitude of the person who receives an anniversary gift and thinks it tactless to find out how much it cost, since that would be to treat the gift as a piece of merchandise, the friend as a tradesman, and the anniversary as a bit of buying and selling. Yet that is precisely the ground on which the verification process deliberately moves.

The reader should not take this analysis as a judgment of comparative value. Its aim is simply to bring out the specific nature of two functions that each have their own aims. Having grasped the specific nature, we will more easily see how difficult it is to harmonize the two, since healing has to do with the freely given, and verification with strict proof. It is very difficult to verify the freely given as such, and Jesus refused to give the scribes the proofs they were seeking when they asked him for a sign from heaven.

The quest for *healing* can foster illusion and credulity, but the quest for *verification,* too, has its danger: It risks losing sight of the essential thing, and doing so the more obstinately inasmuch as the very postulates of science reject the extraordinary event that the verificatory process is supposed to establish.

What harmonization, if any, of these two functions or attitudes is possible?

Dialogue between the representatives of the two approaches is very much to be desired if any progress is to be made, since the two attitudes or approaches are in fact complementary in several respects. The century-long experience of Lourdes can be useful in helping the charismatic movement develop the critical sense in which it is at present somewhat lacking (exaggerated accounts of healings are sometimes hastily published, leading to disillusionment and the discrediting of the healing ministry). On the other hand, the experience of the charismatic movement tends to revive a faith that expects everything, including healing, from God, and that helps to change an atmosphere of reticence, anxiety, and even aggressive opposition when it comes to healing. The charismatic experience of healing gives new importance to God, salvation, and thanksgiving.

We must not exaggerate, to the advantage of one or another side, the contrast that we have been emphasizing in order to draw the lines clearly, for, at Lourdes, the stretcher bearers, nurses, nursing Sisters, and priests in charge of prayer still carry on the original tradition. They exercise on behalf of the sick various ministries concerned with healing. Moreover, an effort is made to reintegrate the sick into society. It begins during the pilgrimages with dialogues between sick and healthy, and these dialogues continue when the pilgrims return home. Finally, it was at Lourdes that the first experiments were made with a view to revising the sacramental liturgy for the anointing of the sick.

On the charismatic side, the publication of embroidered accounts of healings has caused a felt need for documentation and verification. An active effort is being made along these lines at Ann Arbor; when I asked for further information, someone there wrote me recently: "We do intend to publish the fact, but we are still looking for some corroboration. We do not require, of course, what they require at Lourdes, but we do want the testimonies to be solid enough that they will be a source of inspiration and faith for our readers." Here we can see at work a distinction between testimony and canonical proof. The latter should not eliminate the former.

We shall turn now to a further point. It is that modern cultural change is calling for a revision of the classical definition of miracle and, consequently, for a revision of the criteria used in establishing that a miracle has occurred.

## DEFINITION AND CRITERIA OF A "MIRACLE"

Whenever healings are attributed to God in the Gospel, they are described in one or other of three ways: as

1. *signs* (Greek, *sēmeion;* Hebrew, *ôtot*);

2. or *prodigies* (Greek, *teraton;* Hebrew, *môftim*);

3. or *wonders* (Greek *endoxa,* Lk. 13:17, and *paradoxa,* Lk. 5:26, or *thauma,* the more frequent word from which "thaumaturge" is derived). The corresponding verbs, *thaumazo* and *ekthaumazo,* signify (with varying nuances) the astonishment that is also expressed by the verbs *ekplēsso* and *existēmi.* (This last-named verb yields the substantive, ecstasy, which signifies the stupefaction felt by a man who is taken completely out of himself.)

In the Old and New Testaments these nouns do not refer only to miracles in the sense of physical prodigies, but also signify, more broadly, the *signs* of God that the believer recognizes and that he found to be "wonderful" or "prodigious," as the case might be. The idea of a miracle being a defiance of the laws of nature was the response of a Christian rationalism to atheistic rationalism; today, this idea of miracle is as outdated as the rationalism it was meant to counteract.

It is incumbent upon us, therefore, to return to the Bible and learn there the meaning of healings, which can be described as signs, prodigies, or wonders worked by God. The key word, however, is "sign," since the important thing is the *significance* of the healing in relation to God and salvation. It is not, of course, a matter of indifference that a sign should also be something exceptional, marvelous, and astonishing, thus manifesting the transcendence of God and the freedom and liberality with which he acts; but this aspect is secondary and is always overshadowed by the element of mystery.

## TOWARD A RENEWAL OF CRITERIA

What effect will such a return to the sources have on the criteria of verification? The criteria presently used are reducible to three: the fact of the sickness (its organic character); the fact of the cure (complete, sudden, etc.); and the inexplicability of the cure.

The first two criteria fall under the competence of the medical profession. The long experience of the bureau for verification and of the medical commissions at Lourdes has brought to light cures that are marvelous and astonishing.

Today, however, our ideas of both sickness and healing have become relational—that is, medical science tends now to think of illness as something affecting the whole man rather than as a simple organic accident. Health, for its part, is a constantly shifting balance, a perpetual struggle against deficiencies that are more or less successfully integrated into a man's overall condition, more or less successfully compensated for.

The real problem today is with the third point; here we have reached an impasse, for to say that any fact is "inexplicable" is to reject the fundamental methodological principle of all science. Science must never give up in the face of the inexplicable or look to a transcendent cause for its explanation; it must seek the explanation solely within the realm of the phenomenal. Consequently, nothing can be declared "inexplicable" except with the proviso (no matter how explicit or tacit) "in the present state of our knowledge." Once this proviso is added, however, the intention implicit in the question "Is the cure inexplicable?" is rejected. Canonists whose expertise is in the procedures for canonization have told me that the addition of such a proviso would render a medical testimony juridically worthless.

Thus both the Gospels and the norms that hold sway in our contemporary scientific and cultural world bid us rephrase the question. The question must no longer be, "Is this cure inexplicable?" but rather, "Is this cure ordinary or extraordinary? Do we find it baffling? In what way?"

If a cure is extraordinary and baffling, this is enough to confirm its value as a sign, and we can renounce any effort to give scientific proof that the cure represents an exception to the laws of nature. ("Exception to the laws of nature" is nonsense to the very sciences we would have to call on for the proof!)

In this alternative approach, the role of the doctors would be to test whether the cure was beneficial, astonishing, extraordinary. Ecclesiastical authorities could then more comfortably carry out their own proper task, which is to estimate the impact of the event on the sick person and on the community to which he belongs, and, on the basis of these estimates, to judge whether the cure is a beneficial religious sign that is accessible to faith.

This is not the place to push these questions any farther. They are the subject of serious study at Lourdes, in consequence of the lucid and courageous utterances of Dr. Mangiapan, the new president of the verification bureau.[27]

It seemed it would be helpful if the people at Lourdes and the leaders of the charismatic movement could meet and share their thoughts. Such a meeting took place after the Congress in Rome at Pentecost 1975. The chief representatives of the healing ministry in America (Father MacNutt, O.P., author of the first book on the subject, and Father Michael Scanlon, who is interested in healing from the viewpoint of the sacrament of penance and spiritual direction) and in France (Father Regimbal, Father de Monléon, and Father Bertrand Lepesant) journeyed to Lourdes for a meeting with the theological, medical, and pastoral commission that had been discussing these problems for the past year.

The sharing of experiences proved in fact to be very fruitful. The discussion quickly centered on the ongoing experience of healings in the charismatic renewal, and it became increasingly evident that the criteria for verification as well as the predominant role assigned to verification required revision. The basis for such a revision consists of two clear facts. The first is that healing is a moral and spiritual phenomenon and not merely a physical one, and that the relationship of the sick person to other men and to God plays a very important role. The second is that the mission of healing that Jesus gave to his disciples continues in the Church and has recently attained a new vitality.

The important thing was to get the healing activity of the charismatic movement into proper perspective. It is a response to serious questions that are inevitably raised by Scripture, tradition, and contemporary experience. In what sense is healing—moral, psychic, and physical—an integral part of the Gospel? Can the traditional healing function of Christianity be exercised today without giving rise to conflicts with science and without encouraging credulity or magic? How are the various levels of healing to be interrelated: healing for sin, healing for emotional problems (or what MacNutt in a fine phrase calls the "healing of memories"[28]), healing for physical sickness, and even "deliverance" from oppression by demonic powers?[29] How are we to interrelate the hope for healing, the art of integrating sickness into our lives, resignation to the inevitable, and a hope that looks beyond our present world?

## 6. Conclusion

Our concern in this chapter has been with the charism of healing. Let us summarize our conclusions with regard to it.

1. The revival of the healing function that plays so important a role in the Gospel is not retrogressive fantasy but a return to the sources (Scripture and tradition) and a response to contemporary frustrations and needs. The experiences people are having today are shedding light on numerous points of biblical exegesis and early tradition.

2. According to Francis MacNutt, the charism of healing is not to be thought of as extraordinary. Rather, "the extraordinary has become ordinary," and the healing ministry should be "an ordinary, normal part of the life of every Christian community."[30]

This conclusion is identical with one of those we reached concerning glossolalia in the preceding chapter,[31] and cuts the ground from under many objections to the charismatic movement, which find in the movement a tendency to focus on the extraordinary.

"The extraordinary has become ordinary," says Father MacNutt. What Cardinal Suenens calls a "democratization of sanctity"[32] is also a democratization of the charisms. These paradoxical formulas are related to those that are found in the Gospel itself: "The Good News is proclaimed to the poor" (Mt. 11:5).

## Chapter 6

---

# THE CHARISMATIC MOVEMENT
# IN CHURCH HISTORY

Before turning, in the next chapter, to the meaning and importance of the charismatic movement, we must try to give a general impression of how the movement fits into the history of the Church.

## 1. ANTECEDENTS

The charismatic renewal is one of a series of movements that historians use three chief labels to describe.

### REVIVALS

This term is used to characterize the renewals or awakenings that have occurred in great numbers in the post-Reformation period, beginning in the seventeenth century with the movement led by John Wesley (1703–91), the founder of Methodism. While listening to a sermon on the Letter to the Romans, this Anglican pastor underwent an experience that brought great inner warmth and enthusiasm: He experienced his heart being changed by faith in Christ, that is, in the Jesus who is truly a savior.

The experience led Wesley to reinterpret the whole of Christianity in terms of vital Christian life. His movement was a profound reaction to the challenge of rationalism and to a deadening formalism, through a return to direct, lived, sensible experience that was stimulated by contact with the Scriptures. Since rationalism and formalism continued to weigh on the Church through the nineteenth century, other revivals followed. Pentecostalism is the best known of these, and curiously enough it began within Methodism! The Pentecostalists were not accepted by the other Methodists and, to the Pentecostalists' regret, had to break off from the parent Church, just as Wesley's immediate disciples had had to break off, after Wesley's death, from the Anglican Church that rejected them.

### ENTHUSIASM

This term has served as a general descriptive word for all religious movements that are shaped, not by external norms and forms, but by an inspiration directed toward reviving the Christian life and restoring its original dynamism.

In Greek, the word "enthusiasm" meant a "being moved by god" or a "being inspired"; the basic notion was *en theos*, that is, "having the god within oneself" or "being filled with the god." The English word retained this essential meaning, although the corresponding French word lost it after the seventeenth century. Today the word connotes strong feeling of wonder and joyous, fervent dedication, but it can be used unfavorably as well as favorably. In past history, it is a word that has often been used in a derogatory way.

Luther had to enter the lists against the "enthusiasts" who, in the name of the "Spirit," condemned him as a man of the "letter" (that is, of the Scriptures). Luther, of course, rejected any such dissociation. The Formula of Concord (1577) describes as follows those who claim to have knowledge of the Spirit (*Geistgelehrten*) as opposed to knowledge of the Scriptures (*Schriftgelehrten*): "The 'enthusiasts' are those who, without hearing the word of God preached, expect to be enlightened from heaven by the Holy Spirit."[1]

Centuries earlier, Theodoret, bishop of Cyrrhus (c. 393–c. 458), bore witness to a similar conflict when he thus described certain groups of Christians of whom we have little knowledge from other sources: "They are called 'enthusiasts' because, though in fact under the influence of a demon, they interpret his action in them as a sign of the Holy Spirit's presence."[2]

Ronald Knox, drawing on various German scholars, wrote a book about these various movements.[3] He defines them in terms of a break with worldly life and a return, under the impulse of a call from God, to the life of the early Church. Concretely, these movements react against the artificiality of formalistic, decadent, or corrupt societies by returning to the simplicity that marked the apostolic age.

Their desire to regain apostolic simplicity leads them to part company from their coreligionists; the latter react with irony and criticism to the scorn and pity of the enthusiasts. Ecclesiastical authorities begin to feel embarrassed by the high repute of the innovators and feel bound to move against them. This kind of conflict intensified throughout the Middle Ages and the Renaissance, when the enthusiasts could rightly criticize the corruption of ecclesiastical power.

The fervent zeal of the enthusiasts could readily turn into restiveness, and their quest of purity into rigorism. In Knox's view, their attitudes implied a theology of grace according to which grace not only did not perfect nature but also even abolished it, in order to replace it by a new kind of existence equipped with its own new powers. Grace brought divine gifts and powers that were opposed to those of this world, somewhat as young David refused to wear the armor of Saul and confronted Goliath with a minimum of protection. Enthusiasm often aims at direct communication with God through prophecies, oracles, and inspirations; it distrusts intellect and comes down on the side of feeling.

If this tendency is not offset, enthusiasm is in danger of turning into illuminism. This pejorative term is applied to many enthusiastic movements, from the Messalians of the second half of the fourth century (also called *Euchites*, or "praying people," and *Enthusiasts*) to the Quietists of the seventeenth and eighteenth centuries. Illuminism is characterized by a penchant for passivity, for the nonactivity of the soul in the approach to God. It relies excessively on direct interventions of the Holy Spirit and tends to let man be moved rather than to have him freely direct his action by a mind under the influence of faith and its teaching.

## PNEUMATICS, CHARISMATICS

It is possible to apply to all these movements a still broader term, but one that is also more theological and radical. The followers of all these movements rely on the Holy Spirit and his gifts, and can therefore be called "pneumatics" (from *pneuma*, "spirit" or "Spirit") and "charismatics" (from *charisma*, "gift"). Such movements come into existence from time to time when there is a keenly felt nostalgia for the early Church. They try to recapture the experience of a time when the Church had just come into existence through the inspiration of the Holy Spirit, was structured from within by his charisms, and exercised a creative freedom in living according to the words of Jesus.

In their integrated community life these movements are inventive in adapting ministries to varied needs and to an effective preaching, action, and apostolate.

The choice of name makes little difference. In studies of revivals, enthusiasm, and spirit-inspired movements, we find pretty much the same movements passing in review. Certainly, all three descriptive terms are applicable to the Pentecostalists and the Neo-Pentecostalists.

## 2. A TORMENTED HISTORY

These movements, which rise up in imperious reaction against religious dullness and tepidity, the status quo and formalism, have always led a tormented existence.

### OLD AND NEW TESTAMENTS

That statement certainly holds for the prophets, the first men of the Spirit and his gifts. The prophetic schools met with sarcasm and mockery and with repression by the authorities. Yet out of them came Elijah and Elisha, who were hunted by kings and threatened with death; Amos, who was exiled; Jeremiah, who was imprisoned in an underground cell, then thrown into a muddy cistern and left there to die. These men were enthusiasts, in the sense of being truly inspired, and yet they were the spearheads of the messianic movement and splendid forerunners of the Gospel. Jesus expressly aligns himself with them and experiences in his person the tragic fate of the prophets, for which he had reproached Jerusalem.

The early Church likewise passed through some extremely tense situations, the gravity of which is greatly played down in the Acts of the Apostles, written as they were by Luke, the evangelist most inclined to present a picture of peace and tranquillity. His tendency becomes clear when we compare his Gospel with the other three, especially that of Mark.

## MONTANISM

In the postapostolic period the first movement that has left historical memories behind it is Montanism. This movement, with its emphasis on community, prophecy, and glossolalia, came to light in Phrygia, in the second third of the second century; a man named Montanus was its leader.

A strict man to the point of being a rigorist, Montanus fell into schism, although no really significant heresy can be charged against him. In fact the teaching of Tertullian, who was drawn into the Montanist schism, is so irreproachable that it has won him a place of honor among the Fathers of the Church. We find astonishing touches of genius in this theology of the Holy Spirit, where he anticipates key formulations of Catholic doctrine.[4] Generally speaking, it is typical of these movements that they respected the Church's teaching; it took ingenuity or a malicious eye to detect any unorthodoxy in them.

Montanism has always been accused not only of extremism, rigorism, illuminism, and feminism, but also of having established a charismatic hierarchy that set itself up as rival of the official hierarchy. St. Jerome tells us that among the Montanists "the bishop comes third. They give first place to the patriarchs from Pepusa in Phrygia, and second place to those they call the *koinōnous;* thus bishops fall back into the third and almost last place."[5]

But did the Montanists in fact deviate on this point? Despite a concordant reference in the Code of Justinian,[6] we have no real proof that what Jerome says was true. The institution of patriarchs soon became general throughout the East (and has been honored by Vatican II). And if the *koinōnoi* (which means a group characterized by communion or collegiality) were a kind of synod associated with the patriarch, we would again have a situation that prevailed throughout the East and that Vatican II has endeavored to restore in the Church as a whole.

St. Epiphanius attributes to Montanus the monstrous claim "I am the Lord God," and asserts that Montanus regarded himself as the incarnation of the Spirit.[7] In all probability, however, Montanus simply prophesied in the name of the Holy Spirit. This interpretation has seemed evident to me ever since the day when a young woman at Ann Arbor shocked me by the way she spoke. She said, in substance: "Come to me, receive my light, etc." I thought to myself, "Who does she think she is?" However, in fact, she was simply speaking in typically prophetic style, and the words "thus says the Lord" were to be understood. She was the channel of a message that came from God and was spoken in his name. The others at the meeting were used to the exercise of this charism and were in no way misled.

As I indicated a moment ago, the basic deviation with which the Montanists are charged was the transferral of pastoral responsibility from the official hierarchy to the prophets who had overall charge. But this is a tendency we see equally at work in other Christian communities of the early centuries, notably in the community that produced or is reflected in the *Didache*. In this document we read: "Give these first fruits to the prophets, for they are your high priests" (13, 3). Yet we do not therefore regard this community as either dissident or heretical! (Admittedly, there was a great danger that people would ask more of prophecy than it could give; some groups today may be in danger of making the same mistake.)

It is very difficult, then, to know exactly what the Montanists were, especially since, apart from some works of Tertullian, we know them chiefly through their opponents, who had no desire to make distinctions or indicate nuances. The thing that seems most clear is that there was a rift between the Catholic authorities and a prophetic movement whose prophets, once threatened, turned into radical opponents. As a result, the "charismatic" abuses of Montanism undermined the good name of the charisms and caused people to be distrustful of them. This distrust was an important factor in the subsequent history of the charisms in the Church.

At a time where there was little inclination to be indulgent toward "heretics," Dom Henri Leclercq, a well-informed student of antiquity, passed this lenient judgment on Montanism (a judgment in which he uses to some extent language borrowed from Pierre de Labriolle, the foremost authority on the subject):

The hierarchy prevailed over individuals and reduced them to submission and discipline. The charisms had had their day and disappeared. . . . Catholics went too far in attributing to the Montanist manifestations an *originality* and unparalleled novelty. To do so, they had to have forgotten the not too distant past; and if they could forget it, it was because few memories of that past had survived. . . . *Catholics, unaccustomed to the charisms of an earlier day, could not or would not acknowledge them now.*[8]

## RELIGIOUS ORDERS

Within the Catholic Church the most successful revivals of an enthusiastic type have been associated with monasticism and religious life.

In the fourth century St. Anthony felt a call to leave the world and flee into solitude. His rejection of the world and his break with his culture gave birth to the vast movement of the Desert Fathers. This movement was able to preserve its inspired radicalism amid extremes of detachment.

In the sixth century St. Benedict of Nursia decided against solitude (after extensive personal experience of it) and established communities of men who would live and pray together. This marked a return to the common life of the early Christians, with the difference that the monastic community was cut off from the rest of the world. An island replaced the desert.

The Middle Ages brought new aspirations and some dismantling of the cloister walls, as St. Francis of Assisi (1181–1226) established communities that would remain in contact with the people. For centuries, men had fled the world; now Francis remained there to beg his bread and bear witness to the Gospel.

Meanwhile, since the eleventh century, eremitical movements had sprung up all over Europe, though not without encountering problems. We may think, for example, of Robert of Arbrissel (Brittany) who, with disciples of both sexes, went off to lead a penitential life in the forest of Craon and later established the double monastery of Fontevrault, where the abbess governed the men as well as the women.

Such, in very schematic outline, were the renewals that succeeded in the Church. Each involved a break with the past and a new beginning. Each continued in existence after the rise of later forms of a flourishing religious life. The foundation of new communities (hundreds and even thousands of them) that were more or less charismatic in their inspiration went on even despite Church regulations forbidding such new institutions. This was true of the Orders established by St. Francis and St. Dominic, since the Fourth Lateran Council (1215) had forbidden the founding of any new religious Order of any kind. Since this prescription had been ineffectual, the Second Council of Lyons (1274) renewed the prohibition and made it even stricter by eliminating all exceptions and pretexts.[9] The movement, of course, was stronger than any barrier that could be set up against it. But we can see that even in the privileged area of religious life, the relationship between charism and institution has not been without its tensions.

### JOACHIM OF FIORE

Joachim of Fiore (1132–1202) initiated a spiritual renewal that influenced the whole of the later medieval period, but he did not enjoy the same good fortune as his contemporaries who founded religious Orders. Though highly respected during his lifetime and listed by the Bollandists as a Blessed, he fell into such disrepute that Church historians have long presented him as a dangerous dreamer and the prophet of a new age and a new covenant in which the Spirit would replace Christ. A few years after his death, his opponents managed to have his teaching censured.

The censure was the work of the intellectuals of the time, and an act of revenge. Joachim had accused Peter Lombard, the "Master of the Sentences," of setting up a quaternity in God, inasmuch as Lombard spoke of the divine essence as being in some sense prior to the three Persons. Joachim was in fact putting a discerning finger on the most questionable departure of the Latin tradition from the biblical and Eastern tradition on the Trinity; the latter sees as the ultimate principle within the Trinity the Person of the Father, not a prior essence.

The theologians, however, could not tolerate such an attack on the great master of Scholasticism just as the latter's fame was increasing. The condemner must himself be condemned. The theologians therefore accused Joachim of the contrary error: that he reduced the divine unity to the unity of a collectivity. Some of the

Latins leveled this objection against the Eastern tradition as well, yet it seems in Joachim's case to have been simply a pretext. Unfortunately, we cannot reconstruct the debate, since the censure assured the complete disappearance of Joachim's book on the Trinity. But since what he says elsewhere about the Trinity is orthodox, we have every right to be suspicious of his condemnation by the Fourth Lateran Council.[10]

Before ratifying this censure, Honorius III felt bound to say that it could in no way affect the reputation for holiness that the founder of the Order of Fiore enjoyed: "We regard Joachim personally as a true Catholic and an adherent of the orthodox faith."[11]

Joachim's theory of the three ages of the world, the third being the age of the Spirit, responded to the need for restoring the Spirit (already the forgotten Person) to his rightful place. It implied, however, a dangerous inclination to emphasize the age of the Spirit by doing away with the age of the Son. By the same token, it tended to devalue earthly realities and promote an idealism congenial to an elite of the "pure." Such views did undoubtedly encourage aberrations like that of Gerard of San Donnino, who in 1254 announced that the age of the Spirit would begin in 1260, and was rightly condemned in 1255. At the same time, however, authors of renown made prudent use of the theory of the three ages, and no one troubled them on this account. Today, Joachim of Fiore is acknowledged to be "one of the fathers of the theology of history."[12]

## MOVEMENTS SUPPRESSED IN THE MIDDLE AGES

Other charismatic and spiritual movements of the Middle Ages met with a much worse fate. We need only run through the list of movements that, according to Fulbert Cayré, did not deserve the name of "Catholic" because they lacked an all-important virtue, namely, "submission to the authority of the Church."[13] This lack is enough, he says, to rule out "all the false spirituals who were legion in the Middle Ages."

This includes the Waldensians, "disciples of Peter de Vaux or Peter Waldo, a merchant of Lyons who gave away all his possessions and preached poverty about 1173; the heretical and rebellious Waldensians were excommunicated in 1184." The Amalricians, "disciples of Amalric of Benes . . . [who] were pantheists and taught a true divinization of man by the Holy Ghost. They are associated with the Brethren of the Free Spirit." The Joachimites, "disciples of Joachim of Flore. . . . Joachimism is the source of most of the pseudomysticism of the XIII[th] and XIV[th] centuries. One of Joachim's Trinitarian errors was condemned in 1215: He claimed that the unity of essence in God is not *vera* and *propria*."

It includes the Apostolic Brethren, "disciples of an ex-Franciscan, Gerard Segarelli, [who] preached poverty. . . . They fell into Pantheist mysticism." The Spirituals, "followers of the strict Franciscan observance and adepts of the Joachimite mysticism. . . . John Olivi . . . Albertino of Casale." The Fraticelli, "extremists among the Spirituals at the beginning of the XIV[th] century who revolted against John XXII."

It includes, finally, the Beguins, "Franciscan tertiaries who were drawn into the revolt of the Fraticelli." The Beghards, "often confused with the Beguins." The Friends of God, "Rhenish layfolk and clergy, who, in the XIV[th] century, helped to spread a mystical teaching . . . some of them fell into illuminism."

The historian finds it difficult to judge the real nature of these various movements. The chief reason for his predicament is that most of the writings produced by such groups have disappeared and are known only as seen by their opponents. It seems clear now that, in a measure difficult to determine accurately, these movements met with the calumnies that are the lot of the poor and their defenders, of innovators, and of all whose demands make others insecure and rouse the resentment of those in power. Their criticisms of princes of the Church whose lives, if not actually corrupt, bore little resemblance to the Gospel ideal, elicited the same kind of reaction that brought Savonarola to the stake. Obedient and disciplined though he was throughout his life, Joachim of Fiore did not spare the Roman Curia, and with reason.

We are, then, unable to form an accurate idea of the life and aims of these various medieval groups. We do know, however, that they all had in common a love of poverty and of the evangelical life in community. And there is a further fact that bids us avoid hasty and simplistic judgments; it is that for centuries these movements exercised an extensive influence, even on men noted for their orthodoxy, such as Giles of Viterbo in the sixteenth century.

There were certainly excesses and deviations, but did the ill will of the opposition exaggerate these? Were they due to basic defects, or were they peripheral and limited in extent? How far were they due to the radicalization of these groups in response to the continued misunderstanding and defense mechanisms of their opponents? The limited resources available to the historian make it difficult to evaluate the influence of such factors as these, although at times we can see them at work on the contemporary scene.

## THE CASE OF THE ALUMBRADOS

One thing is clear: Historical research has not justified the severity shown for several centuries to the Alumbrados who, from the fifteenth century on, were persecuted by the Holy Office on grounds of illuminism. Even forty-five years ago, Henri Bremond could write:

> The historians and theoreticians of spirituality are constantly warning us about the Spanish *alumbrados* and the danger they represented for the Church. . . . And yet this sinister bogeyman is still hidden in an impenetrable fog! We are constantly being told that a terrible epidemic of illuminism was ravaging Spain at that time. But no one even thinks of tracing for us, text in hand, the origin, exact nature, action, influence, and consequences, or, in a word, the history, of this deadly plague. There are very few proper names, some outrageously sketchy analyses, and not a hint of a statistic.[14]

Bremond's judgment is confirmed by the fact that every person and book of importance in the sixteenth century was at one time or other accused of illuminism.[15] Luis of Granada's *Guía de pecadores* (Guide for Sinners) and *Libro de la oración* (Treatise on Prayer) were put on the Index by Inquisitor General Valdés; this did not prevent them from eventually being regarded as spiritual classics. Blessed John of Avila (1500–69), "the Apostle of Andalusia," was imprisoned at Seville on a charge of illuminism. St. Teresa of Avila (1515–82) was likewise accused of illuminism, but the Inquisition did not dare bring her to trial. St. John of the Cross (1542–91) and St. Joseph Calasanctius (1556–1648) met with difficulties on the same account.

St. Ignatius Loyola (1491–1556) was tried twice: once at Alcalá, where he was imprisoned for forty-two days, and once at Salamanca, where he was detained for twenty-two days with his feet in irons. Although he had been declared innocent in Paris, he was again accused of illuminism at Venice and later at Rome in 1538. St. Francis Borgia, third General of the Jesuits, had his book *Obras del cristiano* (Treatise on the Actions of a Christian) put on the Index in Spain in 1559 and 1583.

We do not mean to say that there were no abuses in this movement as in others. Since Bremond wrote, V. Beltrán de Heredia, M. Bataillon, Mrs. Selke, A. Marquez, and others have shown the historical existence of Alumbrados who went astray to a great or lesser extent. The problem, however, is to distinguish what is valid in their movement from their excesses and relapses, the apparent errors from the real errors, calumnies from genuine deviations, and legitimate condemnations from witchhunts.

## 3. Charism and Institution

The history that we have briefly reviewed sheds some light on a basic problem already mentioned in Chapter 3. People insist that there is no opposition between institution and charisms but, on the contrary, a pre-established harmony grounded in the relation between Christ and the Holy Spirit. This, as we indicated, is certainly true in principle and ideally. But history shows that the peaceful coexistence of institution and charisms has always been beset with difficulties, from the beginning of Church history down to our own time.

Concerning these difficulties, two points must be made. The first is that whenever a fruitful harmony has been achieved between charisms and institution, it has been at the cost of extreme tensions. This is perfectly clear for the early Church, as reflected for us in the Acts of the Apostles and the Letters of St. Paul.

The second point is that the capacity for accepting and integrating the charisms has been progressively lessened over the centuries by a series of events that led always in the same direction. One was the necessary transition from the period of creative improvisation to the period when the transmission and defense of what had been won became more important. Another was the transfer of leadership from itinerant ministers (the apostles) to ministers attached to a specific place—in other words, the passage from nomadism to the settled life. A third was the increasingly hierarchical, juridical, and administrative organization of the ecclesiastical institution as it patterned itself upon the Roman Empire. At the same time there was, within this overall system, the development of clerical power, centralization, and control, along with an emphasis on the apex of the pyramid to the detriment of the base (a criticism repeatedly voiced at Vatican II).

As a result of these factors, the relation between institution and charisms became progressively difficult and marked by conflict. The only exception (a limited one) to this rule was for the purely mystical charisms, that is, the charisms of those people who withdrew to the desert and its solitude or who lived apart in controllable enclosures and had no desire to exercise any influence on social and institutional structures, be they religious or political. This explains the success, which we pointed out a few pages back, of spiritual renewals in monasticism and religious life; it also explains the relative success of various sanctuaries and apparitions, although in this area there have been and continue to be severe strains at times.

We may say, then, that the institution, in its endeavor to grapple with the charisms, has tended to either of two extreme solutions: one is to reject, exclude, excommunicate; the other is to make the charisms part of the organization, to assimilate them into the system, but to the detriment of their vitality, so that the Spirit and his charisms are really "suppressed" (1 Th. 5:19). Assimilation was to some extent the fate of the Franciscan movement in the Middle Ages and of various modern movements such as Catholic Action (which was powerfully charismatic in its beginnings). (An audience with Pius XI saved Canon Cardijn just in the nick of time when he was being attacked.)

These two extreme solutions have their parallels in the chemistry of the body with its mechanisms for rejection, on the one hand, and phagocytosis, on the other. There are also intermediate solutions, such as marginalization, which corresponds to encystment.

The problem that is therefore posed by the history of the groups we have been studying is this: Can evangelical revivals be organically integrated into the life of a Church whose own tradition asserts that it must be constantly renewed and reformed (*semper reformanda*)?

The problem is not peculiar to Catholicism. We saw how Luther was forced to suppress the "enthusiasts" and how classical Pentecostalism was initially rejected by the various confessions that gave birth to it.

## 4. CONCLUSION

In the light of past history, it is striking indeed that Neo-Pentecostalism, a new, dynamic, "enthusiastic" movement that openly admits to Protestant influence, should be accepted in the most institutionalized and "traditional" Christian confessions, notably Catholicism. Is this a sign of the times? A revival of the original ability to live with vital tensions? Does it mark the beginning of an age of reconciliation between institutions (which admittedly have today become rather weak) and revivals of the Spirit and the evangelical life, with all the difficulties their creativity implies for institutions?

It is much too soon to attempt a definitive answer to such questions. The historical picture we have drawn is too sketchy, and the subject of it is too vast and unexplored; but at least it will have helped to shed light on the problem Catholic Pentecostalism faces. The new movement must learn to live with certain tensions, and it must learn to cope with two types of problems that beset the past movements we have been studying.

1. External problems. Charismatic (or enthusiastic, or spiritual) movements necessarily meet with distrust, aggressive rejection, and hostility. They can hardly escape criticism and caricature and the more or less hidden operation of various mechanisms of rejection and repression. Till now, however, the charismatic movement has been sufficiently open, receptive, and modest to prevent the formation of a hard-and-fast opposition.

At the Second International Lutheran Conference on the Holy Spirit, in August 1973, David Wilkerson "prophesied" that the warm welcome extended to the charismatics by the Catholic and Protestant Churches would not last and that the charismatics would be forced to leave their Churches. But he was undoubtedly not really speaking in the name of the Holy Spirit, as Ralph Martin (Catholic) and David du Plessis (Pentecostal) courteously objected.[16] Wilkerson did, however, put his finger on historical forces that operated in the past, and it is truly astonishing that they are not operative today as well. Perhaps these forces were rendered ineffective by the Second Vatican Council when it rejected the old pyramidal view of the relationship between institutions and the people of God. It revised the relationship in keeping with the teaching of Christ, by putting the emphasis once again on the people, equating power once again with service, and rehabilitating the charisms.

2. Internal problems. Illuminism, emotionalism, and elitism have been mentioned in the course of our historical survey. We shall return to them below, in Chapter 8, where we shall see how the charismatic renewal is coping with the problems that accompany "enthusiasm," inspiration, creativity, qualities that can perdure only when they are integrated into an organic order.

## Chapter 7

# SOURCES AND MEANING:
# AN EXPLANATION

*The blasphemy against the Holy Spirit consists in at-
tributing his operations to the contrary spirit, as Basil the
Great tells us. How is such an attribution made? It is
done when, seeing the wonders produced by the Holy
Spirit or the action of some other divine gift in one of
the brothers (for example, compunction, tears . . .) or
any other favor bestowed by the Holy Spirit on those
who love God, a man says that this is a deception of the
devil.*[1]

What is the source, and consequently the meaning, of the charismatic renewal, this remarkable phenomenon now sweeping the
Roman Catholic Church?

## 1. THREE HYPOTHESES

Three types of explanation have been offered:

1. According to the first, the sources of the phenomenon are the
hidden resources of the human psyche itself; this means that we
must go to depth psychology for the explanation. In this view, the
charismatic movement is successful because it applies a set of instru-
ments that liberate certain potentialities lying unrecognized or repressed in the unconscious. That is why charismatics give such a
strong impression of joy, fulfillment, dynamic energy, and improved psychic integration. That is why they can perform such extraordinary acts as healings and tongue speaking. That is why,
finally, they run the risk of emotionalism and illuminism.

2. Others say that the whole business is a delusion created by the devil, who is capable, after all, of leading astray even the elect. Father Molinié has warned charismatics against the possibility of delusion:

> The hypothesis of a more or less morbid, more or less voluntary illusion created by the devil . . . can *never* be totally excluded when there is question of spectacular mystical occurrences, such as we have here. Illusion is even more to be feared when the purpose of a meeting is precisely to stimulate such manifestations or at least to provide a favorable atmosphere for them. . . .
>
> A group that expects such manifestations cannot but desire them, especially if they "do good" to the participants, as the latter enthusiastically assert. Once people are in this frame of mind, there is always danger of a more or less consciously used psychological technique coming into play that will foster not only prayer but the spectacular phenomena which may accompany prayer. . . . The devil and man's imagination can imitate God's works the more easily when those works are of a sensible kind. He who receives these manifestations without having sought them should make a strong and sustained effort to be detached from them and to prefer the darkness of pure faith.[2]

Two of my correspondents, after being utterly disgusted by certain deviations of the Jamaa movement in Zaïre, wrote in categorical terms: "Like the Jamaa movement, Pentecostalism is vitiated in its very source. . . . It manifests a spirit that is not the Holy Spirit." They quote here the words of Father Caffarel: The Pentecostal experience "can overturn the psychological barriers that restrain the action of the Spirit." But, they add, the initiates of the Jamaa movement have also overturned these same "psychological barriers."

> Before enslaving men, Satan first liberates them. That is, he frees them from their psychological complexes. Father Caffarel claims that such an experience "strengthens faith." We see it rather as a drug that eventually causes the degradation of faith.
>
> The discernment of spirits needs to be applied to the very root of Pentecostalism, namely, the experience of the Spirit that is obtained on demand. Once this threshhold is crossed, valid discernment becomes impossible. In the Jamaa movement, a yes

is given, in an act of initiation, to a leader who necessarily remains unknown to the initiate; thereby, the soul crosses a threshhold and is plunged into the occult.

The same occult forces are responsible for the new Pentecost in the Church. For Catholics, there can be no new Pentecost. For occultists, on the contrary, there is indeed a new Pentecost, but it is the Pentecost of Satan as he achieves his supreme influence while continuing to hide himself from the initiate as far as possible. Pentecostalism is an ideal tool for Satan. Once he can imitate the outpouring of the Spirit, he has won the day. . . .

What Satan wants, in the last analysis, is to reduce the "spiritual" to the "sexual." Here both Pentecostalism and the Jamaa are, at bottom, one with the satanic mysticisms that draw their inspiration from the cabala.

This text, an extract from a long document, is based on an assimilation of Pentecostalism to the Jamaa movement. The women who wrote it had resisted the allurements of certain groups within the Jamaa movement, groups that ended up in rather serious deviations: mental derangement due to magic practiced by the leaders, illuminism, and at times group sex orgies. But Pentecostalism and the Jamaa movement are in fact quite different. Concretely, we do not find in the Pentecostal movement the same attitude of self-abandonment and dependence on a leader, the secrets revealed to initiates, the esotericism, and the rest of it.

3. Those who have had the charismatic experience and live under its influence believe quite simply that the Holy Spirit truly exists and is manifesting himself as Christ promised he would (Ac. 1:5, etc.). They believe that he "is healing wounds, melting the ice, straightening the crooked," as the hymn for Pentecost, "Come, Holy Spirit," describes him doing.

## 2. Integration of the "Natural" and the "Supernatural"

Here then are three explanations: natural, satanic, and divine. We cannot simply choose one of the three and eliminate the other two, but we must know how to combine various explanations: "both . . . and," not "either . . . or."

Concretely, this means we must not *oppose* the natural explanation to the supernatural explanation, since the supernatural, as Christianity understands it, does not destroy or denature nature, but respects it. The great evidence for this is the mystery of the incarnation.

The "supernaturalist" heresy consists in opposing or at least dissociating nature and the supernatural, putting a deep moat between them, as it were. But the supernatural is not to be thought of as a hat, or even a crown, set on a man's head. It is not added onto nature from the outside, but completes it from within. It is a new source of life, an in-spiration, a transfiguration. The action of the Spirit is unobtrusive and indistinguishable from the action of the subject whom he, the Spirit, awakens to an awareness of aspirations that are truly his own. One of the most meaningful descriptions of the Spirit's role has been given us by Christ when he tells us that the Spirit makes fountains of living water well up from the innermost depths and recesses (*ek koilias*) of a man (Jn. 7:38–39).

Since the outpouring of the Spirit truly liberates a man, it also involves a free act on man's part whereby he liberates himself. If this were lacking, how could we speak of authentic freedom?

Let us turn now to these various aspects of the problem.

## 3. The Psychosociological Dimension

### LIGHT FROM PSYCHOLOGY

The phenomena associated with Pentecost (the original Pentecost and its renewals today) imply, by any accounting, a liberation of psychic resources that are still not very well known. This liberation, moreover, has a negative and a positive side.

The *negative* side of the phenomenon consists in the elimination of rigidities, inhibitions, and superstructures that dam up vital energies, both spiritual and simply human. To express this aspect of their experience, people use various images. There is a thaw; the ice breaks up and the waters flow. A wall is razed; the interior defenses are dismantled and the subject moves out of his imprisoning egoism into contact with God and his fellow men.

St. Thérèse of Lisieux and Bergson use more dynamic images: The closed circle is broken within which the soul had been moving round and round, the inner drive is allowed to operate, and the soul begins to advance again.[3]

The *positive* side (inseparable from the negative) consists in the liberation and fruitful exercise of resources hitherto unknown or inoperative; this in turn helps to moral and physical balance. The energies thus liberated are applied to prayer, service, and the apostolate. This whole process is stimulated and rendered broader and deeper by the community's contribution in the form of example, mutual help, sharing, and solidarity.

This whole psychological dimension of the Pentecostal phenomenon falls within the purview of the sciences of man; it has been tested and emerged successfully. Numerous tests conducted in America during the past few years have shown charismatics to be basically healthy people from the psychological point of view. There is no positive correlation between tongue speaking and emotionalism or hysteria; in fact, there is even a negative correlation with hysteria. Moreover, the Pentecostal experience implies the overcoming of certain anxieties, inhibitions, rigidities, and neurotic reactions; it fosters a balanced personality. Such are the results of methodical testing.[4]

## ZEN, YOGA, AND CHARISMS

To get a better understanding of the means employed in the charismatic movement, it is helpful to compare them with zen and yoga.

The techniques used in zen and yoga are basically a matter of bodily postures and methods of breathing. Christians have been making extensive use of them in order to offset certain kinds of psychic handicaps and to facilitate spiritual progress. Those who use these disciplines claim, like the Pentecostalists, that they achieve inner pacification, a better integration of their vital powers, and a liberation for prayer.

And yet, according to one leader of the charismatic renewal in France, experience tends to show that one must choose and follow either Pentecostalism or these other ways, not both. Those who really live under the influence of the outpouring of the Spirit renounce, in fact, techniques that are non-Christian in origin. Why so? Because the sources and directions are different on the two sides.

Yoga (like zen) is a way of silence. In Pentecostalism, on the other hand, glossolalia (and the charism of prophecy) effect a liberation through speech. In this respect, glossolalia resembles certain techniques used in psychotherapy.

Furthermore, zen and yoga emphasize interiorization, while the charismatic renewal emphasizes the gift of self, expansiveness, and self-expression. Unlike psychoanalysis, it emphasizes a certain forgetfulness of self, in accordance with the Gospel teaching that "he who loses his life will find it."

Finally, zen and yoga are individual-oriented disciplines, whereas the charismatic renewal aims at communion and communication. From this viewpoint it has something in common with group dynamics, but with the important difference that in the charismatic movement the sharing and communication do not pass through a stage of conflict. In this last respect, Pentecostalism has more in common with the nonviolence of zen and yoga.[5]

A professor of yoga, after finishing psychoanalysis, told me how difficult he found it to harmonize the two experiences. He had managed to integrate them by limiting each to its own proper sphere and not allowing either to interfere with the other, but he would advise others not to engage at the same time in zen or yoga and psychoanalysis. For most people, he thought, the practice of the "way of silence" would hinder the goal aimed at by psychoanalysis, with its techniques of self-awareness and self-expression.

Sociologists have compared the Pentecostal movement with the Jesus movement (many journalists had actually confused the two because they became widespread at the same time). The two movements were in fact a response to the same needs. Both have been described as countercultural reactions to a world that has become a crushing burden for the human spirit, but reactions that move beyond the critical frenzy and rebelliousness of the years 1960–1968 and look for a fuller life and a richer interior experience by shifting the emphasis from "having" (and consumption) to "being," and from the utilitarian to the disinterested.

## THE VIEWPOINT OF THE SOCIOLOGIST

A number of sociologists have tried to situate Pentecostalism as a reaction to contemporary social trends. William McCready, drawing upon Neil Smelser's categories of collective behavior, describes Catholic Pentecostalism as a "craze," that is, a "mobilization for action based on a positive wish-fulfillment belief."[6] Jean Séguy, who has been studying Pentecostalism and sects for a long time, describes it as a "compromise between charismatic innovation and traditionalism, resulting from the uncertainties engendered by Vatican II."[7] He sees it as also a compromise in the struggle between the clerisy (Catholic Pentecostalism started in the universities) and the Church clergy, since the Pentecostal movement is made up of self-regulating lay groups that are independent of the hierarchy. The movement may also be said to represent a compromise position in the struggles underlying ecumenism. On each of these points Séguy points out how Neo-Pentecostalism differs from earlier Pentecostalism.

Psychosociological analyses of this type endeavor to fit the Pentecostal movement into the stream of contemporary social development. But these disciplines, which from the methodological viewpoint are reductive in nature, make no claim to show us the specifically religious element and originality of the movement. The Pentecostal quest of the Holy Spirit within the spirit of man falls within the competence of theology, and to this we shall turn in a moment.

First, however, there is another question that should be asked. Should the Catholic Pentecostal movement be described as a "church" or as a "sect," to use the categories of Max Weber? Ernst Troeltsch provides the following definitions of these two terms:

> The Church is an institution which has been endowed with grace and salvation as the result of the work of Redemption; it is able to receive the masses, and to adjust itself to the world, because, to a certain extent, it can afford to ignore the need for subjective holiness for the sake of the objective treasures of grace and of redemption.
> The sect is a voluntary society, composed of strict and

definite Christian believers bound to each other by the fact that all have experienced "the new birth." These believers live apart from the world, are limited to small groups, emphasize the law instead of grace, and in varying degrees within their own circle set up the Christian order, based on love; all this is done in preparation for and expectation of the coming kingdom of God.[8]

By these definitions, a religious Order is "a sect within a Church," and the Youth Council of Taizé is "a mingling of the two types."[9]

The charismatic movement, too, is neither a sect nor a Church. Like the religious Orders, the movement and its communities show certain characteristics of "a sect within a Church," and, like many religious Orders, they are strongly attached to their Church. The generosity and openness of the movement, where everything is done in broad daylight for everyone to see, are characteristics of a Church which, unlike elitist sects, welcomes all.

## 4. THE HOLY SPIRIT

One of the chief leaders of the movement in France, and a man knowledgeable about group dynamics, told me that in the Pentecostal movement he sees not only the play of psychological mechanisms but also something more that is irreducible to other categories, and "that is the factor that matters to me." He made it his aim, therefore, not to emphasize the role of techniques and the sciences of man but to try to help the charismatics touch a deeper level of reality where God's free gifts (which he himself has experienced) are at work.

### THE MAIN CONCERN

It is one thing to recognize and acknowledge the natural resources on which the charismatic renewal draws. It is another to reduce the renewal to a simple product of such resources. A reduction of this kind would fail to take into account the central focus of the movement on the activity of the Holy Spirit. The renewal's main concern is the spiritual effort to enter into closer communion with

God. The exercise by the Christian of the theological virtues (faith, hope, and charity) makes use, of course, of man's psychological powers and capacities, but the important thing about the exercise of these virtues is their referent and goal: Christ in the Spirit. And they do reach Christ, for faith (like all knowledge) is intentional; faith, according to St. Thomas, terminates not in signs or propositions but in the reality of God.[10]

The charismatic movement is a quest of encounter with God. If the quest were illusory, those who have the experience of it would renounce it, as a traveler in the desert rejects the "water" when he finds it to be a mirage. "If Christ was not raised, your faith is worthless" (1 Co. 15:17, New American Bible). A person seeking someone he loves will not be satisfied with a narcissistic experience, no matter how euphoric.

Our own psychological powers and capacities are simply a means toward the encounter. All knowledge, after all, brings an endlessly complex set of instrumentalities into play. Take the simple act of seeing: It involves the subtle action of the eye muscles, focusing, the impact of vibratory signals on the retina, their transmission by the optic nerve, and the decoding activity of the brain. Yet all these are only the bases of the action, simple in itself, of "seeing" a face or a landscape, for the perception of colored objects is symbolic deciphering of the signals transmitted by the complicated activity just described.

In a similar fashion, various instrumentalities come into play at the level of faith, which in itself is a personal, existential encounter.


## ONE WAY

We learn from history that various ways can be followed and various means used in attaining the goal of faith. Hermits, we noted earlier, sought God through solitude; St. Benedict sought him in a cloistered community, St. Francis of Assisi in the midst of men, the stylites on their column, the Mercedarians by taking the place of prisoners. The means are varied according to differences of times, temperaments, and personal choice. The means chosen can be more or less prudent; what, for example, are we to think of the frenzy of the flagellants?

There is an attrition in this area as in all things human, and so a renewal is needed from time to time in order to regain that fresh and youthful outlook that itself is the work of the Holy Spirit. We saw that youthfulness quite recently in the elderly Pope John XXIII.

The means on which Neo-Pentecostalism concentrates are supplied by Scripture: charisms and charity, the latter being given priority in accordance with 1 Corinthians 13.

God, of course, is like a constant spring of unfailing water. It is for man, then, to replace the meager receptivity proper to decadence with the kind of dynamic, open receptivity that a Francis of Assisi and an Ignatius of Loyola were able to achieve like so many saints of East and West before them.

This quest for God through charity and the charisms requires a high degree of self-commitment on man's part, but men are encouraged in it by a truth that was a basic intuition of, for example, a Thérèse of Lisieux: that God in his infinite love wants to give himself to us. The difficulty is that God is bound and imprisoned, as it were. If he is to be free to act, there must be receptivity, desire, and an urgent summons from the believer. The latter must have the eagerness of the prudent virgins in the parable, who ran out to meet the Spouse as he came to them.

The eagerness and new receptivity that mark the charismatic renewal do not spring from human calculation, nor are they the products of psychological techniques. They are born rather of patient, arduous hope. The origins of the movement are exemplary in this respect, for its history is the story of a fervent, persevering search (Chapter 1, above). The result was the recovery, in new and unexpected ways (as always in God's dealings with men), of basic experiences that are evidenced in Scripture and had been part of Christian tradition but had then become a dead letter.

## CHARISMS

One of the most characteristic marks of the Pentecostal renewal is the acceptance and cultivation of the charisms, that is, those gifts whereby the dynamic energies of the Spirit find expression in the Church (cf. above, Chapter 3, section 2). Charismatics have daily experience of these gifts, but it involves neither magic nor any kind of experimentation with spiritual realities. The point is well made in a letter I received not long ago from a charismatic in the ranks: "Beyond a doubt, everything is possible to him who believes, but at the same time God remains God, Master, and Lord. No one can lay hold of him or force him to intervene by formulas, chants, gestures, or incantations. In our prayers, actions, and lives we are always responding to his calls."

As we saw earlier (Chapter 3), these charisms have their root in love or *agapē*, that is, in love for God. They express and support that love. And the love in turn is from God through the Holy Spirit.

## AN EXPERIENCE OF THE HOLY SPIRIT

In the last analysis, then, the heart of the charismatic movement is an experience of the Holy Spirit, that is, the acceptance of a quiet, interior movement of the Spirit that remains mysterious, since the Spirit himself is One whom we cannot capture with our objectivizing concepts and who proceeds by inspiring us from within. All these characteristics are ascribed to him and his action in Scripture, where life itself provides the only model for understanding him.

The Holy Spirit does not eliminate our spirit, but becomes one with it, St. Paul tells us (Rm. 8:16), so that together we may bear witness (cf. Rm. 9:1). In this witnessing, our being and action are respected, for the Spirit does not work by changing our nature or giving us new faculties. Rather, he unfetters and liberates our human powers and capacities, enabling us to achieve things we did not know ourselves capable of. The Spirit shapes our lives so that we are truly the image and likeness of God. He effects not a perversion but a conversion, not a denaturing but a fulfillment. He makes the Christian one with Christ, but in the process respects his nature and individual characteristics.

The Spirit also shows an unqualified respect for Christ. The Spirit's mission is not to bring any new revelation but simply to recall and actualize Jesus and his word. The Spirit forgets himself, as it were, and manifests only Jesus and the Father. When the Christian has been made one with Christ by the Spirit and says "Abba, Fathers!" (Rm. 8:15; Ga. 4:6), it is not the Holy Spirit that speaks. It would make no sense, in fact, for the Spirit to utter such words, since he is not the son of the Father. No, the Christian who says

"Abba!" is not an instrument of the Spirit but the *sole subject* of words that the Spirit suggests to his consciousness as he inspires him to a full commitment to his vocation as child of God.

The Spirit's basic function, then, is to reveal the Father. But St. Paul glimpses another role the Spirit has, one that is more mysterious, one that is collective, even cosmic in scope: The Spirit changes the tragic, hopeless groaning of creation (Rm. 8:19–23) into the ineffable groaning of hope (8:26). It is not the Spirit who groans, but he brings to a new stage of awareness both man and his human environment in their anxious yearning for salvation.

The Pentecostal experience of the charismatic is fully in accord with this twofold function of the Spirit as revealed to us in Scripture and with the unobtrusiveness that characterizes his action; for the Pentecostal experience is the experience of an interior energy (*dynamis*) and of a breath or inspiration to which no name can be attached, for one knows not whence it comes nor whither it goes (Jn. 3:8). It is the experience of a liberator who does not alienate man from himself but rather enables man to achieve his own liberation.

The experience also makes clear to the individual a point we mentioned earlier in this chapter (section 2): To the extent that a man abandons himself to the action of the Spirit, everything in man proceeds both from the Spirit and from man's own free choice. It is useless, therefore, to attempt to draw a line between the action of the Spirit and the action of the Christian himself. The whole purpose of the Spirit's action is to awaken man's liberty from within and to stimulate it to action within the limits set by the individual's powers and capacities.

# 5. OBSTRUCTIONS

In every authentic work of grace, there is a complete coincidence between the transcendent action of God who moves man (Ac. 17:28) and the action of man who responds to God's call. But this synergy can be disturbed by sin. Man is free to refuse God's action, and the failure is not God's responsibility.

It is very difficult, of course, to conceptualize this lack of harmony between the first cause and the second cause, since the latter has its whole reality from the former, while at the same time the two are not of the same order of being. The one thing clear is that once again we cannot draw a line and separate God's part from man's part in the actions of man—even though we must say that evil is due to man!

Men have elaborated formulas for expressing the coincidence of God and man in man's action, even while respecting both God's transcendence and man's freedom. A Portuguese proverb that Paul Claudel made widely known has it that "God writes straight with crooked lines." The Apostle Paul says, more profoundly, that all things work together for the good of those who love God (cf. Rm. 8:28). To this St. Augustine adds: "even our sins," for the Holy Spirit can make these the occasion for a new start. Then there is also the paradox that God uses the weak to confound the strong.

Evidently, though, this is a problem we cannot master. To do so we would need to stand above the scene, as it were, and be able to separate out and compare the action of God and the action of man.

In view of the history of salvation, we can safely say that grace must take into account the hindrances that human weakness throws in the way of the Spirit's inspirations and action. Analysis of the interplay of nature and grace becomes all the more difficult in the case of the Pentecostal experience, because the latter, as we saw earlier, brings into play the hidden powers and capacities of the psyche. The situation here is ambivalent, and various spirits can come into play:

1. First, the spirit of man himself, with its tendency to egoism and exhibitionism and its attraction to the marvelous or the magical. Thus Christ had to struggle with the spirit of the "world" not only in the scribes and lawyers of his day but even in his own apostles, as when James and John urged him to call down fire from heaven (Lk. 9:51–56), or when Peter sought to turn him aside from his passion and Jesus had to say, "Get behind me, Satan!" (Mt. 16:22–23).

2. The Gospel also tells us that Jesus underwent testing by the "tempter," as Matthew calls him (4:3; cf. Mk. 1:13; Lk. 4:2). Here we can see in action the agent of which we heard Father Molinié speaking earlier: the spirit of darkness, who makes use of human weakness in order to obstruct the action of the Holy Spirit.

At a time when so many Christians no longer believe either in temptation or in a tempter, the charismatic movement takes quite seriously the possibility of Satan's intervention. Those who exercise the charism of healing (Chapter 5, above) endeavor to isolate such cases as call for a charism of "deliverance" or even cases of possession in which there is need of the exorcism provided by the Church. Father MacNutt devotes the fifteenth chapter of his book to the discernment of these various cases.

The vivid awareness of danger from Satan and the exercise of the discernment of spirits (a constant and lively preoccupation in the charismatic movement) are enough to eliminate the danger of demonic influence. The case of those who assert such an influence on the movement is severely weakened by the fact that those who urge it have had no experience of charismatic prayer groups.

In summary:

1. The Pentecostal experience of the charismatic is, in essence, an encounter with God through the Spirit, who effects, in faith, a dynamic conversion of the person's whole being.

2. This conversion liberates interior powers hitherto inhibited or obstructed and new capacities for communication and commitment; it enables the individual to move out of and beyond the dull, conventional, superficial consciousness that ordinarily characterizes men. This gift of God shows its effects in the whole of human life, in an observable, though mysterious, way. The charismatic renewal, which does everything out in the open, makes no effort to elude observation by mankind.

3. The Pentecostal renewal is not secure against temptation and the tempter. It accepts the risks with a clear-eyed humility and a constant effort at discernment. It is aware that it cannot eliminate all ambivalence. But this limitation is not something peculiar to the charismatic movement. It affects everything that is in process, every quest, every history, and specifically the history of the Church between the initial and the final "last times," that is, between the two comings of Christ. Only on the last day will all ambivalence be removed. In the meantime, it is of some importance to look more closely at the dangers in the charismatic renewal and at the way in which they are met.

## Notes on Studies of Psychological Balance
## Among Pentecostalists

V. H. Hine concludes, on the basis of earlier researches and those conducted by L. P. Gerlach and himself at the University of Minnesota: "Quite clearly, available evidence requires that an explanation of glossolalia as pathological must be discarded" ("Pentecostal Glossolalia: Toward a Functional Interpretation," *Journal for the Scientific Study of Religion* 8 [1969], p. 217).

Kilian McDonnell, O.S.B., reaches the same conclusion in an article in *Commonweal* 89 (1968), pp. 201–4, and repeats it in his pamphlet *Catholic Pentecostalism* (Pecos, N.M., 1970), pp. 34–35 and 56.

The Presbyterian Church commissioned a lengthy report some years ago entitled "The Work of the Holy Spirit" (Report of the Special Committee on the Work of the Holy Spirit to the 182nd General Assembly of the United Presbyterian Church in the United States of America; Philadelphia, 1970). The psychological part of the report, prepared by Thomas Foster, M.D., and H. Meisgeier, Ed.D., says: "Older psychological explanations of glossolalia as a concomitant of schizophrenia or hysteria have been found to be no longer defensible or acceptable in the light of recent socio-historical and psychological data."

In some of the studies made, "the glossolalics showed up as having slightly better mental health than the control groups with which they were compared, or the general norms of society," according to Edward D. O'Connor, *The Pentecostal Movement in the Catholic Church* (Notre Dame, 1971), p. 124.

Andrew Greeley, priest and sociologist, took a less favorable view in an article, "Glossolalia: 'It's Rooted in Emotional Disturbance,'" *National Catholic Reporter* (Oct. 2, 1970), p. 17. He classified glossolalia as a pathological phenomenon; in this judgement he was probably influenced by the critical book of a Baptist minister, G. B. Cutten: *Speaking with Tongues* (New Haven, 1927). Edward O'Connor answered Father Greeley in a letter in the October 16, 1970, issue of *National Catholic Reporter*. Father O'Connor says, among other things:

In particular, Van Eetvelt Viiver, a psychiatrist who made one of the most comprehensive studies of Pentecostals, found, using the Cattell Personality Test, that tongue speakers scored *lower* than the control groups on factors associated with hysteria, and were no different as regards suggestibility. These, it will be noted, are the two disorders by which Father Greeley claims that psychologists explain glossolalia. . . .

I have been studying this subject intently for three and a half years, not with the tests and statistics of a psychologist, but through personal contact as a priest and theologian in a pastoral relationship. I have been in direct contact with upwards of 400 glossolalics, at least 30 or 40 of whom I know very intimately. My conclusions could be summarized thus:

1. There is no correlation whatsoever between emotional disturbance and genuine glossolalia. The latter charism is received both by those who are well-adjusted and by those who are disturbed, by the placid and by the intense, by the easygoing and by the energetic, by the dull and unimaginative as well as by those of exquisite sensitivity. It is also found in all ages and walks of life.

2. If a person was emotionally disturbed before receiving the gift of tongues, he will continue to be afterwards, although usually somewhat less so (occasionally much less so). If he was well balanced before, he will continue to be so afterwards, but usually somewhat more so. . . .

5. The number of glossolalics who are outstandingly poised, realistic, productive, successful, happy, loved and respected is so impressive that this remarkable fact itself calls for explanation.

# Chapter 8

---

# DANGERS

The objections raised against the charismatic renewal may not be simply shrugged off, for they point to the dangers inherent in every spiritual quest, especially if the latter be marked by the "enthusiasm" of which we spoke in Chapter 6. We have gathered these various objections and shall discuss them in this chapter. First, however, some general observations are in order.

1. The criticisms come from camps opposed one to the other. Traditionalists fear a new attempt to Protestantize the Church. Progressives, on the contrary, fear a mysticism that will distract from action and allow institutions to gain the upper hand once again. These criticisms tend to cancel each other out. What is really characteristic of the movement is the effort to combine fidelity to institutions with a freedom of initiative that is based on an authentic commitment to Christian life and is open to ecumenism.

2. Criticisms and suspicions often come from outside and are voiced by people who themselves have no experience of the movement. Some of these assimilate the movement to some well-known historical or sociological pattern and thus deny or play down its originality; others are satisfied to repeat the labels that have been attached to revivals for centuries, especially the labels used for sects (elitism, esotericism) and enthusiastic movements (emotionalism, illuminism).

3. Others generalize from particular cases. The movement is quite vulnerable to this sort of attack, since it has not and will not become an organization with official standards of membership or affiliation.

For lack, moreover, of any specific and distinguishing name or title, it is often confused with marginal groups that claim the label "charismatic."

4. The twenty or so objections that we have gathered can be easily reduced to three headings: integration into the institution; authentic Christian life; and involvement outside the specifically religious sphere.

## 1. INSTITUTIONAL INTEGRATION AND UNITY

A first series of criticisms has to do with the dangers that the charismatic movement represents to the order and unity of the Church.

1. The first danger is of the separatism that has characterized classical Pentecostalism. Did not David Wilkerson predict, on August 7, 1973, that the new charismatics will be persecuted and forced to leave their Churches in order to form "a supernatural church of true believers"? But Wilkerson's prestige did not prevent this "prophecy" from rousing strong reactions within the movement.[1] The chief effect of his prediction has been to make the charismatics more watchful and more concerned to establish direct ties with Rome.

The charismatic movement, unlike many other small-group movements, has in fact been marked by a firm attachment to the Church as to a home and a foundation. Catholic Neo-Pentecostalists cultivate close ties with their parish and with the local bishop. One leader told me: "We look to the bishop rather than to the episcopal conference, since the latter is an administrative entity and we would risk being turned into an 'official movement,' with a commission set in charge of us and a bureaucratic framework forced on us that would kill life and liberty, as it has in other cases."

Prayer groups rarely celebrate the Eucharist at their meetings (except in Canada) in order not to withdraw the members from the parish Mass. To avoid any competition with the Sunday celebration in the parish, they avoid having their weekly prayer meetings on a Saturday or a Sunday. In France only five groups out of the fifty listed in the 1974 yearbook meet on one of these two days; but what is involved in these cases are isolated places of retreat to which people come from a distance for a weekend of renewal. The movement avoids, moreover, the unofficial intercommunion that is such a frequent phenomenon in other circles.

In the United States, 76 per cent of the Catholic charismatics attend Sunday Mass.[2]

2. But isn't the movement in danger of turning into a super Church, more universal in membership than the present Churches?

The truth is that the charismatic movement aims at living according to the universal values of the Gospel and thereby becoming a stimulus to reconciliation among the Churches. It has, however, no desire to become itself a Church or even an organized institution. So far indeed is it from seeking to compete with the ecclesiastical institution on the latter's own ground that its wish is to disappear once the leaven it represents has entered into the life of the Churches, like a river disappearing in the sea.[3]

3. Is not the very formation of these small groups a stimulus to disunity? What we have just been saying is already an answer to this objection. Among the small groups that have been multiplying in the Church, hardly any are to be found more faithful to her in teaching, moral doctrine, obedience, and participation in her life.

4. But are not such fervent groups in danger of becoming conventicles, esoteric circles, or at least elites that look down on everyone else?

The danger is there in germ, yes, but the movement guards against it by maintaining an exemplary openness. Everything is done out in the open and in broad daylight, even to the point of making the group's cohesion difficult. The large number of the curious and the passersby is a real burden at the Parisian prayer meetings. I once asked the organizers about this.

"Why don't you close your doors, at least once prayer has begun?"

"No! We can't have any restrictions on our openness."

"But don't you risk attracting a lot of unbalanced people and thus undermining your own reputation?"

"We can have no partiality! And besides, the unbalanced people are probably the ones most in need of help. Why should we discriminate against them?"

"But you'll be overwhelmed with people!"

"At present we can take in more than we have."

The answer really surprised me, but it no longer holds for Paris, where rapid growth has strained openness to its utmost, since the integration of all these varied types of people requires more and more time and resources. I personally know of no movement that has carried disinterestedness to such extremes.

5. Do not the very convictions of the movement risk making it think of itself as a panacea for all problems and as the answer for everyone? For example, many religious men and women belong to the movement. Doesn't this cause problems for them in community life, which is built upon another kind of foundation?

It is true that there have been tensions of this kind, but they are relatively rare and are being resolved. In most instances it is the charismatic movement that either adapts itself or withdraws from the picture. I have had several religious women tell me with a smile: "How we must have tried the patience of our community, when we were in our first fervor as charismatics and looked at everything in the light of our new discoveries!" They could talk this way precisely because a deeper understanding of the movement gave them more objectivity. The conflicts I know of have been peacefully resolved and have not been unprofitable.

At Pecos, New Mexico, an entire abbey is now living according to the spirituality of the charismatic renewal and is dedicating itself to spreading this spirituality. Elsewhere, quite varied kinds of practical arrangements have been worked out; at Rome, for example, where religious communities are usually multinational in composition, the Sisters in some houses attend the prayer meetings of their language group.

There has been a maturing and refining of thought in this area. Robert Wild, of Madonna House, a Canadian community that has been especially receptive to the charismatic renewal, has directly dealt with the question. He warns religious against making invidious comparisons between the prosaic character of the religious Office and the stimulation derived from charismatic prayer. Of religious and the high esteem they have for their weekly prayer meetings he says:

> One reason for the character of these meetings is that this meeting is "all they have," in the sense that during the rest of the week members are cut off from opportunities for this fellowship. Thus the weekly prayer meeting is an opportunity to express themselves—a sort of high point in their week. . . . Life on a daily basis tends to be more subdued, more "low-keyed."[4]

6. Does not a movement based on the charisms run the risk of turning into anarchy?

Yes, the risk is there; it was a problem, for example, in the early Church (cf. 1 Corinthians, etc.). It is being met in the contemporary charismatic movement not with regulations and constraints but by the exercise of discernment and the assignment of responsibilities at every level. Since each meeting and each successive stage through which the movement passes is improvised in openness to the initiatives both of the Spirit and the members, the teams of leaders are undoubtedly facing a constantly demanding task.

The co-operative effort is successful and makes up for any failures along the way. Here is an instance I noted down on the spot, during a prayer meeting at Ann Arbor (June 19, 1974).

About a thousand people are gathered in concentric circles in the huge parish gymnasium. Witnessing, songs, and prophecies (very beautiful) have created a cordial atmosphere. Suddenly a huge fellow in purple dungarees stands up, away up at the top of the stands: a really big fellow with a daft, abstracted air, with a big shock of hair standing up from his head. In this zealous assembly, all the hot ideas boiling up in his brain start coming out. He talks nonstop. At the microphone, Doug, the leader of the meeting, politely reminds him that this is a prayer meeting and asks him to sit down. No response. Then, from three or four parts of the hall, young men start moving toward the fellow casually and carefully. Talking persuasively but quietly, they surround him, like leukocytes engulfing a microbe. But he's tall and stands a head over them. He's confused but convinced in his own mind and continues to talk. Doug asks the whole gathering to stand, and he begins a song. A thousand voices drown out every other sound. . . .

The young men around the purple giant have at last gotten results peacefully. He is seated now, calm like the possessed man at Gennesaret once he had been liberated. From now on he breaks silence only to applaud all by himself during a moment of recollection; he has a genius for the inappropriate. But his neighbors dampen the applause. If I had not come intending to observe everything, I probably would not have noticed this little incident any more than I would a fly buzzing nearby.

All meetings are managed with this kind of flexible organization that fosters improvisation. I was amazed at the light touch and the spontaneity shown at the international conference at Notre Dame (June 1974), in contrast to the usual ponderousness that characterizes meetings on this scale (thirty thousand people). These qualities are the result of careful discernment. Those in the central square near the microphones were selected from among members whose charism of prophecy had been tested and confirmed. Each was to submit the theme of his or her improvised interventions to two others in order to make sure it was of general interest.

After this meeting, as after the previous one, questionnaires were distributed for evaluating the various aspects of the meeting, so that the next meeting might be improved. Moreover, to assure as much balance as possible in the movement, the leaders nationwide meet periodically. A national center for reflection, study, and orientation has been established at the University of Notre Dame. The Ann Arbor community concentrates on liaison at the international level and publishes a magazine as well as guidebooks for initiation and formation.

According to Father Molinié, the charismatic movement embodies a tendency

> to substitute for the authority of the Father that of the group and the Holy Spirit. Group and Holy Spirit coalesce into a single idea in practice, since the Holy Spirit is regarded as fully immanent. He is honored all the more fervently since he is not really thought of as separate from the group and cannot give directives that would be coming as it were. from the outside and be a form of oppression exercised on the group.[5]

Father Molinié's comment is a perceptive one, for the movement does indeed concentrate its attention on life and man's spirit and thus on immanence; it does cultivate a communal self-regulation of the group. In point of fact, however, this attitude does not weaken but, on the contrary, renews the sense of transcendence and *obedience*. I was very much struck by the importance given to the idea of obedience at the international meeting of the leaders of the movement, after the Notre Dame conference (June 17, 1974). Some of the things said even made me afraid that the revitalized cult of obedience might go too far and push an obedience for obedience's sake, as an act of homage to the transcendent God.

A classical Pentecostalist who had been invited to this meeting told of being ordered by the leader of his community to shave his beard and cut his long hair. I asked myself by what right the leader had given such an order. But when I put this question to my neighbor, he was surprised; like everyone else there, he thought the incident quite edifying.

A sociologist has made a diagnosis of the "individualist" tendencies of Pentecostalism. Such tendencies do exist to the extent that Pentecostalism emphasizes personal experience and the demands made upon the individual. Yet the most evident characteristic of the movement, in contrast to the individualism of traditional mysticism, is its stress on the community dimension of the experience, on unlimited sharing, and on the care to sacrifice no aspect of communion.

## 2. BALANCE AND AUTHENTICITY IN SPIRITUAL LIFE

The following objections have been leveled against the spirituality of the charismatic movement. They are mostly a repetition of the objections against classical Pentecostalism and the various sects.

### FUNDAMENTALISM

Fundamentalism means the naïvely literal, material, and "obvious" interpretation of Scripture; it implies an intellectual subservience caused by oversimplification and the fettering of Spirit to letter.

The term "fundamentalism" came into use sixty years ago to describe the antirationalist reaction of American Protestants who looked to the Bible for solid *foundations*. It is a reaction that has been discredited by its excesses. Between the two World Wars the World Christian Fundamentalist Association even sought to have the U. S. Congress prohibit the teaching of evolution as contrary to the doctrine of creation as taught by the Bible; they were willing to cause a new Galileo case, though Protestant this time.

The word "fundamentalism" has thus had a derogatory connotation almost from the beginning. Everyone uses it today as a slogan, though at times without understanding what the word really means.[6]

Catholic Pentecostalism does practice a straightforward reading of the Bible, with emphasis on getting from it food for the soul. But in so doing, it is not looking for doctrinal foundations, but for the means of achieving an encounter, personal and communal, with God, the Spirit helping the community by bestowing divine light. The movement is quite open to contemporary exegesis, and a number of qualified exegetes (Donatien Mollat, Francis Martin, and others) belong to it.

We must look beyond derogatory labels to real problems. Is fundamentalism the greatest danger the faith must face today? Isn't the greater danger the pseudoscientific pretentiousness that denies access to the Bible to anyone who has not thoroughly studied the problems of textual, literary, linguistic, and historical criticism? This is the attitude of the scribes with whom Christ found fault; it is a form of clericalism, with the old claims being put forward in a new guise.

In the current climate of change, exegesis is advancing rapidly at the technical level, but with growing uncertainty about meaning; the crisis of exegesis is all the more intense since some new approaches (especially structuralism) question whether there is any such thing as meaning. The result is uncertainty and perplexity; a seminarian expressed it in a vivid phrase when he said to me about one of his professors: "He's a genius, but when it comes to faith he doesn't know where he's at." The generally reductive nature of analytic methods, the care to draw no conclusions before all the evidence is in, and the crisis within philosophy are combining today to make many exegetes and theologians incapable of providing answers even on essentials. If you push them, they tell you: "We probably won't be able to read the Bible properly until the next century."

But the Gospel or Good News is by definition addressed first and foremost to the simple, the poor. In saying this we do not undervalue the great importance of exact exegetical study, short-term and long-term both, nor do we say that obscurities are to be eliminated at any cost. We are saying only that this labor and its difficulties should not be allowed to break the vital thread of the *lectio divina*, that reading of God's word that speaks to the real life of individual and community. Such a confrontation of the word and the real life of men has been going on from the time of the prophets to our own day, passing by way of the Virgin Mary's meditation, which St. Luke so carefully notes (Lk. 2:19, 51).

It is very likely that we will have to wait for the next millennium for the progress of dietetics to prescribe a less foolish regimen than we follow today, but meanwhile people have to go on eating day after day. So too, men must continue to nourish themselves with the word of God. The charismatics are no more "fundamentalist" than the rest of God's people; in fact, they are less so. In any event, they listen assiduously and fruitfully to the word of God.

### SUBJECTIVISM

The objection is that the intensity of the charismatic experience may tend to turn men away from objective norms.

This is a danger for anyone who sets out to listen to the Holy Spirit! But the danger is seen, accepted, and counteracted by discernment on the part of the community.

### ILLUMINISM

What is meant by this term is the idea of direct communication with God, the expectation of light without making free use of one's own intelligence, and the hasty attribution of all that happens in prayer and life to the transcendent and quasimiraculous action of the Holy Spirit.

The charismatic movement may be tempted to exaggerate in this direction, but it deliberately endeavors to reach a balance between such a divinization of insignificant everyday events and the funereal attitude of those who want a God that is dead and who have given up on attaining any life-giving contact with him.

### EMOTIONALISM

This American term means an attitude of focusing on feeling at the expense of reason.

It is true enough that the movement attributes value to feeling, while allowing for errors and especially for eclipses that can be the occasion for drastic falls (so an airplane in a steep climb quickly loses speed, stalls, plunges, and crashes).

It is also true that the charismatic renewal is a reaction against the excessive frustrating of religious sensibility. There is every justification for the reaction, since the repression of sensibility leads to disillusionment and then, in a backlash, to terrible revenge extorted by the repressed feelings. This is a pattern that has long been observed in the most inflexible classical spiritualities.

The rebirth of sensibility in Christian life should be accounted a merit of the charismatic movement. I have been struck by the knowledge of psychology and the realism that mark the study sessions or seminars of the movement in America.

At Houston (a very mature Episcopalian group that is very close to Catholicism), the weekly prayer meeting in the home where I was staying took up this matter on one occasion. It lasted several hours, and I was much impressed by the understanding, keen preception, and generosity shown. What I saw there was the feeling for Christian life that certain masters of novices and spiritual directors of a former day used to have; there was this difference, however, that here the awareness grew out of the group and its shared dialogue.

## ANTI-INTELLECTUALISM

This objection is connected with the three that have immediately preceded, since relying on direct light from God or on feeling goes with a depreciation of the free exercise of reason.

The charismatic movement, however, rejects neither intelligence nor culture. After all, the charismatic movement originated in the universities. What it is careful to correct is a false intellectualism that is satisfied with words and ideologies. It seeks to put intelligence at the service of life. In this, it shares the vocation of American culture generally, which has little interest in the play of words and ideas that is typical of Latin cultures. Moreover, this reaction is very much called for in an age that often sins through an excessively and corrosively critical application of reason. As St. Augustine once said, echoing St. Paul before him: "Unhappy the knowledge that does not beget love."

There are two further dangers that likewise belong in the catalogue of classical spiritual errors.

## SPIRITUAL PRIDE

The danger here is that the experience of the outpouring of the Spirit may generate a self-satisfaction like that of the Pharisee in the Gospel: "I thank you, Lord, that I am not like the rest of men . . . now that I have received baptism in the Spirit."

But not all thanksgiving means contempt for one's fellows. The thanksgiving of the charismatic movement is also on behalf of the brothers; it is a thanksgiving that resembles that of the Virgin Mary in her "Magnificat" and that of Paul the Apostle.

In actual fact, what we find is rather a sense of inferiority or frustration in those who do not feel the heartwarming grace of "baptism in the Spirit," and especially of glossolalia. But I have found no spirit of self-conceit in those who have received these enriching experiences.

## SPIRITUAL GLUTTONY

By this is meant an excessive liking for favors of a sensible kind and the inclination to retain them through autosuggestion and other superficial or even unhealthy practices.

This classical danger increases with the intensity of fervor, and so it is a serious one for the charismatic renewal. On the other hand, the movement daily cultivates the detachment to which every serious Christian is called, once he has gotten beyond the beginning of a conversion or renewal and the consolations associated with this period. I have already mentioned the spiritual maturity and depth that mark the oldest communities, especially those of Houston and Ann Arbor.

## 3. INFLUENCE AND INVOLVEMENT

We come now to the most frequent and serious criticism: that this movement, with its concentration on mysticism and devotion, turns Christians aside from the struggle for justice and from political involvement. One theologian told me: "The charismatics focus on charity in the narrow sense: the relationship to the neighbor, to individuals, and not on the broader aspects of charity: responsibility at the level of this world's social structures."

Is not Catholic Pentecostalism an alibi? A mysticism that distracts from action? J. Whitney unflinchingly acknowledges the problem: "Many Catholics have come to the charismatic renewal after experiencing the frustration of their hopes in a social involvement that would change the world. . . . The emphasis is on personal renewal rather than social renewal."[7]

Such an emphasis has to do with the nature of the movement, which aims at deepening the practice of the theological virtues. But the movement does not stop there. "Some groups admit they have passed through a period of disinvolvement, a kind of novitiate. Very soon, however, the Spirit had led them to increasingly demanding involvement, especially in defense of the lowly and the poor and in helping marginalized people of every kind."[8]

The truth of this observation can be verified on both sides of the Atlantic, where so many communities are committed to all kinds of social activity in behalf of the economically oppressed, thieves, drug addicts, etc. As we noted earlier, authentic charity always leads to commitments and responsibilities toward others. According to Joseph Fichter's sociological study, 19 per cent of the charismatics "work actively against racism."[9]

Here again we may offer as a concrete example Holy Redeemer parish in Houston, which has matured in a way that may serve as a model for Catholics who are later arrivals in the Pentecostal movement. In this metropolis of the South (four million inhabitants), celebrated from its moon-rocket launchings, the authoritarian promulgation of the edict on racial integration in the schools brought on a severe crisis. Without preparation, hostile groups that were both aggressive and fearful of each other were brought together in the same buildings: 60 per cent black, 34 per cent Mexican American, and 6 per cent white, all of them children aged nine to fourteen. The integration of the Mexican Americans presented even greater difficulty than the integration of the blacks, chiefly for reasons of language.

The school was in an uproar. The teachers applied en masse to be moved to other schools, and the administration firmly refused. The school had become a battleground, with each group taking part out of fear of the others. The parents had enough, and people were tempted to use the resources of the parish for starting a private school. But here is what actually happened, according to the notes I made on June 23, 1974, during a conversation with Nan Pagano, a teacher in this Lantrip Elementary School.

In the parish we prayed and resolved to fast on bread and water for five days. We met each evening after work and finally came to three conclusions:

1. We must think out the problem in terms not merely of our own children, that is, the white children, but of all the children, white, brown, or black.

2. We must trust in the Lord and follow Abraham's example. But note that Abraham did not say to Isaac, "I want to take your life." Rather, he went up the mountain with him. For us, it's a question of going to school with the children, not in order to protect or isolate them, but in order to face the problem with them as companions of Christ.

3. A third saying of the Lord came to mind as we discussed the question: "How are we to go to school with them?" The most important thing was to go to school in a spirit of submission to its director: "to submit to him as to the Lord." Teachers do not like parent participation because it usually creates difficulties. In this case the teachers were even more apprehensive, because the suggestion was coming from a confessional group. The director consented because he was at his wits' end (the situation could not become any worse) and because he understood that we meant the obedience and cooperation we offered. As a result several members of the community were accepted into the school: those with diplomas as salaried employees, the others as volunteers, to serve in areas such as the library.

The first problem was to win acceptance. In the course of the year we won the director's trust, and when school was resumed in 1973 he gave us empty classrooms to use as kindergartens, where we might teach the children to know one another and to work together in a clean and livable atmosphere.

[At this point I interrupted: "Did you have to teach the ghetto children to wash?" Her answer: "We had to teach *all* the children to wash *together*—that was the important thing."]

The first year was a desperate time, unproductive, and marked by distrust of every kind. The Protestant blacks, whether Baptist or from some other denomination, looked upon us as traditionalists. The Mexican Americans thought of us as Protestants; and so on.

Gradually, certain things got through to the children. The first was the fact that of the fifty-five parishioners working in the school, only five were salaried; all the others were volunteers working three hours a week. Another thing that made an impression on them was the fact that all the parishioners embraced one another as friends, without distinction. The children asked why they did this, and we told them: "Because we are brothers and sisters." This spirit of brotherhood and this habit of embracing gradually spread throughout the school.

When school reopened in 1973, we had embarked on a cleanup: a tremendous task that took two hundred parishioners three weeks: washing the walls, cleaning the air-conditioning units, getting all sorts of things in working condition (since the place had been looted over the course of several years). What struck the pupils was all the menial work involved. The result was that there was no more writing on the walls, no more littering; the posters and pictures were not stolen again; in fact, there was almost no stealing. Why? Because the children now thought of it as their house, their school; it was their home.

Now we have won the trust not only of the director and the children, but also of the teachers, who kept their distance for a long time. We are all beginning to work together.

Some of the social and racial evil has been healed, and the healing has even bodily, physical effects. Where remedies fail, love succeeds. The more broken we are, the more we must trust in God's love for us. We trust and we are not disappointed.

In Northern Ireland, "right in Belfast itself, there are six ecumenical prayer groups; the turbulent political situation obliges them to change their place of meeting frequently."[10] We are also told that some groups in Latin America are involved on the political scene, but we have not been able to verify this claim.

Two points are clear. The first is that the charismatic movement contains Christians of differing tendencies; the proportion of those involved in political movements for justice or even in political parties seems greater, however, than in the Christian population generally.

The second is that charismatics have been facing the question of the collective dimension of Christian social and political responsibility. Thus *New Covenant*, the most important periodical published by the movement, devoted a whole issue, not too long ago, to the problem of social concern and the struggle against institutionalized injustice.[11]

The charismatic renewal is seeking to offer its hesitant contribution, in a nonviolent way analogous to that of Taizé, to the crucial and still unanswered question: How unite mysticism and politics, which have now become separated? Almost all Christians today are paralyzed in one or the other of these two areas: men of prayer, when it comes to political commitments; political militants, when it comes to keeping contact with the prayer and the Christian faith that stimulate their involvement. Charismatic groups, like others before them, manifest the normal evolution from charity to action and from action to an involvement in the political area, without which effectiveness is very limited.

In summary, dangers of deviation undoubtedly do exist; some individuals, some groups, and marginal imitators are evidence of this fact. But these inevitable risks are neutralized by communal discernment, which is undoubtedly the most characteristic trait of the movement as a whole.

# Chapter 9

# IMPORTANCE AND FUTURE
# OF THE CHARISMATIC RENEWAL

Now that we have discussed the objections and criticisms brought against the charismatic renewal, it is time to attempt an estimate of its importance and future.

We must be clear on one important point: The renewal is more than simply a trend; it is a movement. The leaders of the renewal are indeed suspicious of this not entirely savory word, which has been taken over by so many political parties and religious organizations as they begin to lose ground and to contain anything you want—except movement! But such an abuse of language should not make us forget the proper meaning of the word: A "movement" is *a spontaneous, collective impulse that arises from the ranks in response to needs and that creates from within its own coherent structure.* The charismatic renewal shows all these characteristics and their consequences.

The quality, importance, and future of any movement depend on the degree to which it satisfies certain requirements: It answers a need; it focuses on essential values; and it effects a tightly structured, coherent, and dynamic synthesis of these values.

Let us examine the charismatic renewal in terms of these three criteria.

# 1. A RESPONSE TO PRESSING CURRENT NEEDS

The charismatic renewal is a remedy for the current crisis of aridity and uncertainty through which so many Christians are passing in our day. It is a crisis that has affected the Church at both the administrative and the doctrinal levels.

On the administrative side, ecclesiastical bureaucracy and budgets are rapidly increasing, while the number of practicing Christians or even of believers, and of priests and religious is lessening. The postconciliar Church exemplifies Parkinson's law that bureaucracies tend to expand, with officials creating work for each other. Since the start of Vatican II, the manpower of the Roman Curia (which was to be decentralized) has almost doubled (1,332 in 1961; 2,260 in 1970); at the same time, every nation has developed its own extensive national administrative force, along with buildings and offices, all entirely new, and with annually increasing budgets. Commissions and officials have been multiplied for the purpose of determining—rather prematurely and at times in a heavy-handed way—the precise ground where the seed is to be sown.

In the area of doctrine, an effort to return to the sources has not prevented an abstract Scholasticism from being replaced by a radical criticism. Coming as it did at a time of cultural change, this criticism has gotten out of hand. Every experience or undertaking of a religious or Christian kind is immediately subjected to a philosophical, historical, psychoanalytical, sociological, or other type of criticism.

As a result of this wave of criticism, suspicion has replaced certainty, and Christian realities have been questioned rather than experienced. Demythologization and secularism make believers feel depressed and frustrated; they also lead to compensatory efforts that give us a "theology" of or a "pastoral approach" to what is just disappearing. This latter reaction is typical of a time of decadence and only increases the anxiety of people as they look into the poorly camouflaged void.

The charismatic renewal does not seek to refute criticism but rather to fill the void with life. It proves there is motion by moving.

Its point of departure is not a discourse of any kind but love and the encounter with God, and on the basis of these, doctrines and institutions regain their meaning. Thus the movement is in no way a movement of rebellion.

By pursuing the course it does, the charismatic renewal restores the joy, confidence, bold assurance (*parrhēsia*), and fervor that are so evident in the community that provides the renewal with its biblical model. The renewal answers the contemporary need for experience and authenticity. It is laying a new emphasis on spontaneous oral expression at the moment when the "Gutenberg galaxy" is being replaced.

The simplicity of the means used by the renewal enables the latter to reach the poor and uneducated. Thus it brings about a real "democratization of sanctity," which does not imply a leveling down but means access to the world of God through God's own gift; in short, it means what the Gospel means.

The charismatic renewal is an answer to the desires that the Jesus movement awakened in American youth: the healing of a diseased intersubjectivity (cf. Chapter 5, above), simplicity, poverty, and a spirit of childhood, but without the reactions typical of the counterculture and without any rejection of doctrinal or institutional foundations. Quite the contrary.

The charismatic renewal also answers the need Christians feel for sensible signs after being too long deprived of them by the excessive spirit of abstraction that theologians and liturgists had fostered. In their hunger, many, of course, grasp at any kind of compensatory nourishment, be it earthly or heavenly: on the one hand, psychedelic experiences and things of that sort; on the other, a burgeoning of sects and of apparitions that the Church does not acknowledge or positively rejects but that remain popular despite ecclesiastical prohibitions.

In this time of uncertainty, the charismatic renewal is performing an immensely valuable service by giving the hungry a food that will restore health. It is providing a haven for the many whom we see going astray where the movement does not exist.

## 2. A RETURN TO ESSENTIAL VALUES

The success of the movement is not due solely to the fact that it meets felt needs. It is also due to the fact that the renewal is helping to restore essential values that are central to revelation itself. The renewal is rediscovering the Gospel as Good News and source of revitalization, Scripture as the word of life, Christianity as the real outpouring of the very Love of God, and charity as not simply a commandment but a way, a life, and a praxis.

The movement is helping to restore the communion which, according to the Council, is the very definition of the Church. It has brought into existence not only prayer groups but also communities in which people live together and share all their possessions and resources.

A report drawn up at the request of the Permanent Commission for Religious (France) tells us that

> prayer groups are almost everywhere giving birth to communities of shared life: Paris, Lyons, Grenoble, Montpellier. . . . In these, young celibates or groups of priests join for a life marked by prayer, sharing, hospitality, joyous poverty, and witness to brotherhood.[1]

This phenomenon is even more striking in Australia. Here, according to Father Gallay's picturesque description, people are forming

> little ecumenical republics in which men and women from various confessions pool their resources as the first Christians did, especially in the slums of Melbourne, where a charismatic prayer group is dedicating itself to the alcoholics; as a result, the lives of the latter have suddenly been transformed.[2]

These are not "republics" in the anarchic sense sometimes read into the word. On the contrary, order and obedience are being reborn in them. Moreover, the leaders, though they operate in a "charismatic" fashion, are attentive to Church norms and to the authorities at every level, from the parish to Rome.

The "little republics" are not always so little. We have seen that the organically federated communities at Ann Arbor number 740 members, with about 1,000 other people joining them for weekly meetings. What we have here is a renaissance of community life and its influence, on the scale of the largest Orthodox monasteries and the largest communities of the Middle Ages. Nor is the sharing any less marked than in the monasteries.

Programs of formation have been established to prepare individuals for the outpouring of the Spirit and for this very demanding type of community life. These programs are widely used, with hundreds of thousands of copies in circulation.

The groups and communities give birth, from within, to new ministries that multiply in a functional way, that is, to meet needs.

This rediscovery of community life has been hailed as a renaissance of religious life, starting from the root of that life and following the primal model that has inspired so many foundations and renewals down the centuries, namely, the first community at Jerusalem. The resurgence of community life is a sign and a source of hope, coming as it does just when so many religious communities are emptying and falling apart. "The oldest religious communities are rediscovering the structure of religious life: period of probation, search for a way of personal commitment before God; link with a community."

One of the things that is different, however, about this renewal of integral community life is that the communities are communities of laymen and laywomen. In this they resemble the first Christian communities and early monasticism, which came into existence as a form of lay, not clerical, life.

Most of the founders of the movement have continued to be totally committed Christians, but not in religious life. They deliberately live a lay life as married people. In so doing, they are following one of the major thrusts of Vatican II: the renaissance of the laity. Often, they are quite conscious of this implication. Pat Gallagher, one of the participants in the weekend of February 1967 at Duquesne, and recently married to the lay leader of the charismatic communities in New Orleans, told me: "Many people are surprised when I say it, but I have never been drawn to any form of religious life." People were surprised because they saw in her a person entirely committed to God and filled with a transparent joy.

The charismatic renewal aims at full holiness as being the vocation of every Christian. In this it takes with complete seriousness a principle established by Vatican II after great effort and difficulty.[3]

In the charismatic communities, celibacy for the sake of the kingdom is spontaneously coming into its own again. At Ann Arbor, a group called The Brotherhood has been founded for the living of this vocation. Steve Clark and four others have made a definitive commitment to it; the commitment is expressed, in part, as follows:

> We want to know and love the Lord as fully as we can and
> to serve him as much as we can, and we want to be as free from

other things as possible for the sake of the Lord and his service. We therefore commit ourselves for the rest of our lives not to marry, to have and to use as little as possible, and to live a common life with brothers who are committed to the same ideal. (610a).[4]

Seven others have made the same commitment, but for a limited period:

We commit ourselves to this group of brothers. . . . (612b). During the period of our commitment, we will not get involved in any relationship that involves erotic attraction or that might lead to marriage. Nor will we do things that are preparatory to entering into such a relationship with someone after the period of our commitment. (621b).

The rediscovery of celibacy for the sake of the kingdom is part of a comprehensive plan for living a completely evangelical life:

We wish to know God as fully as possible, to love him with our whole hearts, and to serve him fervently. (110).
We wish to follow our Lord Jesus Christ. (111).
We wish to offer our lives to the Lord so that he may use us to bring men to him or to help them find a fuller life in him. (112).

The "covenant" implies the necessity of poverty:

To the degree that we can, we wish to have the Lord himself as our only treasure, our portion. We wish to have undivided hearts. We wish to be as free as possible of all distractions from the Lord and his service. We wish to take as little for ourselves as possible that we might have the Lord as fully as possible. . . . (131).
Our life will involve voluntary self-denial, denying ourselves good things in order that we might grow in our love for the Lord. . . . (133).

The poverty aimed at is made concrete in detailed regulations; for example:

We will put our finances in common. (320).
Normally each of us will work enough to pay for his ordinary living expenses, and we will work enough as a brotherhood to pay for all our expenses. (321).

We will never loan money to anyone. When we give money to someone, we will not expect it to be returned. They can return it if they want to. (323).

. . . When possible we will discourage others from giving us gifts. (324).

We will keep only those possessions which are necessary for us to live and to perform the service the Lord gives us. (330).

Our clothing should be as simple and inexpensive as possible without markedly differing from the styles of those around us. We will keep only the clothing that is necessary. (331).

Every six months, we will look over all our possessions and give away everything we do not need. (333).

The commitment to celibacy is likewise spelled out in strict prudential regulations, though these are always subordinated to the requirements of apostolic service. For example: "Whenever possible, no one of us will make trips or go to conferences or on visits that keep him away from home at night without having a partner to go with him." (730).

The renewal has not been lacking in vocations to the priesthood, although the atmosphere of some seminaries is felt by charismatics to be detrimental to faith and thus does not make it easy for charismatics to persevere in a "vocation" to the priesthood. I have met at least one such case at Ann Arbor.

Father de Monléon frequently challenges his audiences: "Name for me a single Christian value that is not lived and practiced in the charismatic renewal: from the Trinity to holy medals, from ecumenism to the rosary!" He is undoubtedly quite safe in issuing the challenge. Nothing is excluded by the renewal: the liking for withdrawal but also zeal for the apostolate; the sense of sin and penance, along with the practice of fasting (very much practiced), but also a spirit of festivity and a love of the sacraments; rediscovery of nocturnal prayer and rediscovery of unbroken prayer in the midst of daily occupations; the development and strengthening of quite varied vocations; a new attraction to the Eucharist and the Blessed Virgin. In short, the renewal is integral without being integrist, that is, without being either pretentious or fearful.

There is no point in dwelling on minor details. Let us concentrate rather on essentials.

## THE HOLY SPIRIT

In the forefront of the charismatic or spiritual renewal stands, of course, the Holy Spirit, the unknown God, who is regaining the place in Christian life that he had in the first community as depicted in the Acts of the Apostles. On one occasion, choosing my words poorly, I said to one of the early leaders of the renewal when I met him in America: "You are one of the founders of the movement." His reply was: "The Holy Spirit is the only founder!"

The function attributed to the Spirit is, as we have seen, the one he has in the most traditional and Scriptural doctrine: to be, not a substitute for Christ, but the revealer of Christ. He links us to and makes us one with Christ; he makes the Good News of Jesus a vital reality. This discovery of the Spirit is not merely verbal; it is a personal experience. In charismatic prayer groups Christ is invoked more often than the Spirit, and this is a proof of authenticity, since the Spirit works essentially in the background, turning men's attention to the incarnate Word.

Here is a significant corroboration of our evaluation of the renewal: Heribert Mühlen, the foremost contemporary theologian of the Holy Spirit, whose work has been profoundly reshaping pneumatology for the past twenty years, has acknowledged that in the charismatic renewal he finds the essentials of what he has been trying to say, but that he finds them there as "a letter written in the heart" (to use St. Paul's phrase in 2 Co. 3:2). Mühlen has himself become personally involved in the movement; his conversion to it took eight months, but a modification of outlook in a theologian of this stature must inevitably be slow and ponderous. Here is how Mühlen speaks of his changed outlook, which will be the subject of his next book:

> I would like simply to say that for 15 years I have known the Holy Spirit with my head, but now I also know him with my heart, and wish the same joy for you. For 15 years people said to me: "What you are writing is speculation, not real." But now I am seeing it come to reality all over the world. The Holy Spirit is real, and is being sent by the Father and the Son to bring the human race to a knowledge of them. I longed for

this, but it was in my head, and an unfulfilled longing. Now it is in my heart, changing my life.[5]

As in the New Testament, the re-emphasis on the Spirit is inseparable from the exercise of the charisms. The charismatic renewal is living in accordance with a principle that was enunciated by Vatican II and that has dominated the postconciliar theology of the Church.[6] This principle is that the Church is not a society shaped from outside by laws and institutional frameworks; it is structured from within by the charisms, and institutions and laws have for their purpose to express and regulate the charisms. What the theologians have been saying in theoretical terms, the communities of the charismatic renewal have been rediscovering in real life. They are proving the validity of the fundamental (and long overlooked) intuition of Johann Adam Moehler, the genius who pioneered the renewal of ecclesiology at the beginning of the nineteenth century.

## LOVE (AGAPE)

At its deepest level, the charismatic renewal is cultivating the gift that is the source of all the charisms and without which the charisms are valueless, as St. Paul clearly states in 1 Corinthians 13. This basic gift is *agapē* or charity, that is, the very life of God as communicated by the Spirit who structures the Church from within.

By its emphasis on charity, the renewal is also faithful to another and even more fundamental insight of Vatican II, the insight that dominates the Dogmatic Constitution on the Church and gave its final shape: that the Church is first and foremost a life and only secondarily an organization. The Church is to be thought of first as the people of God and secondarily as the college of bishops, because authority is meant to take the form of service in and for the people of God.

## 3. A DYNAMIC AND COHERENT SYNTHESIS

The values we have been discussing in the first two sections of this chapter are not simply an impressive garb; they are the fruit of a vital impulse that begets from within this set of coherent though contrasting values.

Because the charismatic renewal, under the inspiration of the Holy Spirit, has rediscovered *agapē* or love at its deepest level, it is able to reconcile charisms and authority, personal prayer and love of the liturgy, obedience and freedom, tradition and creativity, fidelity to the Church's norms and openness to ecumenism, stern demands and openness to all (this last is an especially notable trait), self-expression and inwardness, love of song and love of silence, poverty and effectiveness.

Such an alliance of contrasting qualities would disintegrate in a movement characterized by mediocrity, just as the body breaks down when it becomes a corpse.

What is most striking is that this reconciliation of opposites has not been felt, at least thus far, as a source of tension. The liking for freely exercised initiative is itself rooted in the concern to maintain solid foundations at the level of ecclesiastical authority.

In a similar fashion, the charismatic renewal is able to renew both lay and religious life, both marriage and celibacy, because it goes to the evangelical root of all these things, thus responding to a wish that found expression only after difficulty in the conciliar documents. The depth of this return to the sources explains the union of joy and penance, the expansion without recourse to propaganda, and the extensive membership achieved without advertising or written invitation, but simply through contact and the power of influence.

The movement has succeeded in overcoming limitations and achieving syntheses for which our Church and our world, both of them in a state of disintegration, are still laboriously struggling:

•The overcoming of "grandfather's moralizing ritualism and father's socialist secularism," according to the picturesque expression used by the periodical *Carmel;*

•The overcoming of the religious rationalism in which the Counter-reformation gradually got bogged down, and the secularist ideology that replaced it;

•The overcoming of yesterday's clericalism and today's neoclericalism, yesterday's rigorism and today's laxism, yesterday's institutionalism and today's anti-institutionalism, yesterday's conformism and today's rebellion. Without sacrificing either his authority or the respect due him, a bishop in the movement can ask his brothers to pray for him and lay hands on him that he may undergo the new conversion that is the outpouring of the Spirit.

This kind of harmonious synthesis does not come easily. The radiant joy of the charismatics is the fruit of trials and internal tensions, similar to those we glimpse in the Letters of St. Paul and the Acts of the Apostles: the dispute between Peter and Paul (Ga. 2:11–14), the break between Paul and Barnabas (Ac. 15:37–40), etc. Father Edward O'Connor, one of the early leaders and the chief theologian of the movement, has resigned from the co-ordinating committee (the National Service Committee). His resignation came shortly before the seventh international conference and brought suffering to all concerned; but each side stuck to its position, though in a courteous way and without any loss of mutual esteem and loyalty, as I have been able to verify in my conversations on the subject.

In France there is a similar tension, though without any open conflict, between those who unreservedly accept the risks proper to the Spirit (open doors during prayer meetings, unreserved acceptance of charisms, openness to ecumenism) and groups such as *Feu Nouveau* (New Fire) in which measures are taken to prevent possible deviations and excesses. These latter groups meet behind closed doors and admit only Catholics; they do not list their meetings in the international yearbook, which has for its purpose to make it easy for traveling charismatics to find a ready welcome. The prayer of these groups is less improvised, more organized, etc. Both approaches are still being followed.

## FRUITS

It would be boring to list here all the fruits of the charismatic renewal—such things as the numerous conversions and returns to the faith; the restoration of prayer and the apostolate; the establishment of conditions favorable to a renaissance both of lay life and religious life; etc. Of the more eye-catching results, we have already mentioned healing in all its forms: healing of the will, the memory, the sensibility, the body. Especially striking in this area are the reconciliation of married couples (sometimes far advanced in divorce proceedings), the cure of drug addicts, etc. On my journeys I have met such cases daily.

In such areas as these, the movement is interested in reality, not in statistics. Nonetheless, the results are indeed surprising. Among drug addicts the rate of perseverance is pretty much the same as that achieved by David Wilkerson's Teen Challenge (70 per cent success in forty centers, as contrasted with the less than a 5 per cent rate of cure in federal treatment centers).[7] The movement does not overlook the role of the medical profession; often the addict begins with a medical cure. The different end results of the charismatic renewal and the federal hospitals is that in the former the group helps the individual make the cure permanent, something that medical means alone cannot accomplish. At times, addicts do not even have to have recourse to a medical cure, yet they are healed.

## ORIGINALITY

One leader has summed up the originality of the movement in this way:

1. It has no human founder. The first leaders firmly refuse the title, as we noted above.

2. It sets no stake by administrative organization; it relies more on the Holy Spirit than on human means for attaining the cohesion of the group.

3. It does not emphasize any one special trait (as St. Francis, for example, stressed poverty, or St. Ignatius obedience). Its concern is with the essential Christian life. This is why it has been successful among such widely differing groups: laity and religious of every kind; contemplatives and apostolically active people; people living quietly and people politically committed.[8]

4. It brings together the various generations without showing partiality, even if the leadership and the majority of the members are on the young side.

5. It is not and does not wish to be a competing Church but a leaven that will bring new life to the Church from within and that will promote unity at its source, namely, the Holy Spirit, whose transforming action is much more important than superficial dialogues and negotiations.

## IMPORTANCE

What will prove to have been the importance of the movement? This is hard to say. It is not the only movement that is meeting the needs of our day and rediscovering the role of the Holy Spirit. The Cursillo movement, after all, inspired the first leaders; as one of them said, "That is where we began to experience the baptism in the Spirit." The Focolarini, the Marriage Encounter movement,[9] the Grail movement, the Tower of David movement,[10] and other movements emphasizing community are following convergent paths, as are the Christian groups engaged in various kinds of struggle, political or nonpolitical, for justice and peace, especially in Latin America. Whatever, therefore, the importance of the charismatic renewal may be, it must not make us forget the multiform character or pluralism of the Spirit's action. The Holy Spirit cannot be monopolized.

## DANGERS

What will the future development be like of a movement that relies on no human security or magical method but on God's power to bring to a successful completion what he has started?

Each prayer meeting, each stage in the group's development, is an open-ended improvisation, a happening; things happen, or sometimes fail to happen. Future development may be good or bad, depending on the risky use of human freedom. We must remember here the old saying: "*Corruptio optimi pessima.*" (The worst corruption is the corruption of what is best.) Today, the risks are being properly seen and met through community regulation (cf. Chapter 8, above). But each day is a new adventure, and there is need of ceaseless vigilance.

Though this movement is more cohesive and extensive than others started after the Council, it does not regard itself as its own end. It is well aware that the role of a movement is to disappear for the benefit of the whole Church. As the mission of the biblical movement was to spread an understanding of the Scriptures, which had lost their proper place in Christian life, and then to disappear, and as the mission of the liturgical movement was to renew the official prayer of the Church, which had been afflicted with sclerosis, and then to disappear, so the charismatic renewal aspires to disappear once the whole Church has become charismatic. Cardinal Suenens has stated this explicitly.[11]

The important thing is that the Pentecostal experience, rediscovered by the movement, should not again become the lost paradise it was in centuries past. To this end, the concern for proper order, which is as important today as it was in St. Paul's time, must not be allowed to degenerate into that concern for absolute germ-free purity, which nothing can survive. This is a danger against which the Apostle himself warns us when he says: "Never try to suppress the Spirit" (1 Th. 5:19).

The élan and youthful freshness of the charismatic renewal have caused people to ask: "Can the lightning last?"

It is certainly true that the movement is profiting from the enthusiasm that characterizes all beginnings. The decisive test will be in the desert through which it must pass after the liberation from Egypt. Then there will necessarily be a falling off. To what extent will the charismatic groups be able to accept the need for the patience that achieves its ends amid the detachment of faith? It is by this test, the test of time, that we will be able to gauge the scope and historical importance of the movement. Will it prove to resemble the movements initiated by a St. Francis of Assisi or a St. Ignatius of Loyola? Will it fall victim to an excess of fervor or a loss of fervor? It is too soon to answer these questions. The answers will depend on how those who take part in the renewal use their freedom.

# Chapter 10

# MARY, MODEL
# OF THE CHARISMATIC

[Readers of the first edition of this book were surprised by this final chapter on Mary; they thought it had simply been dragged in. In fact, however, it is an important chapter from the viewpoint both of the charismatic movement and of ecumenism. The role assigned the Virgin Mary in Catholic Neo-Pentecostalism usually does not sit well with classical Pentecostalism. Yet this chapter was well received.

In this portrait of Mary the author defines her essentially as the prototype of the charismatic. It is a portrait that in its broad outlines is quite acceptable to an evangelical Christian. . . . In summary, this is a book that creates and nourishes hope.[1]

A member of the editorial board of the periodical in which the quoted remarks appeared wrote to me: "Though our report was complete by the time we received your book, we have tried to make room for it, especially since it allowed us to moderate somewhat the firm position we had taken" with regard to certain Catholic attitudes toward the Virgin Mary. This is why the paragraph entitled "Mary Was Fully a Charismatic" was added to the report, apparently at the last minute. In it we read:

This is not to say that we underestimate the importance of Mary's role in the history of salvation. Beyond any doubt, she is one of the greatest personages in the New Testament. She was fully a charismatic, and was one of the first to have been baptized in the Spirit on Pentecost. We cannot but have the deepest respect for her who was overshadowed by the power of the Holy Spirit and became the Mother of the Savior.

The following chapter, then, can be regarded as a basis for a constructive dialogue between classical Pentecostalism and the Catholic Pentecostal movement. (I have reflected further on this subject in a paper presented to the International Marian Congress at Rome on May 19, 1975)]

The Virgin Mary, who seemed to have been shunted aside in contemporary Catholicism, has "returned" in the charismatic renewal. This is a point frequently made on the basis of such testimonies as this: "The Virgin Mary is very much present in our group. Initially, her presence was somewhat concealed, but now everyone is keenly aware of it. I recall one prayer meeting in which a real litany to Mary rose from the lips of many participants."[2]

## 1. MARY IN THE CHARISMATIC RENEWAL

Is this rediscovery of Mary widespread in Catholic Pentecostalism? Is it a genuine renewal or simply a regression to a preconciliar stage? These are questions that must be taken seriously and not answered with slogans.

### PRAYER

While the Virgin Mary is enthusiastically invoked at many charismatic prayer meetings in France and Canada, a much greater reserve is shown in the United States. When I inquired as to the reason, Gary Serovik, of Ann Arbor, told me: "In the United States most of our groups are mixed, and we therefore instinctively exercise reserve when it comes to themes peculiar to one or other confession. The Lutherans show the same tact when it comes to points that have been signs of contradiction for Catholics."

This does not mean that the Blessed Virgin is absent from the charismatic renewal in the United States. Rather, the reserve we note there is perceived as a problem; people are beginning to ask:

"How can we give Mary her rightful place, in an authentic and ecumenical way?"

French and Canadian groups are, in some instances, facing an opposite problem. The evocation or invocation of the Virgin Mary in these groups is often simple, matter-of-fact, and biblical in style. At other times, however, fervent individuals seeking to express themselves lyrically revive the ponderous and in some cases questionable formulas of the preconciliar period, to the detriment not only of the ecumenical spirit but of authenticity as well (formulas using the very imperfect terminology of "coredemption," "mediation," "maternity in the order of grace," etc.).

## PUBLICATIONS[3]

In a somewhat parallel way, the initial studies of the subject made some helpful points, the best being contained in the very titles of the first two pamphlets published: *Mary Is Pentecostal* and *Mary, the Model Charismatic*. Unfortunately, the development of the themes is often a patchwork job, in which fervor and improvisation supply us with disparate materials and insufficient reflection on them.

At least the basic problem is clear. The charismatic renewal has made an authentic rediscovery of Mary; now it must learn to express Mary's Spirit-animated presence in the communion of saints in a way that is faithful to the experience of the movement itself, which is so truly biblical and ecumenical and which will not be satisfied with mere words.

## 2. DOCTRINE

The charismatic movement, then, is called upon to shed a life-giving light that is in a special way its own. What it is called upon to illumine, however, is not so much theological constructions, however important ("divine maternity," "Mary, Mother of the Church") as it is the teaching, emphasized in Vatican II, on "Mary, Model of the Church," especially in the mystery of her presence in the Church ever since the first outpouring of the Spirit.

## MARY'S PRESENCE AT PENTECOST

The Blessed Virgin was present in the upper room (Ac. 1:14). Luke mentions her explicitly as part of the community gathered there; she alone of the "several women" is named along with the Twelve.[4]

1. *Mary is the model for the Church in her receptivity to the Holy Spirit*, who forms Christ in the people of God. The New Testament itself provides evidence that Mary is indeed to be seen as a type of and model for the rest of the Church. Luke, historian of the Church's birth (Ac. 1–2), is also the evangelist of Christ's birth (Lk. 1–2). In the Gospel he depicts the Annunciation as a proto-Pentecost, the Pentecost of Mary, using the same language that will be used with reference to the Pentecost of the Church:

| Lk. 1:35 | Ac. 1:8 |
|:---:|:---:|
| The Holy Spirit | when the Holy Spirit |
| will come upon you | comes upon you |

Is the use of the same language intentional? Yes, but more than this, the identity of the language is required by the structure of the two events or, more accurately, by Luke's theology. Both accounts show the same dynamic pattern at work: The supreme Agent, the Spirit who is both transcendent and immanent, plays the essential role, beyond the visible actors on the scene. His coming sets the human actors in motion: Mary goes on her visitation to Elizabeth, the apostles go out on their mission. In both accounts, the individuals leave the enclosed place where the Spirit was manifested to them: Mary's home (Lk. 1:28) and the upper room (Ac. 1:13; 2:2). In both, the coming of the Spirit is followed by witnessing in the form of praise: the "Magnificat" (Lk. 1:46–56), and the outburst of praise on the part of the disciples as they face the crowd (Ac. 2:4–13).

Our comparison is thus not artificial, and has been made by the Second Vatican Council.[5] Mary is indeed a model for the Church in her new relationship to the Holy Spirit, who effects both the interior appropriation of Christ and his birth into the world.

2. *Mary is the model for Christians baptized in the Spirit.* "Baptism in the Spirit" properly describes the gift that the community

received on the first Pentecost, as is clear from Christ's promise: "John baptised with water but you, not many days from now, will be baptised with the Holy Spirit" (Ac. 1:5).

If there still were any doubt that these words are meant as a descripiton of the grace of Pentecost, Chapter 10 of Acts would settle the matter, since it provides the same interpretation of the event. When Cornelius, the centurion, and his household receive the outpouring of the Spirit, Peter expressly states that the same grace is operative here and on Pentecost: "The Holy Spirit came down on them in the same way as it came on us at the beginning. . . . God was giving to them the identical thing he gave to us" (Ac. 11:15, 17). He also states that the phenomenon on this occasion, like that on Pentecost, is a fulfillment of Jesus' words: "I remembered that the Lord had said, 'John baptised with water, but you will be baptised with the Holy Spirit'" (Ac. 11:16).

If one thing is clear, then, from the theology of Acts, it is that the grace of Pentecost was the grace of a baptism "in the Spirit" (Ac. 1:5; 11:16), which might also be described as a "baptism in fire" (Lk. 3:16; Ac. 2:3).

Mary, as object par excellence of God's favor (*kecharitōmenē*, "highly favored": Lk. 1:28) and the first to be moved by the Spirit (Lk. 1:35), is also the model, in the very first Christian community, for the reception of baptism in the Spirit. Here again, she is the Virgin of beginnings.

3. *Mary is also model of the charismatic life.* The first Christian community is offered to us as such a model. It was through the exercise of the gifts Paul calls "charisms" that the coming of the Spirit promised by Christ would be manifested.

## Was Mary a tongue speaker?

The charism that is most evident in the account of Pentecost is glossolalia, in the form of a collective, harmonious speaking in tongues (as we saw earlier). Mary, consequently, is the model not only for the charisms in general but specifically for the praying in tongues that is characteristic of the Pentecostal movement.

No doubt there are ways of evading this conclusion; we noted them earlier. When Luke says "all . . . began to speak foreign languages" (Ac. 2:4), we may invoke his penchant for universal statements and for the poetic use of the word "all." And yet, in the group mentioned in Acts 1:13–14 (a group that 1:15, from another source, estimates as numbering about 120), Mary is the only one to be mentioned by name along with the Twelve. It would seem, then, that she plays an important part in the prayer of collective praise (Ac. 2:4–13), which is something quite distinct from Peter's sermon (2:14–36).

Can we invoke here St. Paul's reminder that "as in all the churches of the saints, women are to remain quiet at meetings" (1 Co. 14:34)? First of all, the Pauline authenticity of this statement is disputed; furthermore, elsewhere in the same letter Paul says that a woman may pray or prophesy in church, provided she keeps her head covered (1 Co. 11:5).

## Was Mary a prophet?

The answer is that she was. This answer is confirmed and made specific by the fact that Luke, using the same Jewish-Christian sources as elsewhere in the Gospel of the infancy and in Acts 1–2, and writing within the same perspective and with the same intention, shows Mary to us in the actual exercise of the charism of prophecy: After the Spirit has come upon her (Lk. 1:35), she sings her "Magnificat" (Lk. 1:45–56)!

It is important to note in this context that her prophecy is a tissue of biblical expressions and thus is analogous to the kind of prophecy that is becoming prominent in our own day. Moreover, both the "Magnificat" and the prophecies of the charismatic renewal are basically poems of praise. Luke presents Mary to us as a "pre-Pentecostal" model of the exercise of the charism of prophecy. She is model and first exerciser of the charism, not its "source" or "mother," since the charism comes from the Holy Spirit.

Luke cautions us, moreover, against thinking of Mary as an isolated figure in the area of prophecy. According to the infancy narrative, she is not the only charismatic, even at this pre-Pentecostal stage. Luke even sets out to show us how the coming and infancy of Jesus gave rise to a first outpouring of the Spirit and how the Spirit caused the gift of prophecy to flourish among those members of God's people whom the Scriptures think of as the "poor of Yahweh."

•Even before Mary, Elizabeth is filled with the Holy Spirit and prophesies: "Of all women you are the most blessed, and blessed is the fruit of your womb. Why should I be honored with a visit from the mother of my Lord?" (Lk. 1:43–44).

•John the Baptist, of whom it has already been said that "even from his mother's womb he will be filled with the Holy Spirit" (Lk. 1:15), now leaps in Elizabeth's womb (1:41) at the approach of Mary, the Mother of the Lord. Luke mentions this movement of the child as a first, preconceptual expression of the prophetic charism John will exercise. Luke's interpretation is mystical indeed and poetical, but Christian tradition has always attached value to it. It is not to be likened to the artificial constructions with which theologians sometimes embellish the Gospel narrative.

•In Luke 1:67, Zechariah, John's father, "was filled with the Holy Spirit and spoke this prophecy." His prophecy is the "Benedictus," which is a parallel to the "Magnificat." The explicit use of the verb "prophesy" to introduce this poem guarantees that we are not going astray in using it of Mary as well. Besides, a weighty tradition originating in the Greek and Latin Fathers attributes to Mary the title of "prophetess."

•The series of prophecies continues with those of Simeon and Anna. This woman is expressly called a prophetess in Luke 2:36, and there is a reason for mentioning her. In Luke 1–2, as in Acts 1:14, Luke (who may be called the most feminist of the evangelists) aims to show that in the new Christian community there is "neither male nor female" (in the emphatic words of Paul, whose companion he had been). At the time when he wrote his Gospel he was well aware that the rite of baptism, which was given to women as well as men, abolished the discriminatory barriers that the initiation rite of circumcision had erected between the sexes in Judaism.

These last observations provide still another reason for thinking that Luke intends to place Mary (precisely as a woman) in the forefront of the charismatic group from the upper room as they exercise the gift of glossolalia for the first time.

We have no intention of exaggerating the importance of this latter charism, which according to St. Paul is quite secondary (cf. above, Chapter 4, section 10). What we do have to do, however, is to resist reductive interpretations. It is rather surprising to see how theologians who are so ingenious at finding Scriptural grounds for much that is not explicit there (including the Immaculate Conception and the Assumption) will raise all sorts of factitious objections in order to avoid facing what is clear and obvious.

The important thing, of course, is that Mary is the prototype of the Church, and, in a special way, the model for the Church's relationship to the Holy Spirit and for the charismatic quality of the whole of the Church's life (a point being emphasized in post-conciliar theology).

## 3. Conclusion

Since the end of Pius XII's pontificate and the start of Vatican II, some Catholics have been disturbed at seeing the Blessed Virgin disappearing from their Church.

In order to allay this disturbance, I have often pointed out an important fact: many theological or pious theories have proved untenable, many honorific titles have been forgotten, and many devotions have been jettisoned, sometimes hastily and in an excessively radical spirit; but amid this collapse of a "Mariology" and a "Marian" devotion that were marked by extremism and an inflated narrowness, something solid and inescapably true has been coming to the fore. It has become clear that Mary, as Mother of Jesus, is at the very heart of revelation and the Church's life. It is essential that Christians make this rediscovery, for Mary's real place has often been mistaken; her true stature has been hidden by too many superstructures.

Various movements—biblical, patristic, ecclesiological (history of salvation), liturgical, missionary, and ecumenical—have taught us to see Mary in a new light, and this at the very time when the first efforts to trim excesses and clear the ground were being made.[6]

When the liberation movement began, a number of Catholics, including Gustavo Gutiérrez and Sergio Méndez Arceo, the latter one of the bishops most involved in the movement, rediscovered the revolutionary impact of Mary's hymn in which she praises God because "he has pulled down princes from their throne and exalted the lowly" (Lk. 1:52).[7] In an earlier generation Charles Maurras perceived quite clearly the radicalism of the "Magnificat" and congratulated the Church on having been able "to kill the virus of revolution" contained in the inspired text![8]

There is an analogous, though more paradoxical phenomenon: Some Christians in the women's liberation movement have discovered in Mary a prototype of the liberated woman, especially because she remained a virgin in conceiving Jesus.[9] Paul VI has acknowledged the justice of their basic intuitions in his Apostolic Exhortation on Devotion to the Blessed Virgin (February 2, 1974).[10]

Now that the most recent movement to arise in the Catholic Church, the Pentecostal renewal, has rediscovered the Blessed Virgin, this time as model for the spiritual person and the charismatic and as prophet and tongue speaker, we are confirmed in our assurance that the Virgin Mary indeed has an important, even if unobtrusive, place at the very heart of Christianity and the communion of saints. That is the "better part" that cannot be taken from her, and it must not be overlooked.

# Chronological Table

*1738*  In May of this year, John Wesley, founder of Methodism and distant forerunner of Pentecostalism, experiences the interior witness of the Spirit and a conversion of heart.

*End of eighteenth century.* The movement reaches the United States, within Wesley's lifetime; from now on, there will be the series of "spiritual awakenings" or "revivals" that have been a main characteristic of Christianity in the United States.

*Middle of nineteenth century.* Numerous reactions, especially among the poor, against formalism.

*1894*  The "Holiness Movement" breaks off from the Methodist charismatic movement. It distinguishes between "complete conversion" and "sanctification" or holiness, and applies the term "baptism in the Spirit" (a term popularized by Charles Finney, Presbyterian theologian) only to the second of these, whereas the Methodists regard the first conversion as the essential thing. This break will give rise to two hundred groups or denominations between now and 1923: Pilgrim Holiness Church, Fire Baptized Holiness Church, etc.

*1900*  In the fall of this year, Charles Parham, a Methodist pastor, starts the Bethel Bible School at Topeka, Kansas, where about thirty persons study God's word, using no book but the Bible.

*1901*  On January 1, at 11 P.M., the first Pentecostal experience at Topeka (Agnes Ozman). During the next few days, the whole school will have the experience.

*1906*  In April, the beginning of the Pentecostal expansion under the influence of a black pastor, W. J. Seymour, who had been a disciple of Parham and who now established a place for prayer in an abandoned Methodist church on Asuza Street in Los Angeles.

*1914*  Establishment of a national organization for American Pentecostalism. Establishment of the Assemblies of God.

*1915*  Expansion in Scandinavia.

*1958*  Appearance of Neo-Pentecostalism among the Episcopalians of California.

*1962*  The Pentecostal movement gets under way in the Lutheran Church of America.

*1966*  In August, the lay professors on the theological faculty of Duquesne University discover the books of David Wilkerson, *The Cross and the Swtichblade*, and of John L. Sherrill, *They Speak in Other Tongues*, and study these in connection with the Acts of the Apostles.

*1967*  On Friday, January 6, the feast of the Epiphany, the group from Duquesne University meets with an Episcopalian lady who tells them about a Pentecostal prayer group.

*1967*  January 13, octave of the Epiphany: the Duquesne group attends the Pentecostal prayer meeting; first charismatic manifestations.

*1967*  In June, first conference at Notre Dame (ninety participants).

*1971*  Beginning of the movement in France.

*1972*  June 20–24: first ecumenical meeting between Catholics and Pentecostals, at Zürich-Horgen. This formal meeting, the first of a series, is preceded by a series of informal meetings (1970–71) between Catholic and non-Catholic Pentecostals.

*1973*  June 18–22: Second meeting of Catholics and Pentecostals, held at Rome, at the Secretariat for Christian Unity; second set of agreements, especially with regard to baptism in the Spirit and the freedom bestowed by the Spirit.

*1973*  October 10: Audience of Pope Paul VI for thirteen leaders of the charismatic movement, on the occasion of the international meeting at Grottaferrata (at which thirty-four nations are represented).

*1974*   June 10–14: Third ecumenical meeting between Catholics and Pentecostals, held at Schloss Craheim, Wetzhausen, Germany, with the participation (as always) of the Secretariat for Christian Unity; the theme is Christian initiation.

*1974*   June 14–16: Eighth international meeting of the charismatic movement, at Notre Dame, with thirty-five thousand attending.

*1975*   May 16–20: Ninth international conference of the charismatic movement, held in Rome on Pentecost.

An exhaustive bibliography would itself fill a volume of several hundred pages. The *Essai bibliographique de langue française*, published by the Bureau de documentation pastorale (publication No. 6) in January 1973 (11 mimeographed pages, 50 titles), had to be supplemented in December 1973 by another *Essai* (publication No. 19 of the Bureau), containing 116 new titles. Yet the movement had been in existence in France for only three years, whereas it was already seven years old in the United States.

We cannot recommend too highly D. W. Paupel, *The American Pentecostal Movement: A Bibliographical Essay* (Wilmore, Ky.: Fisher Library of the Asbury Theological Seminary, 1972).

## 1. General

### BOOKS AND PAMPHLETS

Boisset, L. *Mouvement de Jésus et Renouveau dans l'Esprit.* Meylan: Centre Théologique de Meylan, n.d. Mimeographed, 90 pp.

Caffarel, H. *Faut-il parler d'un Pentecôtisme catholique?* Paris: Editions du Renouveau, 1973. 96 pp.

Eugène de Villeurbanne, O.F.M. Cap. *Illuminisme "67." Un faux renouveau: Le pentecôtisme dit "catholique."* Verjon, Coligny [1974]. This pamphlet, which bears no date or publisher's name or imprimatur, attributes Pentecostalism to the devil.

Gelpi, D. L. *Pentecostalism: A Theological Viewpoint*. New York: Paulist Press, 1971. 234 pp.

McDonnell, K., O.S.B. *Catholic Pentecostalism: Problems in Evaluation*. Pecos, N.M.: Dove, 1970. Reprint of an article that appeared in *Dialog* 9 (1970), pp. 35–54; bibliography added to the reprint.

——. *Statement of the Theological Principles of the Catholic Charismatic Movement*. Pecos, N.M.: Dove, 1973. McDonnell was the chief redactor, but was aided by seven theologians and pastors (H. Mühlen among them).

Martin, R. *Unless the Lord Build the House: The Church of the New Pentecost*. Notre Dame: Ave Maria Press, n.d. 64 pp.

Montague, G. *The Spirit and His Gifts: The Biblical Background of Spirit-Baptism, Tongue-Speaking and Prophecy*. New York: Paulist Press, 1974. 66 pp.

O'Connor, E. D. *The Pentecostal Movement in the Catholic Church*. Notre Dame: Ave Maria Press, 1971. 301 pp. Bibliography (pp. 295–301). A basic work.

——. *Pentecost in the Modern World: The Charismatic Renewal Compared with Other Trends in the Church and the World Today*. Notre Dame: Ave Maria Press, 1972. 48 pp.

Ranaghan, K. *The Lord, the Spirit, and the Church*. Notre Dame: Charismatic Renewal Services, 1973. 64 pp.

Ranaghan, K., and Ranaghan, D. *Catholic Pentecostals*. New York: Paulist Press, 1969. 266 pp.

Regimbal, J. P. *Signes et témoins du Royaume 1: Sous la mouvance de l'Esprit: Le renouveau charismatique dans l'Église catholique*. Quebec: Ralliement pour le Christ, 1971. 48 pp. Regimbal is the founder of the movement in Quebec.

Sauvé, P. *Quand souffle l'Esprit*. Montreal: Beauchemin, 1973. 114 pp.

Tugwell, S. *Did You Receive the Spirit?* New York: Paulist Press, 1972. 144 pp.

Whitney, J. *The Charismatic Renewal: What Is It All About?* Mimeographed pamphlet issued by the Communication Center at Notre Dame, March 4, 1974. 24 pp.

## ARTICLES

Chéry, H. "Catholiques et Pentecôtistes," *Ecclesia* 280 (July–Aug. 1972), pp. 10–12.

Clément, O. "A propos de l'Esprit-Saint," *Contacts* 26 (1974), pp. 85–91 (esp. pp. 88–91).

Ford, J. M. "Pentecostal Catholicism," *The Prayer Life*, ed. C. Duquoc and Cl. Geffré. *Concilium* 79. New York: Herder and Herder, 1972, pp. 85–90.

——. "Pentecostal Poise or Docetic Charismatics?," *Spiritual Life* 19 (1973), pp. 32–47.

Gelpi, D. "American Pentecostalism," *Spiritual Revivals*, ed. C. Duquoc and C. Floristán. *Concilium* 89. New York: Herder and Herder, 1973, pp. 101–10.

Giblet, J. "Le mouvement pentecôtiste dans l'eglise catholique des U.S.A.," *Revue théologique de Louvain* 4 (1973), pp. 469–90.

Gouvernaire, J. "Les charismatiques," *Etudes* 340 (Jan.–June 1974), pp. 123–40.

Grom, B. "Die katholische charismatische Bewegung," *Stimmen der Zeit* 191 (1973), pp. 651–71.

Houdart, Sr. M.-A., O.S.B. "Renouveau dans la prière," *Vie consacrée* 46 (1974), pp. 146–59.

Lebeau, P. "Le renouveau charismatique dans l'Église." Conference to the second meeting of the leaders of charismatic groups, at Magnificat House in Kovenjoel, Belgium, March 2, 1974. Mimeographed, 18 pp.

Lepesant, B., and Fabre, L. "Les oasis de l'Esprit," *Parole et Mission: Dossier 6*. Paris: Editions du Cerf, 1973, pp. 81–84.

McDonnell, K. "Catholic Charismatics," *Commonweal* 96 (1972), pp. 207–11.

Michalon, P. "Témoignages et réflexions sur le mouvement catholique pentecostal," *Unité chrétienne* 28 (Nov. 1972), pp. 60–70.

O'Connor, E. D. "A Catholic Pentecostal Movement," *Ave Maria* 122, No. 105 (June 3, 1967), pp. 6–10. A first explanation by one of the early leaders of the movement.

——. "Pentecost and Catholicism," *Ecumenist* 6 (1968), pp. 161–64.

Regimbal, J. P. "Le renouveau charismatique dans l'Église catholique: Interview avec L. Coutu," *Orient* 21, No. 122 (1973).

Simmel, O. "Die katholische Pfingstbewegung in den Vereinigten Staaten," *Internationale Katholische Zeitschrift* 2 (1973), pp. 148–57.

Sullivan, F. A. "The Pentecostal Movement," *Gregorianum* 53 (1972), pp. 237–66.

Vié, Sr. E. "Le renouveau charismatique," *Christus* 80 (Oct. 1973), p. 497.

Wild, R. " 'It Is Clear That There Are Serious Differences Among You' (1 Cor. 1:11): The Charismatic Renewal Entering Religious Communities," *Review for Religious* 32 (1973), pp. 1,093–1,102.

——. "The Rebirth of Group Prayer," *Cross and Crown* 25 (1973), pp. 379–91.

Woodrow, A. "Le Renouveau charismatique aux États-Unis," *Informations catholiques internationales* 448 (Jan. 15, 1974), pp. 13–20. Cf. Nos. 437–38 (Aug. 1973), pp. 3–5.

## SPECIAL ISSUES OF PERIODICALS

*Courrier communautaire international* 9 (1974), No. 4: *Ces communautés dites charismatiques.* 68 pp.

*Expériences: Document périodique*, 1971, No. 2: *Que faut-il penser des "catholiques pentecôtistes"?* 74 pp. (Published by the Centre Missionaire, Carhaix 29270.)

*Foi et vie* 72, Nos. 4–5 (July–Oct. 1973): *Renouveau charismatique.* 110 pp.

*One in Christ* 10 (1974), pp. 117–205. The papers from the meetings of Catholics and Pentecostalists at Zürich-Horgen, June 20–24, 1972, and at Rome, June 18–22, 1973.

*Prêtre et pasteur* 77, No. 5 (1974): *Libérer l'Esprit: Le Renouveau charismatique*, pp. 225–88. (Published: 4450 rue St. Hubert, Montreal 4450.)

*Vie spirituelle* 128, No. 600 (Jan.–Feb. 1974): *Le mouvement charismatique*, pp. 1–131.

## REPORTS TO EPISCOPAL CONFERENCES

Hocken, P. *Report to the English Episcopate*, published with authorization of the president of the Theological Commission of the Conference of English Bishops, in *Vie spirituelle* 128 (1974), pp. 31–42.

Zaleski, A. M. *Report to the United States Catholic Bishops* meeting in Washington, D.C., November 10–14, 1969. Published in *Theology Digest* 19 (1971), pp. 52–53; in K. McDonnell, *Catholic Pentecostalism: Problems in Evaluation* (Pecos, N.M., 1970); and in E. D. O'Connor, *The Pentecostal Movement in the Catholic Church* (Notre Dame, 1971), pp. 291–93.

## 2. Organs of the Catholic Neo-Pentecostal Movement

### PERIODICALS

*Cahiers du Renouveau.* No. 1 was published in the summer of 1974.

*Feu Nouveau.* A bulletin for liaison and formation, for groups founded by Father H. Caffarel, one of the first leaders of the movement in France.

*Magnificat.* Published quarterly at 2 Byzonder Weg, 3042 Lovenjoel, Belgium.

*New Covenant.* A monthly of increasingly high quality, founded at Ann Arbor, 1971 (P. O. Box 102, Ann Arbor, Mich. 48107).

### PUBLISHING CENTERS

Communication Center, P. O. Drawer, Notre Dame, Ind. 46556. The center has books, records, and a large number of cassettes; it runs a communications network and has charge of the yearbook at the national level (communications at the international level are handled at Ann Arbor, P. O. Box 363).

Dove Editions, Pecos, N.M.

Ökumenischer Schriftendienst, Schloss Craheim, D-8721 Wetzhausen, Germany, publishes and sells Pentecostal books and pamphlets in Germany (including Catholic publications).

### FORMATION

(Under this heading we indicate some books and brochures meant for formation or spiritual development.)

Clark, S. B. *Growing in Faith.* Notre Dame: Charismatic Renewal Services, 1972. 64 pp.

——. *Knowing God's Will.* Notre Dame: Charismatic Renewal Services, 1972. 66 pp.

——. *Spiritual Gifts.* Pecos, N.M.: Dove, 1969. 34 pp.

——. *Where Are We Headed? Guidelines for the Catholic Charismatic Renewal.* Notre Dame: Ave Maria Press, 1973. 80 pp. This is Book 2 in the Servant Series. Book 1 was a *Team Manual of the Life in the Spirit Seminars* (listed below).

Custeau, J., and Michel, R. *Reconnaître l'Esprit.* Montreal: Editions Bellarmin, 1974. 80 pp. Contains the two most notable papers of the Charismatic Renewal Conference held in the summer of 1973 at Loyola College in Montreal.

*Découverte de la vie dans l'Esprit.* Booklet for Life in the Spirit seminars; guide for a seven-week formation period. Montreal: Editions du Renouveau charismatique. 64 pp.

*Life in the Spirit Seminars: Team Manual.* Notre Dame: Charismatic Renewal Services. 184 pp.

McDonnell, K. "Eucharistic Celebrations in the Catholic Charismatic Movement" *Studia Liturgica* 9 (1973), pp. 19–44.

Melançon, O. *Renouveau charismatique: Prophétisme, analyse théologique; Discernement des esprits, signes des temps.* Montreal, 1973. 158 pp.

Mollat, D. *L'expérience spirituelle.* Paris: Editions du Feu Nouveau, 1974.

*Outlines for the Foundations of Christian Living Course.* Mimeographed booklet for the first formation course (Foundation I), ed. The Word of God Community, Ann Arbor (P. O. Box 87). The second course (Foundation II) is now being published.

# 3. LIFE AND ORGANIZATION OF THE MOVEMENT

## YEARBOOK

*Directory of Catholic Charismatic Prayer Groups.* Notre Dame, 1973, 97 pp., and 1974, 106 pp. The yearbook contains the addresses of prayer groups throughout the world, the persons in charge of them, the proportion of Catholics and non-Catholics, etc. A comparison of the two editions enables the reader to gauge the growth of the movement (insofar as it has been inventoried).

## CONGRESSES

*Congrès du Renouveau charismatique catholique.* Participants' brochure for the congress held at Laval University, June 7–9, 1974.

*Jesus Christ Is the Light of the World.* Notre Dame: Charismatic Renewal Services. Participants' brochure for the eighth international congress, held at Notre Dame, June 14–16, 1974.

## DESCRIPTION OF COMMUNITIES

Kosicki, G. *The Lord Is My Shepherd: Witnesses of Priests.* Ann Arbor: Charismatic Renewal Services, 1973. 138 pp. Bishop J. McKinney and thirteen priests testify to what the charismatic renewal has meant to them.

Le Braz, B. M. "Regards sur le Renouveau charismatique," *Cahiers marials* 90 (Nov. 15, 1973), pp. 355–71.

Marc'hadour, G. "L'Esprit-Saint sur le Nouveau Monde," *Impacts* (Angers, France), 1974, pp. 36–64.

Marie-Thérèse, Sister. "Comment si vit une assemblée de prière à Emmanuel?," *Impacts,* 1974, pp. 372–74.

Martin, F. "Un week-end avec le Renouveau (Pau, 22–24 février 1974)," *Notre Dame de Tournay* 124 (July–Aug. 1974), pp. 57–62.

Monléon, A. M. de. "Le Renouveau charismatique aux États-Unis," *Vers l'unité chrétienne* 227 (1970), pp. 81–85. Also in *Cahiers sur l'oraison* (Editions du Feu Nouveau) 122 (Mar.–Apr. 1972), pp. 242–53.

Randall, J. *In God's Providence: The Birth of a Catholic Charismatic Parish.* Plainfield, N.J.: Logos International, 1973.

———. "J'ai reçu le Baptême de l'Esprit," *Expériences* 11 (1971), pp. 11–12. An interview with J. P. Regimbal.

# 4. DISPUTED QUESTIONS

(We have chosen to leave the bibliographical notes in the chapters, since the bibliography on these subjects is necessarily ecumenical and cannot be restricted to Catholic Pentecostalism.)

Baptism in the Spirit: cf. the note at the end of Chapter 2.
Glossolalia: cf. the bibliography at the end of Chapter 4.

Healings: cf. Chapter 5, notes 3, 8, and 10.
Laying on of hands: cf. Chapter 3, note 33.
Mary: cf. Chapter 10, note 4.

## 5. The Viewpoint of the Sciences of Man

Medicine: cf. Chapter 5, notes 1, 3, and 22.
Psychology: cf. Chapter 7, note at the end of the chapter.
Sociology: cf. Chapter 7, notes 6 and 7.

## 6. The Holy Spirit

(The bibliography on this subject is large and scattered. The author will reserve bibliographical listings for a later theological study. For the important works of Heribert Mühlen, cf. Chapter 9, note 5. We shall note here only a few studies that relate more directly to the concerns of the charismatic renewal.)

### THEOLOGY

Congar, Y. M.-J. "Actualité renouvelée du Saint-Esprit," *Lumen Vitae* 27 (1972), pp. 543–60.

———. "La pneumatologie dans la théologie catholique," *Revue des sciences philosophiques et théologiques* 51 (1972), pp. 250–58.

### EXEGESIS

Guillet, J. *Viens, Esprit de Dieu.* Paris: Editions du Feu Nouveau, 1974. A study of the Holy Spirit in the Bible.

Mollat, D. *La révélation du Saint-Esprit chez saint Jean.* Rome, 1971. Notes for the use of students.

Philips, G. *De Spiritu Sancto et Ecclesia in theologia contemporanea* (*Cursus XVI*). Louvain: Louvain University, 1957–58. 140 pp. Mimeographed course. Contains a notable "state of the question" (with an eye on future developments) by the future secretary (and editor) of the Theological Commission of Vatican II.

Rigaux, B. "L'anticipation du salut eschatologique par l'Esprit," *Analecta Biblica* 42 (Rome, 1969), pp. 101–35.


## 7. BIBLIOGRAPHY ON "BAPTISM IN THE SPIRIT"


Cantelon, W. *El bautismo en el Espiritu Santo*, 3rd ed. Springfield, Mo., 1955.

Clark, S. *Baptized in the Spirit*. Pecos, N.M., 1970.

——. *Confirmation and the Baptism in the Holy Spirit*. Pecos, N.M., 1969.

Dunn, J. D. G. *Baptism in the Holy Spirit: A Re-examination of the New Testament Teaching on the Gift of the Holy Spirit in Relation to Pentecostalism Today*. Studies in Biblical Theology, Second Series 15. Naperville, Ill., 1970.

——. "Spirit-Baptism and Pentecostalism," *Scottish Journal of Theology* 23 (1970), pp. 397–407.

Fischer, B. "The Meaning of the Expression 'Baptism of the Spirit' in the Light of Catholic Baptismal Liturgy and Spirituality," *One in Christ* 10 (1974), pp. 172–73.

Garrigues, J.-M. "L'effusion de l'Esprit," *Vie spirituelle* 128 (1974), pp. 73–81.

Giblet, J. "Baptism in the Spirit in the Acts of the Apostles," *One in Christ* 10 (1974), pp. 162–71.

McDonnell, K. *Baptism in the Spirit as an Ecumenical Problem*. Notre Dame, 1972.

McTernan, J. "Water Baptism: A Response to Fr. Kilian McDonnell's Paper," *One in Christ* 10 (1974), pp. 203–5. McDonnell's paper is on pp. 117–28 of the same issue.

Montague, G. T. "Baptism in the Spirit and Speaking in Tongues: A Biblical Appraisal," *Theology Digest* 21 (1973), pp. 342–60. A paper read to the Catholic Biblical Association in New York, August 1, 1973. This serious and well-documented study is reprinted as part of the author's *The Spirit and His Gifts* (New York, 1974); cf. pp. 3–29.

Schneider, H. *Die Bedeutung der Geistestaufe in der charismatischen Erneuerung der Katholischen Kirche*. Wetzhausen, 1974.

Sullivan, F. A. " 'Baptism in the Holy Spirit': A Catholic Interpretation of the Pentecostal Experience," *Gregorianum* 55 (1974), pp. 49–66.

Tugwell, S. *Did You Receive the Spirit?* New York, 1972.

———. "Group Prayer and Contemplation," *New Blackfriars* 52 (1971), pp. 132–38.

Turrano, L. "El bautismo *in Spiritu Sancto et igni*," *Estudios Eclesiásticos* 34 (1960), pp. 807–17.

Wilkens, W. "Wassertaufe and Geistesempfang bei Lukas," *Theologische Zeitschrift* 23 (1967), pp. 26–47. On the distinction between baptism in water and baptism in the Spirit, the latter bestowing the gift of prophecy.

## 8. Chronological Bibliography on Glossolalia

Publication on glossolalia has been extensive during three periods:

1. Second third of the nineteenth century, when tongue speaking in the Irvingite movement (England, 1830 on) attracted a great deal of attention.

2. Beginning of the twentieth century, when interest was roused by the Pentecostalist revival in Germany (where it was called "The Glossolalic and Pentecostal movement," *Zungen- und Pfingstbewegung*), and by similar movements in Australia (1902) and Wales (1904). This led to the first essays on the psychology of the phenomenon (Mosiman, 1911) and on the linguistic aspect, with an attempt at establishing a topology (Lombard, 1908-11).

3. Beginning in 1963, with the appearance of Neo-Pentecostalism within the traditional confessions (first among the Episcopalians).

### PREHISTORY

For the period before 1829, we shall mention only five titles; even these are of limited interest.

Scaramelli, G. B. *Direttorio mistico*. Venice, 1754. Treatise 3, Chap. 7, links glossolalic phenomena to a "spiritual intoxication" (an allusion to Ac. 2:13).

Ernesti, G. A. *De doni linguarum natura ad illustrandum 1 Co. 14*. Leipzig, 1765.

Less, G. *De doni linguarum indole disquisitio*. Göttingen, 1771.

Klein. *De loquendi formula "glôssais lalein."* Jena, 1816.

Melville. *Observationes theologico-exegeticae de dono linguarum.* Basel, 1816.

## 1829–99

Bleek, F. "Über die Gabe des *glôssais lalein* in der ersten christlichen Kirche," *Theologische Studien und Kritiken* 2 (1829), pp. 3–79, with the critical remarks of J. Olshauzen, pp. 538–49.

Baur, F. C. "Über den wahren Begriff des *glôssais lalein*," *Zeitschrift für Theologie* 3 (1830), pp. 78–133.

Bleek, F. "Noch ein Paar Worte über die Gabe des *glôssais lalein*," *Theologische Studien und Kritiken* 3 (1830), pp. 45–64, with the rest of Olshauzen's remarks, pp. 64–66 and 566–80.

Baur, F. C. "Kritische Übersicht über die neuesten des *glôssais lalein* in der ersten christlichen Kirche betreffend der Untersuchung," *Theologische Studien und Kritiken* 11 (1838), pp. 618–702.

Wieseler. "Über das *glôssais lalein*," *Theologische Studien und Kritiken* 11 (1838), pp. 703–72.

Kollner, W. H. *De formula "glôssais lalein" in Novo Testamento.* Göttingen, 1841.

Bauer, W. *Über die Sprachengabe und über das "glôssais lalein."* Denkschrift des Seminars zu Herborn, 1842.

Hilgenfeld, Ad. *Die Glossolalie in der alten Kirche.* Leipzig, 1850. Bibliography of earlier literature, p. 15, n. 1.

Rooteuscher, E. *Die Gabe der Sprachen im Apostolischen Zeitalter.* Marburg, 1850.

Reuss, Ed. "La glossolalie: Chapitre de psychologie évangélique," *Revue théologique de Strasbourg* 3 (1851), pp. 65–97. The opening words show the extent of contemporary interest in the question: "Fifty-four special dissertations [on glossolalia] published in Germany alone since the beginning of the century, several dozen commentaries, and countless critical articles in twenty different periodicals would seem to be more than enough. . . ."

Corluy, J. "Langues," *Dictionnaire apologétique de Jaugey* (Paris, 1889), cols. 1,785–1,800. Reproduced verbatim in the *Dictionnaire apologétique de la foi catholique* 2:1,810–19.

Simon, Th. *Die Psychologie des Apostels Paulus.* Göttingen, 1897. Pp. 114–15 contain a bibliography of Protestant works since 1665.

Clemen, C. "The Speaking with Tongues of the Early Christians," *Expository Times* 10 (1898–99), pp. 344–52.

1901–63

Henry, V. *Le langage martien.* Paris, 1901. A study of the successive forms (Martian, ultra-Martian, Uranian, lunar) of glossolalia heard from Hélène Smith, a spiritualist, from 1896 to 1899.

Lombard, E. "Essai d'une classification des phénomènes psychologiques," *Archives de psychologie* 7 (1907), pp. 1–51.

Wolf, J. E. *Pentecost and Tongues.* Toronto, 1907.

Anderson, W. B. *Speaking with Tongues.* New York, 1908.

Feine, P. "Zungenreden," *Realencyclopädie für Protestantische Theologie und Kirche* 21 (1908), pp. 749–59, with bibliography.

Lesêtre, H. "Langues (Don des)," *Dictionnaire de la Bible* 4 (1908), pp. 74–81.

Prat, F. *La theologie de saint Paul* 1 (Paris, 1908), pp. 177–79. In English: *The Theology of St. Paul,* tr. J. L. Stoddard (London, 1938), 1:129–33.

Henke, Fr. G. "The Gift of Tongues and Related Phenomena at the Present Day," *American Journal of Theology* 13 (1909), pp. 193–206.

Lombard, E. "Le parler en langues à Corinthe d'après les textes de saint Paul et les analogies modernes," *Revue de théologie et de philosophie* 42 (1909), pp. 5–52.

Beauclerc, J. [P. Rousselot, S.J.]. "A travers les revues," *Études* 123 (1910), pp. 867–71, on glossolalia in Germany and Norway; comments on T. Flournoy, *Nouvelles observations sur un cas de glossolalie* (Geneva, 1902), which dealt with Hélène Smith, the spiritualist (cf. Henry, V., 1901 above).

Fonck, L. *Quaestiones Paulinae* 9/5 (Rome, 1910). Reproduced as the article "Charismata," *Lexicon Biblicon.* Fonck did good service by providing a patristic dossier; his references are summarized by A. Michel (below, 1924).

Lombard, E. *De la glossolalie chez les premiers chrétiens et phénomènes similaires: Études d'exégèse et de philologie.* Lausanne and Paris, 1910. Preface by T. Flournoy, who, in addition to his book on Hélène Smith (see under Beauclerc, above), had published *Des Indes à la planète Mars,* a systematic study of a case of somnambulant glossolalia.

Reilly, T. à K. "The Gift of Tongues: What Was It?" *American Ecclesiastical Review* 43 (July–Dec. 1910), pp. 3–25.

Sheppard, W. T. C. "The Gift of Tongues in the Early Church," *American Ecclesiastical Review* 42 (Jan.–June 1910), pp. 513–22.

Bovet, P. "Le parler en langues des premiers chrétiens," *Revue d'histoire des religions* 63–64 (1911), pp. 292–310.

Lombard, E. "La glossolalie à notre époque," *Journal de Genève* (Dec. 3, 1911).

Mosiman, E. *Das Zungenreden geschichtlich und psychologisch untersucht.* Tübingen, 1911. A historical and psychological study. The same book in an incomplete form had been published earlier in the year at Leipzig, in preparation for defense of it as a dissertation.

Pfister, O. *Die psychologische Enträtselung der religiösen Glossolalie und der automatischen Krytographie.* Leipzig, 1912.

Reilly, T. à K. "Tongues," *Catholic Encyclopaedia* 14 (1912), pp. 776–77.

Hayes, D. A. *The Gift of Tongues.* Cincinnati, 1913.

Haensler, P. B. "Nochmals zu Apg 2, 4," *Byzantinische Zeitschrift* 12 (1914), pp. 35–44, 269–74.

McCrossan, T. J. *Speaking with other Tongues: Sign or Gift? Which?* Harrisburg, 1919.

Shumway, C. W. "A Critical History of Glossolalia." Boston, 1919. Unpublished doctoral dissertation, Boston University.

Mackie, A. *The Gift of Tongues: A Study in the Pathological Aspects of Christianity.* New York, 1921.

Rust, H. *Das Zungenreden: Eine Studie zur kritischen Religionspsychologie.* Tübingen, 1923.

Fonck, L. "Coeperunt variis linguis loqui (Act. 2, 4)," *Verbum domini* 4 (1924), pp. 163–69.

Leclercq, H. "Glossolalie," *Dictionnaire d'archéologie chrétienne et de liturgie* 6 (1924), cols. 1,322–27.

Michel, A. "Langues," *Dictionnaire de théologie catholique* 8 (1924), cols. 2,591–2,601. Sums up data of tradition, which, in his view, take New Testament glossolalia to be an "ecstatic speaking in a foreign language."

Jacquier, E. *Les Actes des Apôtres.* Paris, 1926. Cf. commentary, pp. 54–57, 336–37, and *Excursus* 7, pp. 187–95.

Thomson, W. S. "Tongues at Pentecost," *Expository Times* 38 (1926–27), pp. 284–86.

Cutten, G. B. *Speaking with Tongues, Historically and Psychologically Considered.* New Haven, 1927. Defends idea that glossolalia is pathological; the thesis has been disproved by further investigation of Neo-Pentecostalist groups.

Lemonnyer, A. "Charismes," *Dictionnaire de la Bible: Supplément* 1 (1928), cols. 1,233–43.

Taylor, R. "The Tongues of Pentecost," *Expository Times* 40 (1928–29), pp. 300–3.

Bell, H. "Speaking in Tongues." Unpublished dissertation defended at the Evangelical Theological College, Dallas, 1930. There is another dissertation by a J. Graber at the same college, undated.

Jacquier, E. "Zungenreden," *Die Religion in Geschichte und Gegenwart.* Tübingen, 1931. Cols. 2,142–43.

Behm, J. "Glōssa," *Theologisches Wörterbuch zum Neuen Testament* 1 (1933), pp. 719–26. In English, tr. G. W. Bromiley: *Theological Dictionary of the New Testament* 1 (1964), pp. 719–26.

Allo, E. B. *Première Epître aux Corinthiens.* Paris, 1934. Cf. pp. 319–27, 333–34, 354–84.

Cerfaux, L. "La symbolique attachée au miracles des languages," *Ephemerides Theologicae Lovanienses* 13 (1936), pp. 256–59. Repr. *Recueil Lucien Cerfaux* (Gembloux, 1954), 2:183–87.

Richstätter, K. "Die Glossolalie im Lichte der Mystik," *Scholastik* 11 (1936), pp. 321–45.

Grossouw, W. "Glossolalie," *Bijbelsch Woordenboek.* Turnhout, 1941. Cols. 537–38 (where a distinction is made between the glossolalia of Acts 2 and that of 1 Corinthians 14).

Schlauch, Margaret. *The Gift of Tongues.* New York, 1942.

Haanapfel, B. G. "A glossolalia no Novo Testamento," *Revista Ecclesiastica Brasileira* 3 (1944), pp. 51–66.

Lyonnet, S. "De glossolalia Pentecostes eiusque significatione," *Verbum domini* 24 (1944), pp. 63–75. Rightly maintains that the same glossolalia is meant in Acts 2 and 1 Corinthians 14.

Martin, I. J. "Glossolalia," *Journal of Biblical Literature* 63 (1944), pp. 123–30. Comparison of New Testament glossolalia with similar pagan phenomena.

Dalton, R. C. *Tongues Like As of Fire.* Springfield, Mo., 1945.

Horner, K. A. "A Study of the Spiritual Gifts with Special Attention to the Gift of Tongues." Unpublished dissertation, Faith Theological Seminary, Wilmington, 1945.

Mayeda, G. *Le langage de l'Evangile.* Geneva, 1948. A new explanation: the miracle of Pentecost was that the Apostles spoke Greek and thus achieved their first missionary success!

Dupont, J. *Gnosis.* Paris, 1949. Pp. 21–410.

White, A. *Demons and Tongues.* Zarephath, N.J., 1949.

Alvarez de Linera, A. "El glosolalo y su interprete," *Estudios bíblicos* 9 (1950), pp. 193–208.

Davis, J. C. "Pentecost and Glossolalia," *Journal of Theological Studies,* n.s., 3 (1952), pp. 228–31.

Clavier, H. "Langues," in A. Westphal (ed.), *Dictionnaire Encyclopédique de la Bible* 2 (1956), pp. 7–21. A well-informed analysis of the various aspects and forms of the phenomenon: exegetical, historical, psychological, and linguistic.

Gewiess, J. "Glossolalie," *Lexikon für Theologie und Kirche*[2] 4 (1960), cols. 972–73.

Martin, I. J. *Glossolalia in the Apostolic Church.* Berea, Ky., 1960.

Vivier, L. M. "Glossolalia." Unpublished dissertation, University of the Witwatersrand, Johannesburg, South Africa, 1960. Summary in Kelsey (infra), pp. 204–6.

Diocese of Chicago. "Report on Spiritual Speaking," *The Living Church* 144 (1961), pp. 10–11, 18.

Amiot, F. "Glossolalie," *Catholicisme* 5 (1962), cols. 67–69. Concludes to an ecstatic, incoherent, inarticulate utterance.

Dupont, J. "Le problème des langues dans l'Église de Corinthe," *Proche-Orient Chrétien* 12 (1962), pp. 3–12.

Lovekin, A. A. "Glossolalia: A Critical Study of Alleged Origins in the New Testament and the Early Church." Unpublished dissertation, University of the South, Sewanee, Tenn., 1962.

Christenson, L. *Die Gabe des Zungenredens in der Lutherischen Kirche.* Marburg, 1963.

Dollar, G. W. "Church History and the Tongues Movement," *Bibliotheca Sacra* 120 (1963), pp. 316–21.

Farrell, F. "Outburst of Tongues: The New Penetration," *Christianity Today* 7 (Sept. 1963), pp. 3–7.

Fuller, R. H. "Tongues in the New Testament," *American Church Quarterly* 3 (1963), pp. 162–68.

Hodges, Z. C. "The Purpose of Tongues," *Bibliotheca Sacra* 120 (1963), pp. 226–33.

Oman, J. B. "On Speaking in Tongues: A Psychological Analysis," *Pastoral Psychology* 14 (Dec. 1963), pp. 48–51.

Pike, J. "Glossolalia," *The Living Church* 146 (1963), p. 11.

Study Commission on Glossolalia, Episcopal Diocese of California, *Preliminary Report*. Division of Pastoral Services, 1963.

## 1964–73

Beare, F. W. "Speaking with Tongues: A Critical Survey of the New Testament Evidence," *Journal of Biblical Literature* 83 (1964), pp. 93–96.

Hess, H. "A Study of Glossa in the New Testament," *Biblical Translator* 15 (1964), pp. 93–96.

Johnson, S. L. "The Gift of Tongues and the Book of Acts," *Bibliotheca Sacra* 121 (1964), pp. 309–11.

Kelsey, M. T. *Tongue Speaking: An Experiment in Spiritual Experience*. Garden City, N.Y., 1964. One of the best-informed studies in English.

Nida, E. *Preliminary Report on Glossolalia* (for the Linguistic Society of America). New York, 1964.

Rice, R. F. "Christian Glossolalia through the Centuries," *View* 1 (1964).

Sadler, A. W. "Glossolalia and Possession," *Journal for the Scientific Study of Religion* 4 (1964), pp. 84–90.

Sherrill, J. L. *They Speak in Other Tongues*. Westwood, N.J., 1964.

Van Elderen, B. "Glossolalia in the New Testament," *Bulletin of the Evangelical Theology Society* 7 (1964), pp. 53–58.

Bergsma, S. *Speaking with Tongues*. Grand Rapids, Mich., 1965.

Currie, S. D. "Speaking in Tongues: Early Evidence Outside the New Testament Bearing on *glôssais lalein*," *Interpretation* 19 (1965), pp. 274–94.

Goldsmith, H. "The Psychological Usefulness of Glossolalia in the Believer," *View* 2 (1965), pp. 7–8.

Lapsley, J. N., and Simpson, J. H. "Speaking in Tongues," *Princeton Seminary Bulletin* 58 (1965) pp. 3–18.

Lester, A. D. "Glossolalia: A Psychological Evaluation." Unpublished report, Southern Baptist Theological Seminary, Louisville, 1965.

Banks R. M. "Speaking in Tongues: A Survey of the New Testament Evidence," *Churchman* 80 (1966), pp. 287–94.

Charlier, J.-P. *L'Evangile de l'enfance de l'Église: Commentaire de Actes 1–2*. Brussels-Paris, 1966. Cf. pp. 126–32: "Le miracles des langues."

Chevalier, M. A. *Esprit de Dieu, paroles des hommes*. Neuchâtel-Paris,

1966. Cf. pp. 171–200: "Mises au point de Paul concernant la glossolalie."

Douglas, J. "Tongues in Transition," *Christianity Today* 10 (July 8, 1966), p. 34.

Gundry, R. H. "Ecstatic Utterance: *glôssais lalein*," *Journal of Theological Studies*, n.s., 17 (1966), pp. 299–307.

Harpur, T. W. "The Gift of Tongues and Interpretation," *Canadian Journal of Theology* 12 (1966), pp. 164–71.

Hoekema, A. *What About Tongue Speaking?* Grand Rapids, Mich., 1966.

Horton, W. H. *The Glossolalia Phenomenon.* Cleveland, O., 1966.

Stibb, A. "Putting the Gift of Tongues in Its Place (1 Co. 12–14)," *Churchman* 80 (1966), pp. 295–303.

Wolfram, W. A. "The Sociolinguists of Glossolalia." Unpublished M.A. thesis, Hartford, 1966.

Cleveland, L. D. "Let's Demythologize Glossolalia," *The Baptist Program* 45 (June 1967), pp. 8, 11.

Dicharry, W. F. "Gift of Tongues," *New Catholic Encyclopedia* 6 (1967), cols. 472–73.

Maly, K. *Mündige Gemeinde.* Stuttgart, 1967. Cf. *Excursus* 3: "Zur Überschätzung der Glossolalie," pp. 237–39; and pp. 182–228.

Sweet, J. P. M. "A Sign for Unbelievers: Paul's Attitude to Glossolalia," *New Testament Studies* 13 (1967), pp. 240–57.

Betz, O. "Zungenreden und süsser Wein: Zur eschatologischen Exegese von Is. 28 in Qumran und Neuen Testament," in S. Wagner (ed.), *Bibel und Qumran: Beiträge zur Erforschung zwischen Bibel- und Qumranwissenschaft.* Berlin, 1968. Pp. 20–36.

Christenson, L. *Speaking in Tongues.* Minneapolis, 1968.

Mills, W. E. "Theological Interpretation of Tongues in Acts and 1 Corinthians." Unpublished dissertation, Baptist Theological Seminary, Louisville, 1968.

Pattison, E. M. "Behavioral Science Research on the Nature of Glossolalia," *Journal of the American Scientific Affiliation* 20 (1968), pp. 73–86.

Spoerri, Th. "Ekstatische Rede und Glossolalie" in his *Beiträge zur Ekstase. Bibliotheca Psychiatrica et Neurologica* 134. Basel, 1968.

Barbarie, T. J. "Tongues, Si! Latin, No!" *Triumph* (Apr. 1969), pp. 20–22.

Bittlinger, A. *Glossolalie.* Wetzhausen, 1969.

Hine, V. "Pentecostal Glossolalia: Toward a Functional Interpretation," *Journal for the Scientific Study of Religion* 8 (1969), pp. 212–26.

Dismisses Cutten's interpretation of glossolalia as pathological (cf. Cutten above, 1927).

Samarin, W. J. "Glossolalia as Learned Behavior," *Canadian Journal of Theology* 15 (1969), pp. 60–64.

Mills, W. E. "Reassessing Glossolalia," *Christian Century* 87 (1970), pp. 1,217–19.

Engelson, N. I. "Glossolalia and Other Forms of Inspired Speech According to 1 Co. 12–14," *Parole di Vita* 6 (1971), pp. 376–87.

Ford, J. M. "Toward a Theology of Speaking in Tongues," *Theological Studies* 32 (1971), pp. 3–29.

Gillespie, T. W. "Prophecy and Tongues." Unpublished dissertation, Claremont Graduate School and University Center, 1971. Résumé in *Dissertation Abstracts* 32 (1971), No. 5887A.

McKay, J. R. "A Critique of Pentecostalism," *Church Quarterly* 3 (1971), pp. 311–17.

Unger, M. F. *New Testament Teaching on Tongues*. Grand Rapids, Mich., 1971.

Bittlinger, A. *Und sie beten in anderen Sprachen: Charismatische Bewegung und Glossolalie*. Ökumenischer Schriftendienst 2. Wetzhausen, 1972. French translation: "Et ils prient en d'autres langues," *Foi et vie* 72 (1973), pp. 97–108.

Goodman, F. D. *Speaking in Tongues: A Cross-cultural Study of Glossolalia*. Chicago, 1972.

Kidahl, J. *The Psychology of Speaking in Tongues*. New York, 1972.

Mills, W. E. *Understanding Speaking in Tongues*. Grand Rapids, Mich., 1972.

Samarin, W. J. *Tongues of Men and Angels: The Religious Language of Pentecostalism*. New York, 1972.

Fernández del Rio, P. "Hablar en lenguas: Precedentes histórico-literários e interpretación exegética en el Nuevo Testamento." Unpublished dissertation, Pontifical Biblical Institute, Rome, 1973, dir. I. de la Potterie, S.J. Studies the antecedents in the Old Testament (Is. 28:11; 66:18b–21; Gn. 11:9; Zp. 3:9–10; Ps. 80:6; Si. 51:22), at Qumran (1 QH IV, 15–19; II, 15), in the Targums, Philo, and Hellenistic literature (pp. 1–136); then takes up 1 Co. 14 (pp. 144–270), Mk. 16:17 (pp. 271–301), and Acts (pp. 302–543).

Montague, G. T. "Baptism in the Spirit and Speaking in Tongues: A Biblical Appraisal," *Theology Digest* 21 (1973), pp. 342–60. Pp. 349–60 are on glossolalia.

Tugwell, S. *Did You Receive the Spirit?* New York, 1973.

——. "The Gift of Tongues in the New Testament," *Expository Times* 84 (1973), pp. 137–40.

# 9. Connected Topics

## PENTECOSTALISM IN GENERAL

Bloch-Hoell, N. *The Pentecostal Movement: Its Origin, Development and Distinctive Character*. London: Allen and Unwin, 1964.

Bruner, F. D. *A Theology of the Holy Spirit: The Pentecostal Experience and the New Testament Witness*. Grand Rapids: Eerdmans, 1970.

Hollenweger, W. J. *Enthusiastisches Christentum: Die Pfingstbewegung in Geschichte und Gegenwart*. Zürich: Rolf Brockenhaus Wuppental, 1966. Tr. as *The Pentecostals: The Charismatic Movement in the Church*. Minneapolis: Augsburg, 1972.

Kendrick, Klaude. *The Promise Fulfilled: A History of the Modern Pentecostal Movement*. Springfield, Mo.: Gospel Publishing House, 1961.

Nichol, J. T. *Pentecostalism*. New York: Harper & Row, 1966.

Séguy, J. "Pentecôtisme," *Encyclopaedia Universalis* 12 (1968), p. 754.

## ENTHUSIASTIC MOVEMENTS

(Cf. Chap. 6, n. 3, 5, 7, 8, and 11 for pertinent references.)

## HOLY REDEEMER PARISH, HOUSTON

(On this Episcopalian parish, which was a pioneer in the charismatic renewal, and has been close to Catholicism and in close touch with Catholics, cf. the following:)

Harper, M. *A New Way of Living: How the Church of the Redeemer, Houston, Found a New Life-Style*. Plainfield, N.J.: Logos International, 1973. 144 pp.

Pulkingham, W. G. *Gathered for Power: Charisma, Communalism, Christian Witness*. New York: Morehouse-Barlow, 1972. By the founder of the parish.

——. *They Left Their Nets: A Vision for Community Ministry*. New York: Morehouse-Barlow, 1973. Continuation of the story.

# Notes

## Exergues

[1] Prayer of Pope John XXIII to the Holy Spirit for the Success of the Ecumenical Council, tr. in W. M. Abbott (ed.), *The Documents of Vatican II* (New York, 1966), p. 793.

[2] Jacques Maritain (Dec. 1970).

[3] Pope Paul VI, Address to the College of Cardinals (Dec. 21, 1973), tr. in *The Pope Speaks* 18 (1973–74), p. 334.

## Introduction

[1] The title of a book by J. L. Sherrill (Westwood, N.J., 1964).

[2] Judgment expressed in *Present Truth* (Fall Brook, Calif.), p. 28.

## Chapter 1

[1] The best account is by K. and D. Ranaghan, *Catholic Pentecostals* (New York, 1969). For the "Notre Dame experience," cf. E. D. O'Connor, *The Pentecostal Movement in the Catholic Church* (Notre Dame, 1971), pp. 39–110.

[2] D. Wilkerson, with J. and E. Sherrill, *The Cross and the Switchblade*.

[3] Ranaghan, op. cit., p. 15.

[4] Father Regimbal, a Canadian, who came into very early contact with the movement in the United States, subsequently started it first in his own country and then in many others. On his international tour, he influenced two abbeys (especially the Abbey of Bec) and acted as catalyst for scattered individuals who likewise had come into contact with the movement on visits to the United States.

[5] E. D. O'Connor, "A Catholic Pentecostal Movement," *Ave Maria* 105, No. 22 (June 3, 1967), pp. 6–10.

[6] Report submitted to the semiannual meeting of the United States Catholic Bishops in Washington, D.C., by Bishop Alexander M. Zaleski of Lansing, Michigan, chairman of the Committee on Doctrine of the National Conference of Catholic Bishops (United States Catholic Conference Documentary Service Press Release, Nov. 14, 1969). The report may be found in *Theology Digest* 19 (1971), pp. 52–53; O'Connor, op. cit., pp. 291–93; K. McDonnell, "Catholic Pentecostalism: Problems in Evaluation," *Dialog* 9 (1970), pp. 35–54 (repr. Pecos, N.M., 1970).

[7] In *La Croix* (Jan. 19, 1974).

# Chapter 2

[1] E. D. O'Connor, "Pentecost and Catholicism," *Ecumenist* 6 (1968), p. 161.

[2] O'Connor, *The Pentecostal Movement*, p. 22.

[3] H. Caffarel, *Faut-il parler d'un Pentecôtisme catholique?* (Paris, 1973), p. 40.

[4] A. N. (Ozman) LaBerge, *What God Hath Wrought* (Chicago, n.d.), pp. 28–29.

[5] Quoted in O'Connor, *The Pentecostal Movement*, p. 22.

[6] W. J. Hollenweger, "Pentecostalism: Contribution to the World Church," *Theology Digest* 19 (1971), p. 56. (This is an abstract of Hollenweger, "Das Charisma in der Ökumene: Der Beitrag der Pfingstbewegung an die allgemeine Kirche," *Una Sancta* 25 [1970], pp. 150–59.)

[7] Hollenweger, op. cit., p. 55.

[8] Cf. H. Chéry, "Catholiques et Pentecôtistes," *Ecclesia*, No. 280 (July–Aug. 1972), pp. 10–12.

[9] The reports of the first meeting (at Zürich-Horgen, June 20–24, 1972) and of the second (at Rome, June 18–22, 1973) have been published; cf. "The Roman Catholic-Pentecostal Dialogue," *One in Christ* 10 (1974), pp. 105–215. "Christian Initiation" was the theme of the third meeting, held at Schloss Craheim, Wetzhausen, Germany, June 10–14, 1974.

[10] O'Connor, "A Catholic Pentecostal Movement," p. 10.

[11] This observation applies chiefly to the United States, and would have to be qualified for England and France, where the "Low Church" and the "Evangelicals" have been more receptive.

[12] As reported in *New Covenant* (Nov. 1973), p. 11.

[13] Cf. R. Martin, "David Wilkerson's Vision," *New Covenant* (Jan. 1974), pp. 11–12.

[14] *Theology Digest* 19 (1971), pp. 52–53. (Cf. Chap. I, n. 6, above).

[15] French translation in *Vie spirituelle* 128 (1974), pp. 31–48.

[16] Cf. "An Interview with Cardinal Suenens," *New Covenant* (June 1973), pp. 1–5; an adapted version appeared in *Logos Journal* (Mar.–Apr. 1974), pp. 14–16. Cf. also R. Ackermann, interview in *La Croix* (Apr. 20, 1974); R. Laurentin, two interviews, in *Le Figaro* (June 3, 1974), and *Famiglia Mese* (Nov. 1974), pp. 24–30; A. Vimeux, interview in *Hebdo-TC* (Sept. 1, 1974), pp. 17–18.

[17] "Redécouvrir le Saint-Esprit: Lettre du cardinal Suenens pour le Pentecôte 1973," *Documentation catholique* 70 (1973), pp. 687–90.

[18] *Une nouvelle Pentecôte?* (Paris, 1974); tr. English F. Martin, *A New Pentecost?* (New York, 1974).

[19] The address was published in *Osservatore Romano* (Oct. 11, 1973) and tr. in *New Covenant* (Nov. 1973), p. 5. Archbishop Hayes of Halifax and Bishop McKinney, auxiliary of Grand Rapids, were at the audience. Cardinal Suenens, who attended the meeting at Grottaferrata, but in a private capacity, did not attend the audience so as to avoid publicity. He played a major part, however, at the international meeting in Rome on Pentecost 1975. The Pope even invited him to celebrate Mass at the altar of the Confession on Pentecost Monday, a Mass the Pope himself had been thinking of celebrating.

[20] *Osservatore Romano* (Dec. 22, 1973); tr. in *The Pope Speaks* 18 (1973–74), p. 334.

# Chapter 3

[1] Ranaghan, op. cit., p. 16.

[2] Op. cit., pp. 16–17.

[3] Op. cit., p. 16.

[4] "Témoignages: Une malade," *Vie spirituelle* 128 (1974), p. 99.

[5] O'Connor, "Pentecost and Catholicism," p. 161.

[6] O'Connor, "A Catholic Pentecostal Movement," p. 10.

[7] J. H. Fichter, *The Catholic Cult of the Paraclete* (New York, 1975), pp. 64–65.

[8] O'Connor, "A Catholic Pentecostal Movement," p. 9.

[9] Op. cit., pp. 70–71.

[10] O'Connor, "A Catholic Pentecostal Movement."

[11] Testimony in B. M. Le Braz, "Regards sur le Renouveau charismatique," *Cahiers marials* 90 (Nov. 15, 1973), pp. 355–71. The qualifications added in the next issue of the *Cahiers* did not bear on the point mentioned here.

[12] Ranaghan, op. cit., p. 28.

[13] Cf. J. Giblet, "Baptism in the Spirit in the Acts of the Apostles," *One in Christ* 10 (1974), p. 163.

[14] Epiphanius of Salamis, *Haereses* 66:42 (*PG* 42:91).

[15] "Group Prayer and Contemplation," *New Blackfriars* 52 (1971), pp. 137–38.

[16] F. A. Sullivan, " 'Baptism in the Spirit': A Catholic Interpretation of the Pentecostal Experience," *Gregorianum* 55 (1974), p. 61.

[17] Cardinal Suenens, for example, uses it in his book *A New Pentecost?*, while also providing a good explanation of it (cf. esp. Chap. 7).

[18] E. S. Williams, *Systematic Theology* (3 vols.; Springfield, Mo., 1953); cf. 3:39–61 (cited by R. Wild in a work to appear shortly).

[19] J. D. G. Dunn, *Baptism in the Holy Spirit: A Re-examination of the New Testament Teaching on the Gift of the Holy Spirit in Relation to Pentecostalism Today* (Studies in Biblical Theology, Second Series 15; Naperville, Ill., 1970), pp. 224–29.

[20] Cf., e.g., Giblet, op. cit., p. 169.

[21] Cf. Sullivan, op. cit., pp. 52–53, for these views, with bibliographical references. Sullivan shows (p. 57) that it is worth studying the expression "baptism in the Spirit" in connection with interchangeable expressions found in similar contexts: The Spirit is *sent* by Christ; he *comes* or *falls* upon Christians; the latter are *clothed* (Lk. 24:49) or *filled* (Ac. 2:4) with the Spirit who is *poured out* on them (Ac. 2:17, 23).

[22] G. T. Montague, "Baptism in the Spirit and Speaking in Tongues: A Biblical Appraisal," *Theology Digest* 21 (1973), p. 349, and R. Wild, "Baptism in the Holy Spirit," *Cross and Crown* 25 (1973), pp. 147–61, emphasize the notion of "experience." Its importance is shown in D. Mollat, "The Role of Experience in the New Testament Teaching on Baptism and the Coming of the Spirit," *One in Christ* 10 (1974), pp. 129–37.

[23] L. Bouyer has some good observations on charismatic experience and the night of the spirit in his "Charismatic Movements in History within the Church Tradition," *One in Christ* 19 (1974), pp. 160–61.

[24] *Summa Theologiae* I, q. 43, aa. 5 and 6; tr. in Sullivan, op. cit., p. 64.

[25] *Summa Theologiae* I, q. 43, a. 6, ad 2; tr. ibid.

[26] Op. cit., p. 66.

[27] Cf. his article in *La Croix* (Jan. 19, 1974).

[28] On prophecy in the charismatic movement, cf. L. Dallière, "Le charisme prophétique," *Foi et vie* 72 (1973), pp. 90–96; M. C. Harper, *Prophetie: Eine Gabe für die Kirche Christi* (Wetzhausen, 1974); Montague, *The Spirit and His Gifts* (New York, 1974), pp. 30–50 (this little book is a reprint of the article mentioned above in n. 22, with the addition of a chapter on prophecy).

[29] The results of the consultation on the conduct of the 1973 conference were mimeographed by the Notre Dame center, in the form of a set of tables. The percentages of those who in varying degrees approved or disapproved of the management of the conference show that enthusiasm

and general satisfaction were matched by a critical spirit bent on improvement. For example, there were 376 responses to the question, "Was the conference useful to me personally, in my situation?": 37 per cent a strong yes; 46 per cent no; 15 per cent somewhat; 2 per cent no (half of these a strong no).

[30] A basic bibliography on the charisms would include the following (in chronological order): Heinz Schürmann, "Les charismes spirituels," in Y. M.-J. Congar (ed.), *L'Eglise de Vatican II* (Unam Sanctam 51; Paris, 1966), pp. 541–73; Hans Küng, *The Church,* tr. Ray and Rosaleen Ockenden (New York, London, 1967), pp. 105–203, esp. pp. 179–91 on "The Continuing Charismatic Structure of the Church"; G. Hasenhüttl, *Charisma, Ordnungsprinzip der Kirche* (Ökumenische Forschungen 1/5; Freiburg, 1970), with Yves Congar's review in *Revue des sciences philosophiques et théologiques* 55 (1971), pp. 341–42.

Küng's and Hasenhüttl's books are illustrative of the postconciliar effort to reconstruct ecclesiology on the basis of the charisms. Johann Adam Moehler projected such a reconstruction when the renewal of ecclesiology began in the early nineteenth century.

[31] Tr. in Abbott, op. cit., p. 30.

[32] "Charismes et institution," *Nouvelle revue théologique* 96 (1974), pp. 3–19.

[33] Bibliography: J.-C. Didier, "Imposition des mains," *Catholicisme* 5: 1356–61; P. Galtier, "Imposition des mains," *Dictionnaire de théologie catholique* 7:1302–1425; G. Lafont, "Pour un discernement," *Vie spirituelle* 128 (1974), 82–97.

# Chapter 4

[1] See the historical note on glossolalia at the end of this chapter.

[2] "A Catholic Pentecostal Movement," pp. 8–9.

[3] A. Bittlinger, *Und Sie Beten in anderen Sprachen: Charismatische Bewegung und Glossolalie* (Wetzhausen, 1972); tr. as "Ils prient en d'autres langues," *Foi et vie* 72 (1973), pp. 97–108. References henceforth will be to this French version.

[4] Ed. of 1950, p. 1,166.

[5] Cf. H. Jaschke, "Lalein," *Biblische Zeitschrift* 15 (1971), pp. 109–14.

[6] Bittlinger, op. cit., p. 99.

[7] Quoted ibid., p. 108.

[8] Ibid., p. 100.

[9] W. J. Samarin, *Tongues of Men and Angels: The Religious Language of Pentecostalism* (New York, 1972), pp. 107–8.

[10] Ibid., pp. 114–15.

[11] Cf. V. Synan, *The Holiness-Pentecostal Movement in the United States* (Grand Rapids, 1971), pp. 102–3, cited by Montague, op. cit., p. 360, n. 80.

[12] Cf. S. Tugwell, *Did You Receive the Spirit?* (New York, 1972): "Prayer is the normal and principal purpose of the gift of tongues. But, on occasion, it is used also as a gift for preaching, and this is the use with which the scholastic theologians of the Middle Ages were familiar, and it is fairly widely attested among missionaries, ancient and modern, though it is often unclear whether the miracle is to be situated strictly in the speaking or in the hearing. St. Vincent Ferrer, for instance, and St. Francis Xavier both preached in languages they did not know, and the same thing is reported now from the mission field in our own century, though chiefly among Protestants, as far as I know" (pp. 73–74).

[13] The testimonies for the canonization process were collected twenty to thirty years after his death. They do not say that Vincent spoke in tongues, but, on the contrary, assert that he spoke only "the Catalan of a man from Valencia, the old 'Limousin' language of the Avignon curia" (M.–M. Gorce, "Vincent Ferrer [Saint]," *Dictionnaire de théologie catholique* 15:3,041) and yet was understood by large crowds of people who spoke Breton or Italian. Historians continue, however, to inquire into the nature and mechanism of the communication; since we know nothing about it, we are unable to exclude natural explanations.

We are justified in asking whether the reports concerning Protestant missionaries in Chapter 9 of Sherrill's *They Speak in Other Tongues* have any better foundation. They are even more difficult to control than the testimonies regarding St. Vincent Ferrer.

St. Augustine, St. Gregory the Great, and the Scholastics after them were indulging in pure deduction when they maintained that the purpose of glossolalia in the early Church was to spread the Gospel among the pagan nations. Scripture and tradition speak against this view, since they see glossolalia as meant for a nonutilitarian mysterious form of praise, not for communication.

[14] For St. Francis Xavier, Tugwell refers to the readings in the old Breviary. But as everyone knows, scholars long before Vatican II used to say: "as false as a Second Nocturn reading." U. Miliez, S.J., writes: "He [Xavier] did not in fact have the gift of tongues. He himself tells us of the difficulty he had in making himself understood by the peoples to whom he preached. In order to preach at all, he had to have interpreters translate for him some texts on prayer and the basics of the Christian religion; then he learned these by heart and repeated them" ("François Xavier [Saint]," *Catholicisme* 4:1,548).

[15] Op. cit., p. 370 (cf. above, Chap. 3, n. 11).

[16] Interview published in *Expériences* 2 (1971), pp. 12–14.

[17] *Die Seherin von Prevorst* (2nd ed.; Stuttgart, 1832), tr. in Bittlinger, op. cit., pp. 101–2.

[18] *Die geistige Entwicklung des Kindes* (Jena, 1930), p. 221, tr. ibid., p. 102, n. 2.

[19] *Tongue Speaking: An Experiment in Spiritual Experience* (Garden City, N.Y., 1964), p. 199.

[20] Op. cit., p. 99.

[21] Samarin, op. cit., pp. 73, 81, 124.

[22] Ibid., p. 83.

[23] Ibid., p. 227.

[24] Loc. cit.

[25] Op. cit., p. 99; and cf. the interview in *Le Figaro* (June 3, 1974).

[26] E. Lombard, *De la glossolalie chez les premiers chrétiens et phéno-mènes similaires: Études d'exégèse et de philologie* (Paris and Lausanne, 1910), p. 3.

[27] According to the testimony of Dom F. Martin, "Un week-end avec le Renouveau," *Notre Dame de Tournay* 124 (July–Aug. 1974), p. 60.

[28] Op. cit., p. 199.

[29] "Some Cultural Group Abreaction Techniques and Their Relation to Modern Treatments," *Proceedings of the Royal Society of Medicine* 77 (1949), pp. 367ff.

[30] Op. cit., p. 231.

[31] According to W. Meyer, *Der erste Korintherbrief: Prophezeiung* (1945), 2:22, cited in Bittlinger, op. cit., p. 106.

[32] Op. cit., p. 104.

[33] This is Samarin's conclusion, op. cit., p. 227.

[34] Charismatics often speak of the gift of tongues, but not of the gift of tears. Yet when I broached the subject, several of them, well-balanced individuals, acknowledged that they had experienced the gift of tears while praying, usually in private. They would probably have restrained their tears in public; the gift of tongues, on the other hand, is accepted and used.

"Do you want the gift of tongues? Then you will have it," I heard one of the most experienced leaders of the movement answer someone who asked him, in a tone of frustration, "Why don't I have the gift of tongues?"

[35] See the historical note on the gift of tears at the end of this chapter.

[36] *The Doctrine of Reconciliation*, Part II (Church Dogmatics IV/2), tr. G. W. Bromiley (Edinburgh, 1958), p. 829.

[37] *Predigtlehre* (Munich, 1971), p. 332, quoted by Bittlinger, op. cit., p. 104.

[38] *Adversus haereses* V, 6, 1 (PG 7:1,137).

[39] *In Epistolam Primam ad Corinthios Homiliae* 29, 1 (PG 61:329).

[40] *Poetics*, Chap. 20 (1457b3).

[41] *Vita S. Hilarionis*, 22 (PL 23:41).

[42] *Rituale Romanum*, Titulus XI, Caput 1, No. 3.

[43] See the historical note on glossolalia at the end of this chapter.

[44] *The Spiritual Journal of St. Ignatius Loyola*, tr. W. J. Young, S.J. (Woodstock, Md., 1958), pp. 43, 45.

[45] Quoted by E. B. Allo, *Première épître aux Corinthiens* (Paris, 1934), pp. 377, 379.

[46] Cf. E. Jacquier, *Les Actes des Apôtres* (Paris, 1926), *Excursus* 7, pp. 187–95, and the commentary, pp. 44–57, 336–37, 568–69; and Allo, ibid., pp. 319–27, 333–34, 354–84.

[47] Cf. J. Dupont, *Les Actes des Apôtres* (3rd ed.; Paris, 1964), p. 42.

[48] Quoted in Allo, op. cit., p. 377.

[49] We shall not touch here on Mark 16:17, which we mentioned above: Those who believe "will have the gift of tongues" (or, according to another reading, "will speak in new tongues"). Kelsey, op. cit., mentions other passages that allude to glossolalia: Romans 8:26–27 [cf. 8:14–15; Ga. 4:6]; Acts 4:23–32; 8:9–24; Colossians 3:16; Ephesians 5:18. The allusion seems clearest in the first and last of these passages; these two texts deal with inspired speech and are of interest at least to the theology and spirituality of glossolalia.

[50] Our contemporary experience confirms the view of the better exegetes that the glossolalia on Pentecost (Ac. 2) is the same as the glossolalia mentioned in other passages of Acts and in 1 Corinthians 12:14. It is an inspired, disinterested, mysterious prayer of praise, not an intelligible communication in a foreign language. It is a charism given by the Spirit. The gibes of the mockers in Acts 2:13 may be illustrated by Paul's remark that "any uninitiated people or unbelievers, coming into a meeting of the whole church where everybody was speaking in tongues, would say you were all mad" (1 Co. 14:23).

[51] And cf. 10:45: "The Jewish believers . . . were all astonished that the gift of the Holy Spirit should be poured out on the pagans too."

[52] Compare Philo, *De Decalogo*, 32–33: God the Creator "who fashions the air . . . and transforms it into flames of fire, produced this articulated sound, like the breath (*pneuma*) passing through a *trumpet* that rings out and is heard far and near." The passage is quoted in A. Laurentin, "Le pneuma dans la doctrine de Philon," *Ephemerides Theologicae Lovanienses* 27 (1951), p. 417.

[53] As A. Laurentin has shown, ibid., pp. 417–19.

[54] Cf. Allo, op. cit., p. 379.

[55] Cf. Bittlinger, op. cit., p. 98.

# Chapter 5

[1] Dr. T. Mangiapan, chairman of the medical board, has courageously faced the problem of the crisis of belief in miracles, in a series of articles entitled: "Jalons . . . Lourdes et les malades," *Bulletin de liaison de l'hospitalité de Lourdes* 3 (July 1973), pp. 14–18; 4 (Oct. 1973), pp. 15–20; 5 (Jan. 1974), pp. 13–20; 6 (Apr. 1974), pp. 11–20; 7 (July 1974), pp. 9–13. These five *Bulletins* are a supplement to *Recherches sur Lourdes* 43–47. The articles analyze the changed conditions: fewer of the seriously ill come to Lourdes, and practically none of those on whom the doctors have given up; almost all who come are being treated (and the treatment must be presumed to be the cause of any cure that occurs; hardly anyone now practices the abstention from all medical care that used to be habitual among the sick who came to Lourdes). In this chapter, we cannot enter into all aspects of this complicated problem, which is now being studied at Lourdes.

Father M. de Roton, rector of the sanctuaries, introduced and concluded Dr. Mangiapan's series of articles with two of his own, entitled "Réflexions par rapport à notre foi," *Bulletin* 3 (July 1973), pp. 19–20, and 7 (July 1974), pp. 13–16. The articles of the doctor and the priest have been reprinted in an abridged form in *Association médicale internationale de Lourdes* 165–66 (May 1974), pp. 24–33.

[2] Op. cit., p. 163.

[3] Bibliography on healing in the charismatic movement: M. T. Kelsey, *Healing and Christianity* (New York, 1973); F. MacNutt, O.P., *Healing* (Notre Dame, 1974); M. Scanlon, *The Power of Penance* (Notre Dame, 1972), and *Inner Healing* (New York, 1974), Cf. also *New Covenant*, issues of Nov. 1973 on "Healing," and May 1974 on "Inner Healing." Cf. also n. 8 and 10 below.

[4] "I would make a rough estimate that about half of those we pray for are healed (or are notably improved) of physical sickness and about three fourths of those we pray for are healed of emotional or spiritual problems. . . . The extraordinary has become ordinary. And that's the way I think the healing ministry should be: an ordinary, normal part of the life of every Christian community."

[5] L. D. Weatherhead, *Psychology, Religion and Healing* (Nashville, 1951), pp. 196–97.

[6] Pastor Wohlfahrt adds here: "I learned later on that she is seventy." This is what was commonly said, but Kathryn Kuhlman herself pointed out the real source of the rumor, in an interview with Glenn Gilbert in

the Ann Arbor *News*. She recalled that at a meeting in Chicago a reporter seized her by the arm and asked her her age; she broke away saying "seventy," and he took her seriously. As a matter of fact, she kept only one secret concerning her ministry: her age. It continued to be a secret during the press conference at Ann Arbor on June 1, 1974, although she was generally taken to be in her fifties.

[7] Interview in *Foi et vie* 72 (1973), pp. 5–7.

[8] Old Tappan, N.J., 1962. Cf. also her book *God Can Do It Again* (Englewood Cliffs, N.J., 1969).

[9] Op. cit., p. 9.

[10] Op. cit., p. 9. With regard to this same point, Weatherhead, op. cit., pp. 158–59, has some hard words to say about Lourdes as presented in Vernon Johnson's Catholic Truth Society pamphlet, *Suffering and Lourdes* (London, 1950). "He [Johnson] tells us that suffering is a beautiful thing ordained from all eternity, and then tells us that God did not mean it. . . . Having assured us on p. 44 that suffering is the result of the fall of man, he doubles back on p. 50 and writes this: 'The pain, the suffering, the death which lies before you is simply the chalice which your Heavenly Father has given you.' Having said that suffering was due to sin, he says on p. 54, 'Our Lord Jesus wants our suffering for the completion of His work for souls.' It is impossible to make sense of such confused statements" (p. 159). And: "Roman Catholic teaching about Lourdes is to me incomprehensible" (p. 158).

Though poorly informed about Lourdes, Weatherhead does present the history of the therapeutic element in religion, concentrating chiefly on the Christian forms of healing that came on the scene beginning with F. A. Mesmer (1734–1815). Within this field he focuses mainly on Christian Science. In reaction to numerous abuses, he elaborates balanced norms for the exercise of healing in Christianity.

[11] MacNutt, ibid., p. 74.

[12] Second Council of Lyons (174), Profession of Faith required of Emperor Michael Paleologos, in Denzinger-Schönmetzer, *Enchiridion symbolorum* (32nd ed.; Freiburg, 1963), No. 860 (cited henceforth as *DS*, with number of document).

[13] Decree on the Sacraments, Canon 1 (*DS*, No. 1601), and Decree on Extreme Unction, Canon 1 (*DS*, No. 1716).

[14] For the history and evolution of this sacrament, cf. the notable synthesis of R. Béraudy, "Les sacrement des malades: Etude historique et théologique," *Nouvelle revue théologique* 96 (1974), pp. 600–34.

[15] G. Jacquemet, "Guérisseurs," *Catholicisme* 5:341.

[16] *Bulletin de l'Union Catholique des Scientifiques Français* 13 (Mar.–Apr. 1953).

[17] M. Colenon, *Essai sur les causes du succès des guérisseurs* (Paris, 1954).

18 MacNutt, op. cit., p. 24.

19 Vatican Council I, Dogmatic Constitution on the Catholic Faith, Chap. 3 (*DS*, No. 3009).

20 [The issue of *Concilium*, planned for late 1974, has been delayed, but will appear (tr.).]

21 *Time* (Aug. 19, 1974), p. 14.

22 Cf. M. Balint, *The Doctor, His Patient and the Illness* (2nd ed.; London, 1968); M. and E. Balint, *Psychotherapeutic Techniques in Medicine* (London, 1961).

23 MacNutt, op. cit., p. 267.

24 Cf. the Ann Arbor *News* (June 2, 1974), p. 53.

25 Cf. R. Laurentin et al., *Lourdes: Documents authentiques 5: Procès de Lourdes* 1 (Paris, 1959), p. 398. Here the reader will find the documents on the first inquiry conducted at Lourdes and on its circumstances, along with the medical notes of M. Bariety (Academy of Medicine), P. Mauriac, F. Thiébaut, and L. Cornet, all members of the International Medical Commission of Lourdes.

26 Dr. A. Olivieri and Dom B. Billet, *Ya-t-il encore des miracles à Lourdes? 30 dossiers de guérisons* (Paris, 1972).

27 Cf. n. 1 for this chapter.

28 Op. cit., p. 163.

29 Ibid., pp. 208–31.

30 Ibid., p. 15.

31 Cf. Chap. 4, sec. 11, conclusion No. 4.

32 Op. cit., p. 108.

## Chapter 6

1 Cited in H. Siegert, *Griechisches in der Kirchensprache* (Heidelberg, 1950), p. 57.

2 *Historia ecclesiastica* IV, 10 (PG 82:1,144).

3 *Enthusiasm: A Chapter in the History of Religion* (New York, 1950).

4 More clearly than any other Father before Nicaea, Tertullian affirms the divinity and personality of the Spirit, two points on which there will be hesitation and uncertainty until the Council of Constantinople in 381 (for the latter cf. *DS*, No. 150). Tertullian is the first to express the doctrine of the divine processions according to the Greek schema: *A Patre per Filium* ("From the Father through the Son"), and according to the Latin schema as well: *Ex Patre Filioque* ("From the Father and the Son"). Tertullian uses an almost identical formula: *A Patre Filioque*, and does so in a context that counteracts the inconveniences of this formula: "The Spirit is a third, from the Father and the Son, as the fruit from the blossom is third from the root, and as the

tip of the ray is third from the sun" (*Adversus Praxean*, 8, 7, in *PL* 2:187 or *CCL* 2:1,168).

Tertullian is also the first to say that the Son and the Spirit are "sharers in the Father's substance" (op. cit., 3, 5, in *PL* 2:181 or *CCL* 2:1,162). A brilliant use of the resources of the Latin neuter and masculine genders enables him to express the relation between nature and person in a definitive formula that is not easily translated into French or English: "The connection of the Father in the Son and of the Son in the Paraclete effects the cohesion of the three, each proceeding from the other. And the three are one [neuter, that is, 'thing,' or being], not one [masculine, that is, person] (*Qui tres unum sunt, non unus*)" (op. cit., 25, 1, in *PL* 2:211 or *CCL* 2:1,195).

In view of these anticipations and definitive formulations, it is impossible to understand how a substantial encyclopedia article on the Holy Spirit can say of Tertullian only that "he has but a few allusions to the Holy Spirit" (M.-J. Le Guillou, "Esprit-Saint," *Catholicisme* 4:482).

[5] *Epist.* 41, 3 (*PL* 22:476); cf. G. Bardy, "Montanisme," *Dictionnaire de théologie catholique* 10:2,368.

[6] Code of Justinian, I, v, 20, ed. P. Krueger (Berlin, 1877), p. 58; cited by Bardy, loc. cit.

[7] Oracles 1 and 2, cited in P. de Labriolle, *La crise montaniste* (Paris, 1913), p. 38.

[8] H. Leclercq, "Glossolalie," *Dictionnaire d'archéologie chrétienne et de liturgie* 6 (1924), cols. 1,326–27. The italicized words are from P. de Labriolle, ibid., pp. 171–72.

[9] Cf. Fourth Lateran Council, Constitution 13, in *Conciliorum Oecumenicorum Decreta*, ed. J. Alberigo et al. (3rd ed.; Bologna, 1973), p. 243, and Second Council of Lyons, Constitution 23 (ibid., p. 326). The latter Council deplores the failure to enforce the prohibition passed by the Fourth Lateran Council and revokes the authorizations that religious Orders had managed to "extort" in the interim. But the revocation itself remained ineffective, since among the authorizations that had been "extorted" were those given to Francis and Dominic.

[10] For the text of the censure, cf. Constitution 2 (ibid., p. 231), or *DS*, No. 803.

[11] Letter of Dec. 27, 1220, quoted in B.-D. Dupuy, "Joachim de Flore," *Catholicisme* 6:880. Basic now are the works of M. E. Reeves, *The Influence of Prophecy in the Later Middle Ages: A Study in Joachimism* (Oxford, 1969) and (with B. Hirsch-Reich), *The Figurae of Joachim of Flora* (Oxford, 1972).

[12] Dupuy, ibid., col. 887.

[13] F. Cayré, *Manual of Patrology and History of Theology*, tr. H. Howitt, 2 (Paris, 1940), p. 691. The following list is taken from p. 692, n. 1–9.

[14] Op. cit., 8 (Paris, 1928), p. 219.
[15] Cf. J. Morienval, "Illuminés," *Catholicisme* 5:1,223–24, for the following examples.
[16] *New Covenant* (Jan. 1974), pp. 11–14.

# Chapter 7

[1] Symeon the New Theologian, *Catechesis* 32, in *Catéchèses 23–34* (Sources chrétiennes 113; Paris, 1965), pp. 238–40.
[2] Circular Letter No. 16 (Christmas 1973), pp. 2–3 (mimeographed). Father Molinié offered further explanations in the next circular, No. 17.
[3] St. Thérèse, Manuscrit A. 46v, and Bergson, *The Two Sources of Morality and Religion*, tr. R. A. Audra and C. Brereton (New York, 1935). Chap. 1.
[4] Cf. the note at the end of this chapter on "Studies of Psychological Balance among Pentecostals."
[5] For the sake of clarification we are here emphasizing the differences from zen and yoga, but we must not oversimplify the contrast or opposition between these and the charismatic renewal.

It is true enough that the practice of zen and yoga is much less common among charismatics than it is among Carmelites, Benedictines, or Trappists, yet some not untypical charismatics do make use of these disciplines. It seems, however, that they do not go as far with the Asian methods as the monks do and use them rather as ways simply of achieving bodily equilibrium and concentration.

The integration of zen and yoga (as techniques of non-Christian origin) into a properly Christian experience raises problems that become more pressing the farther one advances in the use of them. The Christian monks who employ them often have a highly intelligent and alert consciousness of the nature of the techniques and show this by the way they use them.

When all is said and done, Pentecostal spirituality does provide an opportune alternative, namely the cultivation of the charisms, that draws upon specifically Christian sources
[6] W. McCready, "The Pentecostals: A Social Analysis," in H. Schmidt (ed.), *Liturgy: Self-Expression of the Church* (*Concilium* 72; New York, 1972), p. 113. The purpose of this article is to describe Catholic Neo-Pentecostalism in terms of social change. With Neil Smelser, McCready describes five types of collective behavior that happen when ordinary normative structures disappear: panics, crazes, hostile outbursts, norm-oriented movements, and value-oriented movements. Neo-Pentecostalism is a "craze" because it appeals to an "outside force" and is a "mobilization of opinions towards the creation of a positive wish-

fulfillment belief" (p. 115). The author makes this rough classification without ever having participated in a Pentecostal prayer meeting (p. 112).

[7] J. Séguy, "Pentecôtisme et néo-Pentecôtisme: Pour une interprétation macrosociologique," in *Actes de la 12ᵉ Conférence Internationale de Sociologie Religieuse* (The Hague, Aug. 26–30, 1973), pp. 271–83. Séguy analyzes Pentecostalism (especially in Protestantism) as an expression of social conflict. His study is a prolongation of his earlier "La dynamique interne des groupes informels," in the collection of essays *Les groupes informels dans l'Eglise* (Strasbourg, 1971), pp. 37–71, and his *Les conflits du dialogue* (Paris, 1973), pp. 74–77. In this last-named book he sees as the specific note of (interconfessional) Pentecostal ecumenism its experiential character—that is, persons from the various confessions gather not to discuss differences but to share experiences in the exercise of the charisms.

[8] *The Social Teaching of the Christian Churches*, tr. O. Wyon (New York, 1931). Quoted from the Harper Torchbook edition (1960), 2:993.

[9] According to the analyses of M. Magnificat, "Prophétie et oecuménisme, Une expérience contemporaine: Taizé" (unpublished dissertation, Ecole Pratique des Hautes Etudes, 1972), p. 162.

[10] "The act of faith has for its term not a proposition but the reality (*actus fidei non terminatur ad enuntiabile sed ad rem*)" (*Summa Theologiae* II–II, q. 1, a. 2, ad 2; I–II, q. 13, a. 1)

# Chapter 8

[1] For the "prophecy" and the reactions to it, cf. *New Covenant* (Nov. 1973), pp. 11; (Jan. 1974), pp. 11–14.

[2] *Informations catholiques internationales*, No. 443 (Nov. 1, 1973), p. 18.

[3] Cf. below, Chap. 9, n. 11, and corresponding text.

[4] R. Wild, "'It Is Clear That There Are Serious Differences Among You' (1 Cor. 1:11): The Charismatic Renewal Entering Religious Communities," *Review for Religious* 32 (1973), p. 1,097. We might note here the influence of American culture with its empiricism and realism and its distrust of the ideologies and superstructures that have always enjoyed a greater prestige in the world of Latin culture.

[5] Circular Letter No. 16, p. 11.

[6] The word has been ignored in the *Dictionnaire de théologie catholique* (Paris, 1903–50) and its *Supplément*.

[7] *The Charismatic Renewal*, mimeographed document (dated Mar. 4, 1974) issued by the Communications Center at Notre Dame, p. 6. [I have not been able to locate this document and have been forced to translate back from Father Laurentin's French version of it (tr.).]

[8] "Une session du Renouveau charismatique à Aix," *Cahiers de l'actualité religieuse et sociale* (Oct. 1973), p. 544.

[9] *Informations catholiques internationales* 443 (Nov. 1, 1973), p. 18.

[10] J. Whitney, op. cit., p. 4. Cf. J. McCarthy, "The Charismatic Renewal and Reconciliation in Northern Ireland," *One in Christ* 10 (1974), pp. 31–43; R. D. Wead, "Healing of a Country: A Beginning," *New Covenant* (June 1974), pp. 16–17, who observes that "Irish Catholic and Protestant prayer groups are meeting, though cautiously" (p. 16); caution is needed in such an atmosphere of threats and death.

[11] *New Covenant* (June 1974). Several articles deal with involvement in racial and social problems and with institutionalized injustice: T. D. Parham, "Removing Racial and Social Barriers through Charismatic Renewal" (pp. 14–15); J. F. Maxwell, "The Reform of Institutionalized Injustice" (pp. 42–45); The Chicago Declaration of Fifty Evangelicals, "Evangelical Social Concern" (pp. 56–57).

# Chapter 9

[1] Report of Feb. 1974, p. 3.

[2] In *Le Point*, No. 92 (Apr. 15, 1974), p. 79.

[3] Cf. the Dogmatic Constitution on the Church, Chap 4.

[4] This and the following numbered quotations are from a mimeographed document *The Covenant of a Brotherhood*, from the sections entitled "Our Way of Life" and "Our Commitment as a Brotherhood." [I wish to thank the Word of God Community for supplying a copy of this document (tr.).]

[5] R. Martin, "An Interview with Fr. Heribert Mühlen, Theologian of the Holy Spirit," *New Covenant* (July 1974), p. 6. Father Mühlen's major works are: (1) *Der Heilige Geist als Person* (The Holy Spirit as a Person) with the subtitle "Contribution to the Question of the Proper Role of the Holy Spirit Within the Trinity, in the Incarnation, and in the Covenant of Grace" (Münster, 1963; 2nd, enlarged ed., 1967). The purpose of the book is to describe the Holy Spirit in terms of the function proper to him rather than of a function appropriated to him but belonging in fact to the whole Trinity (Scholasticism remained more or less faithful to the latter approach). Because the Holy Spirit has this function proper to himself, Christians acquire a special relation to him through grace. (2) *Una Mystica Persona* (One Mystical Person), with the subtitle "The Church as the Mystery of the Salvation-historical Identity of the Holy Spirit in Christ and in Christians: One Person in Many Persons" (Paderborn, 1964; 2nd, enlarged ed., 1966). The book deals with the relation between the theology of the Church and the theology of the Holy

Spirit. (3) *Entsakralisierung* (Desacralization) (Paderborn, 1971, on the status of the sacred in view of the doctrine of the Spirit as expounded in the two earlier works; (4) *Morgen wird Einheit sein* (Tomorrow There Will be Unity), with the subtitle "The Coming Council of All Christians—Goal of the Separated Churches" (Paderborn, 1974). [This is the "next book" to which Father Laurentin and the interview in *New Covenant* refer (tr.).]

6 Cf. again the Dogmatic Constitution on the Church, Chap. 4.

7 Cf. MacNutt, op. cit., p. 96.

8 I would ask, however, whether the importance attached to the gift of tongues is not an emphasis on a particular spiritual technique and whether a particular style of human relationships, of feeling, and even of nonviolence is not characteristic of the movement.

9 Cardinal Suenens uses these two as examples of "new communal experiences" that bear witness to the stirrings of the Holy Spirit (op. cit., pp. 154–58).

10 As I studied the communities of North America, I was particularly impressed by this young and interesting movement, which is hearing significant witness to the values of popular Catholicism in Canada.

11 Interview in *Le Figaro* (June 3, 1974).

## Chapter 10

1 J.-Y. Carluer, "Un livre courageux: Pentecôtisme chez les catholiques!," *Expériences* 16 (4th qtr. 1974), p. 74.

2 *Cahiers marials* 90 (Nov. 15, 1974), p. 374.

3 Bibliography on Mary in the charismatic renewal:

A. The first two pamphlets alluded to in the text: L. Pfaller and J. Alberts, *Mary is Pentecost: A Fresh Look at Mary from a Charismatic Viewpoint* (Pecos, N.M., 1973); D. E. Rosage, *Mary, the Model Charismatic* (Spokane, n.d.).

B. Two helpful chapters: G. T. Montague, *Riding the Wind: Learning the Ways of the Spirit* (Ann Arbor, 1974), Chap. 7: "Mary and Learning the Ways of the Spirit" (pp. 91–98); Cardinal Suenens, *A New Pentecost?*, Chap. 11: "The Holy Spirit and Mary" (pp. 196–211).

C. *Croyons-vous au Saint-Esprit?* is the title of a special issue of *Cahiers marials* 90 (Nov. 15, 1973). In addition to some testimonies it contains an article by A.-M. de Monléon, "Les apparitions de Lourdes et le renouveau spirituel" (pp. 333–42).

4 The bibliography on Acts 1:14 is extremely sparse. The exhaustive bibliographies of G. Besutti, which cover 1948–66, do not mention a single monograph on this verse. The only two we know of are: Augustin Bea,

*"Erant perseverantes . . . cum Maria Matre Iesu . . . in communicatione fractionis panis* (Ac. 1, 14; 2, 42)," *Alma Socia Christi* 6: *De B. V. Maria et SSma Eucharistia* (Rome, 1952), pp. 21–37 (this article is superficial from an exegetical viewpoint and deals only with Mary and the Eucharist); B. Prete, "Il sommario dei Atti 1, 13–14 e suo apporto per la conoscenza della Chiesa delle origini," *Sacra Doctrina,* 69–70 (June 1973), pp. 64–124 (a well-informed study; on Mary's presence in the first Christian community, cf. esp. pp. 94–103 and the notes on pp. 120–24).

[5] Cf. the Dogmatic Constitution on the Church, No. 59, and the Decree on the Missionary Activity of the Church, No. 4.

[6] Cf. R. Laurentin, *La Vierge au Concile* (Paris, 1965), pp. 56–81.

[7] Cf. G. Gutiérrez, *A Theology of Liberation: History, Politics and Salvation,* tr. and ed. Sister Caridad Inda and John Eagleson (Maryknoll, N.Y., 1973): "The Magnificat . . . is one of the New Testament texts which contains great implications both as regards liberation and the political sphere" (p. 207).

[8] S. Méndez Arceo, sermon in the Basilica of Our Lady of Guadaloupe, published in *Excelsior* (May 28, 1971) and reprinted in *CIDOC* 71, p. 319. This text and that of Maurras, with other references, may also be found in R. Laurentin, "Bulletin sur la Vierge Marie," *Revue des sciences philosophiques et théologiques* 56 (1972), p. 481 and n. 124.

[9] Cf. R. Laurentin, "Bulletin sur la Vierge Marie," *Revue des sciences philosophiques et théologiques* 58 (1974), pp. 298–301.

[10] Tr. in *The Pope Speaks* 19 (1974–75), pp. 49–87. Mary is presented as "a mirror of the expectations of . . . the modern woman, anxious to have a share in community affairs. . . . Mary of Nazareth . . . was far from being a timidly submissive woman or one whose piety was repellent to others; on the contrary she did not hesitate to proclaim that God vindicates the humble and oppressed, and removes the powerful people of this world from their privileged positions" (pp. 74–75).